Statistics Canada

1991 Census Highlights

W9-AGN-887

CAI
CS9,6
304
1991

Published by authority of the Minister responsible for Statistics Canada

March 1994

Price: Canada: $10.00
United States: US$12.00
Other Countries: US$14.00

Catalogue 96-304 E

ISBN 0-660-14311-9

Ottawa

La version française de cette publication est disponible sur demande.

Note of Appreciation

Canada owes the success of its statistical system to a long-standing cooperation involving Statistics Canada, the population of Canada, its businesses and governments. Accurate and timely statistical information could not be produced without their continued cooperation and goodwill.

Canadian Cataloguing in Publication Data

Main entry under title:

1991 census highlights

Issued also in French under title:
Faits saillants du recensement de 1991.
ISBN 0-660-14311-9
CS96-304E

1. Canada -- Census, 1991. I. Statistics Canada.
II. Title.

HA741.5.1991 N56 1994   304.6'0971
C94-988024-8

Preface

When the first modern census was conducted by Jean Talon in 1666, it recorded 3,215 habitants by age, sex, marital status, occupation and relationship to the head of family. In 1991, some 325 years later, the Census of Canada enumerated more than 27.3 million people and was the source of a wealth of information on the social, economic, demographic and cultural life of Canada.

The 1991 Census Highlights provides readers with the leading stories from the 1991 Census of Population, the Census of Agriculture and the Post-censal Survey Program. These stories cover the major data releases from each program and paint an up-to-date portrait of Canada and Canadians.

I would like to express my appreciation to the millions of Canadian who participated in the 1991 Census of Canada and made it possible for a nation to better know and govern itself.

Ivan P. Fellegi
Chief Statistician

Acknowledgements

I would like to acknowledge the contribution of the small team of individuals who played the key role in the production of this publication.

This team included Anne-Marie Fleury who was instrumental in coordinating all production phases, Nicola Paterson and Christian Carbonneau who did the editing and proofreading while Elaine Brassard and Natacha Cousineau were responsible for the input, format and design of the text and tables. Without the efforts of this team, this publication would not have been possible.

Dale Sewell
Manager, Census Communications

TABLE OF CONTENTS

CENSUS OF POPULATION

CENSUS OF AGRICULTURE

POST-CENSAL SURVEYS

Census of Population

Catalogue 11-001E (Français 11-001F) ISSN 0827-0465

The Daily

Statistics Canada

Tuesday, April 28, 1992

POPULATION AND DWELLING COUNTS

HIGHLIGHTS

- The 1991 Census recorded a population of 27,296,859 on June 4, 1991, up 7.9% from 1986

- British Columbia, Ontario, Yukon Territory and the Northwest Territories all had population growth rates between 1986 and 1991 exceeding the national average

- 61.1% of Canada's population lived in census metropolitan areas

- There were over 10 million occupied private dwellings in Canada

---

A National Overview: Population and Dwelling Counts
Census Divisions and Census Subdivisions: Population and Dwelling Counts
(100% data)

A National Overview (93-301, $20) contains 11 tables with 1991 population and dwelling counts for Canada, the provinces and territories, federal electoral districts, census divisions, census metropolitan areas, census agglomerations as well as counts of the urban and rural populations. Census subdivisions appear in three tables, ranked by size, greatest percentage population growth and greatest percentage population decline.

Census Divisions and Census Subdivisions (93-304, $50) presents population and dwelling counts for 1991 and, in some cases, 1986, and land area and population density for these two types of geographic areas. Census divisions include counties and regional districts; census subdivisions include cities, municipalities, towns, townships, and villages. A geographic index is included and census divisions and subdivisions are grouped by province and territory.

Census Divisions and Census Subdivisions is also available on diskette.

 Statistics   Statistique
Canada   Canada

Canada

On June 4, 1991, Statistics Canada conducted the 17th Census of Population and Housing since Confederation. With the information reported by more than 27 million people in over 10 million households, Statistics Canada has developed a new statistical portrait of Canada and Canadians. This first release provides information on population and dwelling counts.

Population grew 7.9%

Canada's population was enumerated at 27,296,859 on June 4, 1991, an increase of 7.9%, or nearly two million persons, since the 1986 Census.

Getting bigger faster

The 1991 Census recorded the first increase in the intercensal population growth rate since the 1951

Total Population and Growth Rate

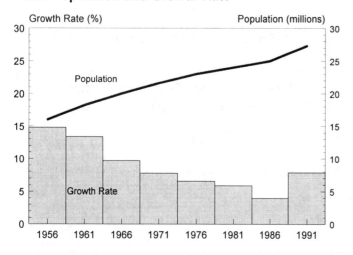

Census. Although Canada's population continued to increase, its rate of growth declined steadily throughout most of the last four decades. The recent increase was due to a combination of increased immigration, decreased emigration and stable natural increases (increases in both births and deaths).

How we've grown

British Columbia, Ontario, the Yukon Territory and the Northwest Territories all had population growth rates exceeding the national rate of 7.9%.

British Columbia, the only province which has had a growth rate above the national average since it joined Confederation, was the fastest growing province. British Columbia's population increased by 13.8%. Ontario was close behind with an increase of 10.8%.

The Yukon Territory, which had the country's smallest total population (27,797), had a growth rate for the 1986-1991 period of 18.3%. This is a significant increase over the 1.5% growth rate during the previous five-year period. The population of the Northwest Territories increased by 10.4% to 57,649. While not as high as the 14.2% population increase recorded by the 1986 Census, the growth rate of the Northwest Territories continued to be higher than the national five-year growth rate.

Quebec's population growth rate was 5.6%, up from 1.5% between 1981 and 1986. This is the first time since the 1956 Census that Quebec's growth rate increased from one census period to the next.

Alberta's population increased by 7.6% between 1986 and 1991, up from the 5.7% increase for the previous five-year period, but slightly lower than the national rate of 7.9%. This is the first time since the 1951 Census that Alberta's five-year growth rate did not exceed the national average.

Population Growth

Year	Total Population	Population Increase	Population Growth Rate (%)
1951	14,009,429	...	...
1956	16,080,791	2,071,362	14.8
1961	18,238,247	2,157,456	13.4
1966	20,014,880	1,776,633	9.7
1971	21,568,311	1,553,431	7.8
1976	22,992,604	1,424,293	6.6
1981	24,343,181	1,350,577	5.9
1986	25,309,331 *	966,150	4.0
1991	27,296,859 *	1,987,528	7.9

*   *Excludes data from incompletely enumerated Indian reserves and settlements; see note on Data Comparability on page 183.*

Population Change

	1986 Population	1991 Population	Absolute Change	% Change 1981-1986	% Change 1986-1991
Canada	25,309,331	27,296,859	1,987,528	4.0	7.9
Newfoundland	568,349	568,474	125	0.1	- -
Prince Edward Island	126,646	129,765	3,119	3.4	2.5
Nova Scotia	873,176	899,942	26,766	3.0	3.1
New Brunswick	709,442	723,900	14,458	1.9	2.0
Quebec	6,532,461	6,895,963	363,502	1.5	5.6
Ontario	9,101,694	10,084,885	983,191	5.5	10.8
Manitoba	1,063,016	1,091,942	28,926	3.6	2.7
Saskatchewan	1,009,613	988,928	-20,685	4.3	-2.0
Alberta	2,365,825	2,545,553	179,728	5.7	7.6
British Columbia	2,883,367	3,282,061	398,694	5.1	13.8
Yukon Territory	23,504	27,797	4,293	1.5	18.3
Northwest Territories	52,238	57,649	5,411	14.2	10.4

- - *amount too small to be expressed*

Newfoundland's total population in 1991 differed little from what it was in both 1981 and 1986. Nova Scotia and New Brunswick experienced slight increases in their population growth rates between the 1981-1986 and 1986-1991 periods. Two provinces, Prince Edward Island and Manitoba, experienced slower growth for the 1986-1991 period than during the previous period, 1981-1986.

Saskatchewan was the only province with a population drop – declining by approximately 21 thousand from an all time high of slightly over one million in 1986 to below one million in 1991.

Population distribution – 40 year trend continued

Decennial censuses taken since Newfoundland joined Confederation in 1949 showed that the distribution of Canada's population among the provinces and territories shifted in favour of British Columbia, Alberta and Ontario.

Of all the provinces, only Alberta and British Columbia experienced continuous increases in their percentage share of Canada's population over the last 40 years. In 1951, 15% of Canada's population lived in Alberta and British Columbia. By 1991, this proportion

Population Growth Rate

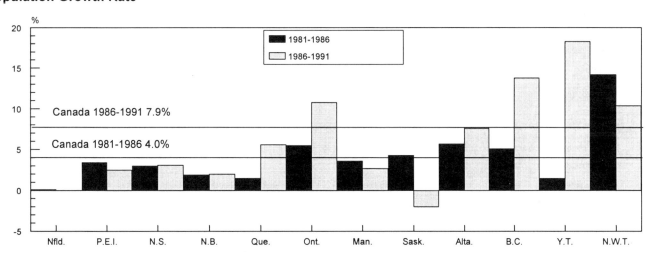

Population Distribution

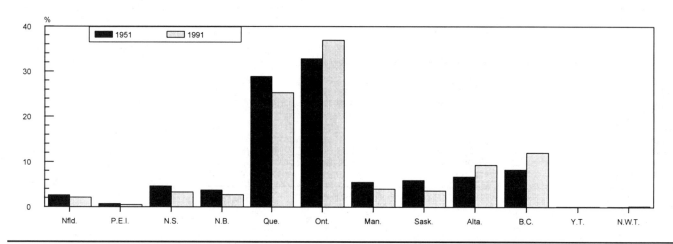

had increased to 21.3%. Despite a slight decrease in its share of the population in the 1970s, Ontario's share of the population increased from 32.8% in 1951 to 36.9% in 1991.

After two decades of slight change, the shares of Prince Edward Island and the Northwest Territories have remained stable since 1971. Yukon's share of the population has not changed since 1951.

New Brunswick, Nova Scotia, Newfoundland, Manitoba and Saskatchewan all experienced small but continuous declines in their shares of the population between 1951 and 1991. Over the same period, Quebec's proportion declined from 28.9% to 25.3%.

Population Distribution

	% Distribution				
	1951	1961	1971	1981	1991
Canada	**100.0**	**100.0**	**100.0**	**100.0**	**100.0**
Newfoundland	2.6	2.5	2.4	2.3	2.1
Prince Edward Island	0.7	0.6	0.5	0.5	0.5
Nova Scotia	4.6	4.0	3.7	3.5	3.3
New Brunswick	3.7	3.3	2.9	2.9	2.7
Quebec	28.9	28.8	27.9	26.4	25.3
Ontario	32.8	34.2	35.7	35.4	36.9
Manitoba	5.5	5.1	4.6	4.2	4.0
Saskatchewan	5.9	5.1	4.3	4.0	3.6
Alberta	6.7	7.3	7.5	9.2	9.3
British Columbia	8.3	8.9	10.1	11.3	12.0
Yukon Territory	0.1	0.1	0.1	0.1	0.1
Northwest Territories	0.1	0.1	0.2	0.2	0.2

The biggest get bigger – Canada's census metropolitan areas

The 1991 Census revealed that 61.1% of Canada's population lived in census metropolitan areas – more than ever before. Between 1986 and 1991, every one of Canada's 25 metropolitan areas grew, with the result that there were 1.5 million more people living in these areas in 1991 than in 1986.

Ten census metropolitan areas – Toronto, Vancouver, Ottawa-Hull, Edmonton, Calgary, London, Kitchener, Halifax, Victoria and Oshawa – had higher rates of growth than Canada as a whole. The country's fastest growing metropolitan area was Oshawa, with a growth rate of 18%. Vancouver was next, with 16.1%, followed by Kitchener with 14.5%.

Over the five-year census period, the population of metropolitan Montréal increased by 7%, bringing it above three million for the first time. During the same period, Halifax was the fastest growing census metropolitan area in the Atlantic provinces and its population climbed by 8.3% to pass the 300,000 mark. Saint John, with a growth rate of 3.1%, became the 24th largest metropolitan area in 1991, up from 25th place in 1986.

Census Metropolitan Areas

| | Rank | | 1986 Population | 1991 Population | Absolute Change | % Change |
	1986	1991				
Toronto	1	1	3,431,981 A	3,893,046	461,065	13.4
Montréal	2	2	2,921,357	3,127,242	205,885	7.0
Vancouver	3	3	1,380,729	1,602,502	221,773	16.1
Ottawa-Hull	4	4	819,263	920,857	101,594	12.4
Edmonton	5	5	774,026 A	839,924	65,898	8.5
Calgary	6	6	671,453 A	754,033	82,580	12.3
Winnipeg	7	7	625,304	652,354	27,050	4.3
Québec	8	8	603,267	645,550	42,283	7.0
Hamilton	9	9	557,029	599,760	42,731	7.7
London	11	10	342,302	381,522	39,220	11.5
St. Catharines-Niagara	10	11	343,258	364,552	21,294	6.2
Kitchener	12	12	311,195	356,421	45,226	14.5
Halifax	13	13	295,922 A	320,501	24,579	8.3
Victoria	14	14	255,225 A	287,897	32,672	12.8
Windsor	15	15	253,988	262,075	8,087	3.2
Oshawa	16	16	203,543	240,104	36,561	18.0
Saskatoon	17	17	200,665	210,023	9,358	4.7
Regina	18	18	186,521	191,692	5,171	2.8
St. John's	19	19	161,901	171,859	9,958	6.2
Chicoutimi-Jonquière	20	20	158,468	160,928	2,460	1.6
Sudbury	21	21	148,877	157,613	8,736	5.9
Sherbrooke	22	22	129,960	139,194	9,234	7.1
Trois-Rivières	23	23	128,888	136,303	7,415	5.8
Saint John	25	24	121,265	124,981	3,716	3.1
Thunder Bay	24	25	122,217	124,427	2,210	1.8

A - Adjusted figure due to boundary change

Bright lights, bigger cities – Canada's 25 largest municipalities

Montréal retained its position as Canada's largest municipality, the only one with a population of over one million. Calgary, the second largest, had a population slightly over 710,000.

Of Canada's 25 largest municipalities, Surrey, British Columbia, with a growth rate of 35.1% was the fastest growing between 1986 and 1991. Markham, Ontario, was a close second with 34.2%. Windsor, Ontario, was the only municipality of the top 25 whose population declined; but the decrease was slight – less than 2,000 people.

Mississauga, Ontario, Canada's ninth largest municipality, experienced the largest absolute population increase of just over 89,000 people. Calgary was second with an increase of over 73,000 people.

In terms of ranking, the 10 largest municipalities in 1986 retained their positions in 1991. However, there was considerable change in those ranked 11th to 25th.

Laval, Quebec, passed two slower growing Ontario communities (Etobicoke and Ottawa) in its jump from 13th largest in 1986 to 11th in 1991. Surrey, British Columbia, with the highest population growth rate of the top 25, went from 17th to 15th. Markham, Ontario, vaulted from 28th in 1986 to 23rd – dropping Oshawa, Ontario, the 25th largest in 1986, to 27th in 1991.

Growth Rates of Canada's 25 Largest Municipalities, 1991

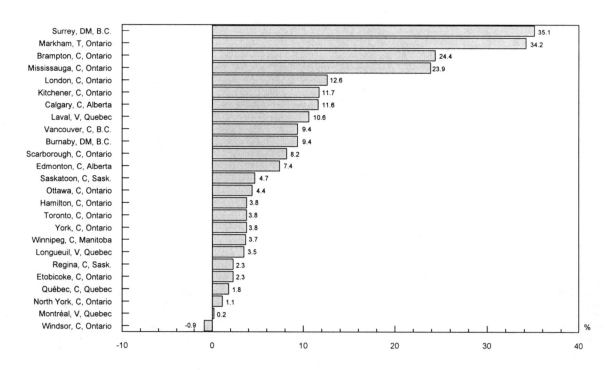

Note: T = Town   V = Ville   C = City   DM = District Municipality

Twenty-five Largest Municipalities

	Rank		1986 Population	1991 Population	Absolute Change	% Change
	1986	1991				
Montréal	1	1	1,015,420	1,017,666	2,246	0.2
Calgary	2	2	636,843 A	710,677	73,834	11.6
Toronto	3	3	612,289	635,395	23,106	3.8
Winnipeg	4	4	594,551	616,790	22,239	3.7
Edmonton	5	5	573,982	616,741	42,759	7.4
North York	6	6	556,297	562,564	6,267	1.1
Scarborough	7	7	484,676	524,598	39,922	8.2
Vancouver	8	8	431,147	471,844	40,697	9.4
Mississauga	9	9	374,005	463,388	89,383	23.9
Hamilton	10	10	306,734 A	318,499	11,765	3.8
Laval	13	11	284,164	314,398	30,234	10.6
Ottawa	12	12	300,763	313,987	13,224	4.4
Etobicoke	11	13	302,973	309,993	7,020	2.3
London	14	14	269,202 A	303,165	33,963	12.6
Surrey	17	15	181,447	245,173	63,726	35.1
Brampton	16	16	188,498	234,445	45,947	24.4
Windsor	15	17	193,122 A	191,435	-1,687	-0.9
Saskatoon	18	18	177,659 A	186,058	8,399	4.7
Regina	19	19	175,064	179,178	4,114	2.3
Kitchener	21	20	150,604	168,282	17,678	11.7
Québec	20	21	164,580	167,517	2,937	1.8
Burnaby	22	22	145,161	158,858	13,697	9.4
Markham	28	23	114,597	153,811	39,214	34.2
York	23	24	135,401	140,525	5,124	3.8
Longueuil	24	25	125,441	129,874	4,433	3.5

A - Adjusted figure due to boundary change

Municipalities with Populations over 25,000 in 1991 but not in 1986

	1986 Population	1991 Population	% Increase
Aurora, T, Ontario	20,905	29,454	40.9
Georgina, T, Ontario	22,486	29,746	32.3
Mascouche, V, Quebec	21,285	25,828	21.3
Mission, DM, British Columbia	21,985	26,202	19.2
Penticton, C, British Columbia	23,588	27,258	15.6
Fort Erie, T, Ontario	23,253	26,006	11.8
Orillia, C, Ontario	24,141	25,925	7.4
Cape Breton Subd. B, SCM, Nova Scotia	24,626	25,385	3.1

Note: T = town   V = ville   C = city   DM = district municipality   SCM = subdivision of county municipality

Fastest Growing and Declining Municipalities with Populations over 25,000 in 1991

% Decrease   % Increase

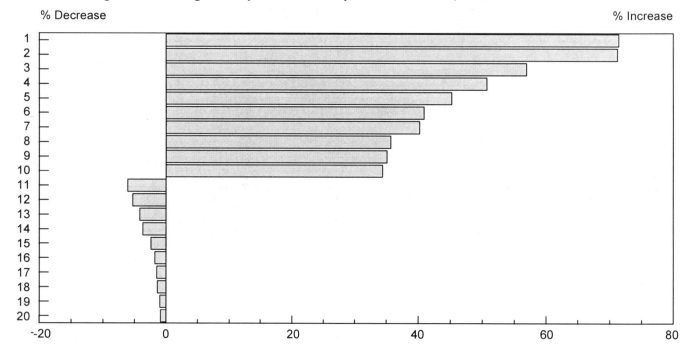

1. Richmond Hill, T, Ontario, 71.4
2. Vaughan, C, Ontario, 71.2
3. Ajax, T, Ontario, 56.9
4. Cumberland, TP, Ontario, 50.7
5. Newcastle, T, Ontario, 45.2
6. Aurora, T, Ontario, 40.9
7. Pickering, T, Ontario, 40.2
8. Kanata, C, Ontario, 35.7
9. Surrey, DM, British Columbia, 35.1
10. Maple Ridge, DM, British Columbia, 34.4

11. Sydney, C, Nova Scotia, -6.1
12. Montréal-Nord, V, Quebec, -5.3
13. Moose Jaw, C, Saskatchewan, -4.2
14. Saint-Léonard, V, Quebec, -3.7
15. LaSalle, V, Quebec, -2.4
16. Saint John, C, New Brunswick, -1.8
17. Drummondville, V, Quebec, -1.5
18. Trois-Rivières, V, Quebec, -1.4
19. Salaberry-de-Valleyfield, V, Quebec, -1.0
20. Windsor, C, Ontario, -0.9

Note: *T = Town*   *C = City*   *TP = Township*   *DM = District Municipality*   *V = Ville*

Suburban municipalities still growing strong: population growth in census subdivisions of over 25,000

In 1986, there were 145 municipalities (census subdivisions) with a population of over 25,000. By 1991, of the 6,006 municipalities in Canada, 153 had achieved a population level of over 25,000. The municipalities new to this category were distributed across the country – one in Nova Scotia, one in Quebec, four in Ontario and two in British Columbia.

The 10 fastest growing large municipalities were in urban areas. Richmond Hill and Vaughan, two municipalities located in the Toronto census metropolitan area, were the fastest growing large municipalities in the country. Over the five-year census period, Richmond Hill grew by 71.4% and Vaughan by 71.2%. Ajax, another Toronto area municipality, was third, with a population growth rate of 56.9%.

Ups and downs of Canada's small municipalities: census subdivisions with populations between 5,000 and 24,999

The 1991 Census found great variation in the population growth rates of the 560 municipalities with populations between 5,000 and 24,999 people. Thirty-six of the 50 fastest growing and 46 of the 50 fastest declining municipalities with populations over 5,000 had populations under 25,000.

The two fastest growing municipalities with populations over 5,000 were small municipalities – Saint-Lazare, Quebec, had a population increase of 78.9%, or 3,993 people, and La Plaine, Quebec, had a growth rate of 76.4%, or 4,580 people. Of all municipalities with populations over 5,000, the one with the greatest percent decline in population was also a small municipality – Elliot Lake, Ontario, with a population decline of 21.7%, or 3,895 people.

Fastest Growing and Declining Municipalities with Populations Between 5,000 and 24,999 in 1991

% Decrease   % Increase

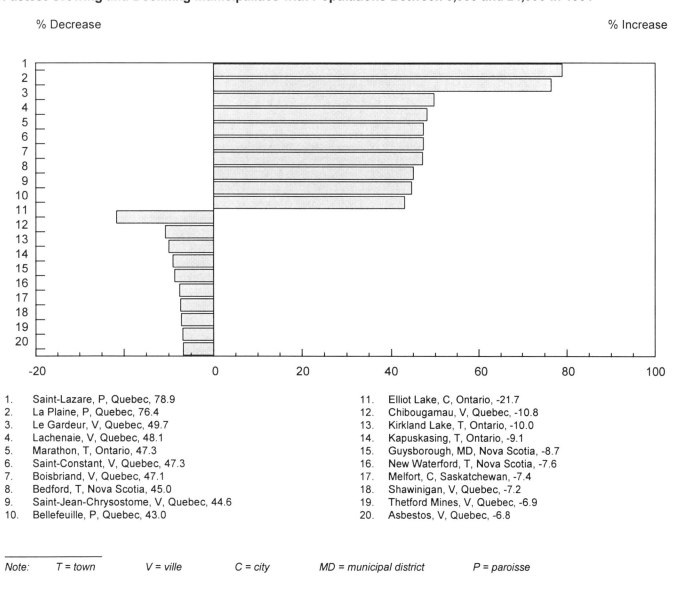

1. Saint-Lazare, P, Quebec, 78.9	11. Elliot Lake, C, Ontario, -21.7
2. La Plaine, P, Quebec, 76.4	12. Chibougamau, V, Quebec, -10.8
3. Le Gardeur, V, Quebec, 49.7	13. Kirkland Lake, T, Ontario, -10.0
4. Lachenaie, V, Quebec, 48.1	14. Kapuskasing, T, Ontario, -9.1
5. Marathon, T, Ontario, 47.3	15. Guysborough, MD, Nova Scotia, -8.7
6. Saint-Constant, V, Quebec, 47.3	16. New Waterford, T, Nova Scotia, -7.6
7. Boisbriand, V, Quebec, 47.1	17. Melfort, C, Saskatchewan, -7.4
8. Bedford, T, Nova Scotia, 45.0	18. Shawinigan, V, Quebec, -7.2
9. Saint-Jean-Chrysostome, V, Quebec, 44.6	19. Thetford Mines, V, Quebec, -6.9
10. Bellefeuille, P, Quebec, 43.0	20. Asbestos, V, Quebec, -6.8

Note: T = town   V = ville   C = city   MD = municipal district   P = paroisse

Number of dwellings continued to grow faster than population

While Canada's population increased by 7.9% over the five-year census period, the number of occupied private dwellings increased by 11.4%, or more than one million units. There were over 10 million occupied private dwellings in Canada in 1991.

The growth in occupied private dwellings for the 1986-1991 period was larger than the 9.4% increase recorded between 1981-1986, but fell short of the increases recorded during the previous four census periods.

Population and Dwelling Growth

Census Period	% Increase Dwellings	% Increase Population
1961-66	13.7	9.7
1966-71	16.5	7.8
1971-76	18.7	6.6
1976-81	15.1	5.9
1981-86	9.4	4.0
1986-91	11.4	7.9

Catalogue 11-001E (Français 11-001F) ISSN 0827-0465

The Daily
Statistics Canada

Tuesday, July 7, 1992

AGE, SEX, MARITAL STATUS, FAMILIES, DWELLINGS AND HOUSEHOLDS

HIGHLIGHTS

- Three million Canadians were over age 65

- Average family size remained at 3.1 persons

- Number of lone-parent families continued to grow faster than the number of husband-wife families

- 1.5 million Canadians were living in common-law unions

- 2.3 million people lived alone

- Close to 60% of all people living alone were women

Age, Sex and Marital Status
Dwellings and Households
Families: Number, Type and Structure

Age, Sex and Marital Status (93-310, $40) provides 1991 age, sex, and marital status data for Canada, provinces, territories and census metropolitan areas (CMAs). Two tables contain age, sex and marital status data from censuses since 1921.

Dwellings and Households (93-311, $40) contains data on dwelling type and tenure as well as household size and type for Canada, provinces, territories and CMAs. Demographic data are available for those living in private and collective dwellings and for household maintainers. Some historical data are included.

Families: Number, Type and Structure (93-312, $40) provides information on census families, family persons and non-family persons. Demographic data for now-married and common-law couples are presented along with data on family size, structure and type for Canada, provinces, territories and CMAs. Some 1986 Census data are included.

These three products are also available on diskette. The diskette versions contain some data for CMAs not presented in the publications.

 Statistics Statistique
Canada Canada

 Canadä

This release describes how our age structure is changing, how many of us are young and how many are old, what our families are like, who lives alone and who owns their homes.

More youngsters...

The size of the preschool (under five years) and primary-school-age (aged 5 to 14) populations grew during the 1980s, mainly due to baby-boomers in their 30s and 40s having children and a slight increase in general fertility rates.

While there were still fewer preschool-age children in 1991 than there were in 1961, the number of children in this age group increased. Between 1986 and 1991, the preschool population grew by 5%, from 1.8 million in 1986 to 1.9 million in 1991.

Growth in the preschool-age population was not evenly distributed across the country. Newfoundland, Prince Edward Island, New Brunswick, as well as Saskatchewan, which was the only province to lose population between 1986 and 1991, all had fewer preschoolers in 1991 than in 1986.

Canada's primary-school-age population grew by 200,000 (6%) over the 1986-1991 period, bringing the number of children aged 5 to 14 to 3.8 million.

...But they're a smaller part of the population

Despite the increasing size of the preschool-age and primary-school-age populations, these groups continued to represent a smaller proportion of Canada's population. Combined, the preschool-age and primary-school-age groups represented 21% of the population in 1991, down from 23% in 1986.

Fewer young adults

While the population aged 14 and under increased during the 1980s, the population aged 15 to 24 declined by 18%. Between 1981 and 1991, the secondary-school-age population (aged 15 to 19) declined by 19%, or almost half a million people. Over the same period, the number of youths (aged 20 to 24) decreased by 16%, from 2.3 million to 2.0 million.

Persons aged 15 to 24 in 1991 were born during the "baby-bust" era of the late 1960s and 1970s, when the number of births dropped after the post-war baby-boom. As this group proceeds through the 1990s, their small numbers will have a considerable impact on university enrolment, the number of new entrants to the labour market and the number of new families and households.

Population by Selected Age Groups

	Pre-school Age 0-4	Primary School Age 5-14	Secondary School Age 15-19	Young Adult Age 20-24	Adult Working Age 20-64	Junior Working Age 20-44	Senior Working Age 45-64	Seniors 65+	Seniors 75+
Number ('000)									
1981	1,783	3,698	2,315	2,344	14,186	9,528	4,658	2,361	883
1986	1,810	3,582	1,925	2,253	15,295	10,421	4,874	2,698	1,047
1991	1,907	3,786	1,869	1,962	16,566	11,200	5,366	3,170	1,275
% of Total Population									
1981	7.3	15.2	9.5	9.6	58.3	39.1	19.1	9.7	3.6
1986	7.2	14.2	7.6	8.9	60.4	41.2	19.3	10.7	4.1
1991	7.0	13.9	6.8	7.2	60.7	41.0	19.7	11.6	4.7
% Change Over Specified Period									
1981-1986	1.5	-3.1	-16.8	-3.9	7.8	9.4	4.6	14.3	18.6
1986-1991	5.4	5.7	-2.9	-12.9	8.3	7.5	10.1	17.5	21.8
1981-1991	7.0	2.4	-19.3	-16.3	16.8	17.5	15.2	34.3	44.4

Population by Age and Sex

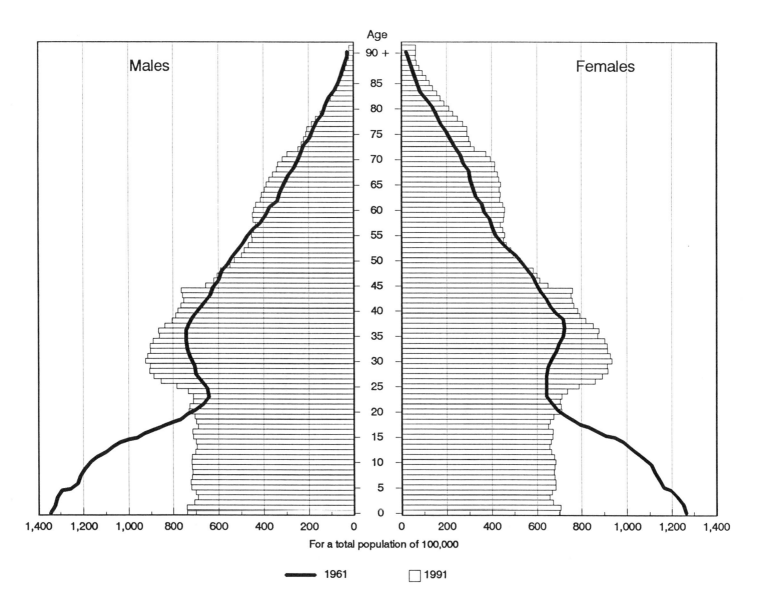

For a total population of 100,000

1961   1991

Our greying work force

The number of adults aged 20 to 64 increased by 8% between 1986 and 1991, bringing the total number of working-age adults to 16.6 million, up from 15.3 million in 1986.

The majority (68%) of working-age people were between the ages of 20 and 44 in 1991. As these people grow older, the working-age population will become increasingly concentrated in the older age groups. For the next decade, however, the current age distribution indicates a continuing high concentration of the labour force in the traditionally most productive age groups.

Three million now over age 65

The population aged 65 and over reached 3.2 million in 1991. Since 1981, the proportion of Canada's population aged 65 and over increased from 10% to 12%. This aging of the Canadian population was primarily the result of the decline in fertility rates since the 1960s, although increases in life expectancy have contributed as well.

Living Arrangements of Seniors, 1991

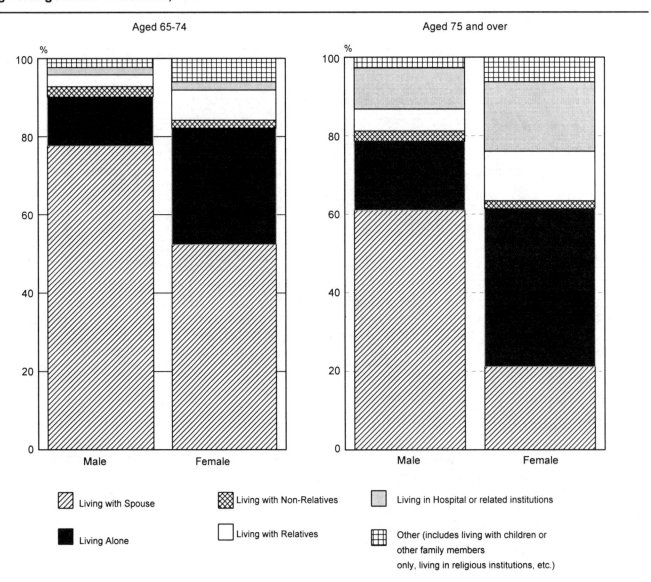

Differences in the mortality rates for men and women result in women outnumbering men by large numbers. In the 65 and over age group, there were 138 women for every 100 men. Among the population 85 years and over, women outnumbered men by more than two to one.

Living arrangements among Canada's seniors

The different mortality rates for men and women were reflected in the living arrangements of Canada's population aged 65 and over. Women, who tended to live longer, were less likely to live with a spouse and more likely to live alone in a private household, a hospital or related institution. These differences between men and women became even more pronounced in the 75 and over age group.

For those aged 65 to 74, almost 78% of the men were living with their spouse in a private household, compared with just over half of the women.

However, for those 75 years and older, the majority of men (61%) were still living with a spouse; less than one-quarter (21%) of women were living with a spouse. Both men and women 75 years and older were more likely to live in a hospital or related institution than those aged 65 to 74.

Delaying marriage...

Over the past decade, there was a dramatic increase in the proportion of younger adults, those aged 20 to 34, who remained unmarried. Among women aged 20 to 24, almost 65% were single in 1991, compared to 51% in 1981. During the same period, the proportion of men aged 20 to 24 who had never been married

rose from 72% to 82%. Similar patterns were observed for men and women in the 25 to 29 and 30 to 34 age groups.

Families in Canada...

In 1991, more than five out of every six (84%) Canadians in private households lived within a family as a spouse, lone-parent or child. This is down slightly from 1986, and marks the continuation of a downward trend in the proportion of the population living in families. In 1971, 89% of the population in private households lived in families.

Average Family Size

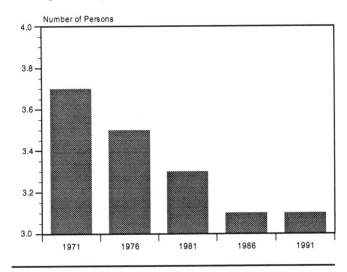

...Larger in numbers

Although the proportion of the population living in families had been gradually declining, the number of families continued to increase. Between 1986 and 1991, the number of families increased by 9% – from 6.7 million in 1986 to 7.3 million in 1991. In comparison, the number of families increased by 7% between 1981 and 1986 and by 10% between 1976 and 1981.

These increases were due to a combination of elements – population growth, immigration, child-bearing outside of marriage and slow but steady increases in marriage and fertility rates.

...And stable in size

Over the last twenty years, average family size declined – from 3.7 persons in 1971 to 3.1 persons in

Population that has Never Married

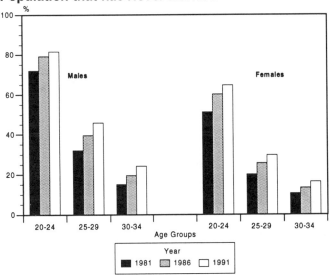

1991. For the first time since the 1971 Census, average family size did not decrease, with both the 1986 and 1991 Censuses recording a family size of 3.1 persons.

Past decreases in family size were attributed to declining fertility rates and increasing numbers of lone-parent families.

More families without children at home...

There has been dramatic growth in the number of husband-wife families without any children living at home. These may be childless families or families whose children had left home. Between 1986 and 1991, the number of families without children at home rose by 378,000 (17%), primarily due to an increase of 257,000 in the number of married-couple families without children at home.

...But families with children still the majority

Although the number of families without children at home grew faster than the number of families with children at home, the majority (65%) of families in Canada still had at least one child living at home.

...Eight out of ten children live with two parents

Most children (86%) under the age of 15 lived in a family with two parents present. An additional 14% lived in a family with one parent present.

Family Structure, 1991

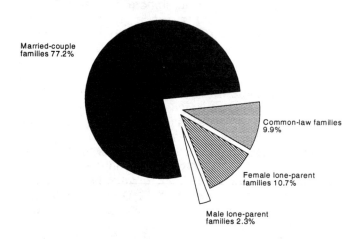

Married-couple families 77.2%

Common-law families 9.9%

Female lone-parent families 10.7%

Male lone-parent families 2.3%

Average number of children per family declining

The average number of children living at home decreased from 1.3 per family in 1986 to 1.2 in 1991. This average was smallest for common-law families, at 0.7 children, compared with 1.2 for married-couple families and 1.6 for lone-parent families.

Several factors, including lower fertility during the 1970s and early 1980s, delayed marriage and delayed child-bearing contributed to the decrease in the number of children living at home.

Family Structure by Number of Children Living at Home

| | 1986 | | 1991 | | |
	Number of Families	% of Total	Number of Families	% of Total	% Change 1986-91
Total Families	**6,734,980**	**100.0**	**7,356,170**	**100.0**	**9.2**
Husband-wife families	5,881,330	87.3	6,401,455	87.0	8.8
with children at home	3,679,780	54.6	3,821,610	52.0	3.9
without children at home	2,201,545	32.7	2,579,845	35.1	17.2
Married-couple families	5,394,390	80.1	5,675,510	77.2	5.2
with children at home	3,495,855	51.9	3,519,610	47.8	0.7
without children at home	1,898,535	28.2	2,155,900	29.3	13.6
Common-law families	486,940	7.2	725,950	9.9	49.1
with children at home	183,925	2.7	302,005	4.1	64.2
without children at home	303,010	4.5	423,950	5.8	39.9
Lone-parent families	853,645	12.7	954,705	13.0	11.8
male	151,740	2.3	168,240	2.3	10.9
female	701,905	10.4	786,470	10.7	12.0

One or two children most common

For families with children living at home, one or two children was the norm. Over 80% of all families with children had either one or two children living at home. Large families were becoming rare – in 1991 only 1% of families with children at home had five or more children living at home.

Married-couple families with children living at home were the most likely to have two at home. This was true for almost 44% of married couples with children, 33% for common-law families, 31% for female lone-parent families and 28% for male lone-parent families.

Male lone-parent families were the most likely to have one child living at home. Almost two-thirds (62%) of all male lone-parent families had one child living at home, compared with 58% for female lone-parent families, 54% for common-law families, and 35% for married-couple families.

Families with Children Living at Home by Number of Children, 1991

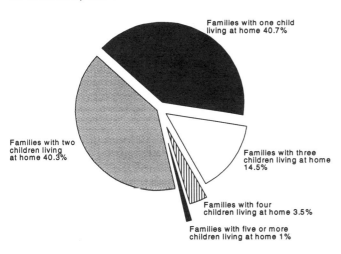

Married-couple families in Canada...

In 1986, married-couple families represented 80% of all families. By 1991, this proportion had dropped to 77%. This drop could be partly attributed to the increase in common-law families between 1986 and 1991. Over the same period, the number of married-couple families grew by 5%, bringing the total number of married-couple families to almost 5.7 million.

...And around the country

Between 1986 and 1991, the number of married-couple families decreased by less than 1% in Quebec and by almost 4% in Saskatchewan. The Yukon Territory, with the smallest number of families, experienced the largest percentage increase in the number of married-couple families (17%).

The highest proportions of married-couple families were found in Newfoundland, Prince Edward Island, Saskatchewan and Ontario, where slightly more than 80% of all families were married-couple families. These families were less common in the Northwest Territories, the Yukon Territory and Quebec, where they represented 62%, 65% and 69% of all families, respectively.

More and more lone-parent families...

Lone-parent families, though fewer in number than married-couple families, had increased at a much faster rate. Between 1986 and 1991, lone-parent families increased by 12%, with lone-parent families headed by women increasing at a slightly faster pace (12%) than lone-parent families headed by men (11%).

There were considerable regional variations in the growth of male and female lone-parent families during the 1986-1991 period. While the number of male lone-parent families did not increase in either of the territories, the Yukon had the greatest increase in the number of female lone-parent families (25%). Ontario followed with an increase of 19% and was tied with Alberta for the largest increase in the number of male lone-parent families (14%).

In 1991, lone-parent families represented 13% of all families, up from 12.7% in 1986. This proportion was highest in the Northwest Territories, where 16% of all families were lone-parent families, followed by the Yukon Territory (15%), and Quebec (14%). In Saskatchewan and Newfoundland, the proportion of families who were lone-parent families was the lowest – slightly under 12%.

...Headed by women

Lone-parent families headed by women continued to outnumber those headed by men by four to one. In 1991, 82% of all lone-parent families were headed by women; little changed from 1986 and 1981. Female lone-parents tended to be younger than their male counterparts, with 61% of female lone-parents aged less than 45, compared to 46% of male lone-parents.

Families in Private Households by Family Structure and Selected Characteristics, 1991

	All Families in Private Households	Husband- Wife Families	Married- Couple Families	Common- Law Families	Male Lone- Parent Families	Female Lone-Parent Families
Total number of families	**7,356,170**	**6,401,455**	**5,675,510**	**725,950**	**168,240**	**786,470**
Total number of families without children at home	2,579,850	2,579,845	2,155,900	423,950	N/A*	N/A*
Total number of families with children at home	4,776,320	3,821,610	3,519,610	302,005	168,240	786,470
all aged 18 years and over	1,163,740	817,425	792,435	24,990	70,710	275,610
some aged 18 years and over and some 17 years and under	499,705	428,095	412,515	15,580	13,975	57,630
all aged 17 years and under	3,112,880	2,576,095	2,314,655	261,440	83,555	453,230
all aged under 6 years	955,655	816,535	698,005	118,530	14,805	124,320
Total number of children at home aged 24 years and under	**8,128,245**	**6,884,340**	**6,395,550**	**488,795**	**210,160**	**1,033,735**
Families by number of never- married children at home						
one	1,944,865	1,384,995	1,222,185	162,805	104,705	455,170
two	1,926,805	1,640,065	1,540,815	99,250	47,000	239,740
three	690,700	608,140	578,510	29,625	12,685	69,875
four	165,235	146,065	138,280	7,785	2,870	16,305
five	33,215	28,580	26,860	1,720	675	3,960
six and over	15,500	13,770	12,960	805	310	1,425
Average number of children per family - 1986	1.3	1.2	1.3	0.6	1.6	1.6
Average number of children per family - 1991	1.2	1.1	1.2	0.7	1.5	1.6

*   N/A - all lone-parent families have children at home

Families in Private Households by Family Structure, 1991

	All Families (%)	Husband- Wife (%)	Married- Couple (%)	Common- Law (%)	Male Lone- Parent (%)	Female Lone- Parent (%)
Canada	**100.0**	**87.0**	**77.2**	**9.9**	**2.3**	**10.7**
Newfoundland	100.0	88.1	81.5	6.6	2.3	9.6
Prince Edward Island	100.0	87.1	81.1	6.0	2.2	10.7
Nova Scotia	100.0	86.5	78.2	8.2	2.2	11.3
New Brunswick	100.0	86.6	78.6	8.0	2.3	11.1
Quebec	100.0	85.7	69.4	16.3	2.6	11.7
Ontario	100.0	87.4	80.7	6.7	2.2	10.4
Manitoba	100.0	86.9	79.5	7.5	2.3	10.8
Saskatchewan	100.0	88.3	81.4	6.9	2.1	9.7
Alberta	100.0	87.6	78.6	9.0	2.2	10.2
British Columbia	100.0	87.9	78.3	9.6	2.2	9.9
Yukon Territory	100.0	85.4	65.4	19.9	3.3	11.3
Northwest Territories	100.0	83.9	61.7	22.2	4.1	12.0

One in ten families were common-law

An increasing number of Canadian families were common-law families. Since 1986, there was a 49% increase in the number of common-law families identified by the Census. In 1991, common-law families represented 10% of all families, up from 7% in 1986.[1]

Persons Living Common-law, 1991

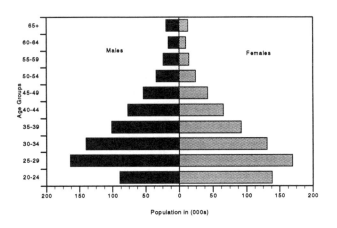

Population in (000s)

Among the provinces and territories, the proportion of families which were common-law families varied considerably. In the Northwest Territories, common-law families represented 22% of all families, followed by the Yukon Territory at 20% and Quebec at 16%. In comparison, common-law families represented 7% of all families in Newfoundland and 6% in Prince Edward Island.

Two of every five common-law families lived in Quebec

Although common-law unions represented a higher proportion of families in the territories in absolute numbers, common-law families were concentrated in the larger provinces. In 1991, 87% of all common-law families lived in the provinces of Quebec (42%), Ontario (25%), British Columbia (12%) and Alberta (8%).

More, but smaller, households

The number of private households in Canada increased 11% between 1986 and 1991, from nine million to 10 million. This increase in the number of households was significantly greater than the increase (7.9%) in the size of the population.

Substantial increases in the number of smaller households (one or two people) combined with decreases in the number of larger households (six or more people) resulted in a small but significant decline in average household size – from 2.8 persons in 1986 to 2.7 persons in 1991.

People living alone

More and more people in Canada live alone. In 1961, less than 10% of all private households were one-person households. Three decades later, over 2.3 million people lived alone, some 23% of all private households.

Factors contributing to the growth in the number of one-person households were the aging of the population and increases in marriage breakdown. Differences in mortality rates have continued to result in rising numbers of elderly widows living on their own.

Who Lived Alone?

In 1991...

The majority (60%) of people living alone were aged 45 or older.

Only 15% of people living alone were under the age of thirty.

The percentage of young people aged 15 to 24 living alone had declined, from 4% in 1986 to 3% in 1991.

Almost 40% of all people aged 75 and over who lived in private households were living alone.

Among those aged 65 and over, 38% of the women and 15% of the men lived alone.

Close to 60% of all people living alone were women.

---

1   *For information on the collection of common-law data, see note on page 22.*

One-person households and home ownership

Overall, nearly two-thirds (63%) of Canadian householders owned their own homes in 1991. Compared to family households, one-person households were much less likely to own their own home. In 1991, 72% of family households were homeowners, while this was true for only 37% of one-person households.

The rate of home-ownership for one-person households varied considerably among Canada's census metropolitan areas. Home ownership was highest in St. Catharines-Niagara, Ontario, where almost half (49%) of people living alone owned their home. One-person households in Montréal were the least likely to own their home – only 19% of those living alone owned their own homes.

Common-law Unions

In 1991, almost 1.5 million people in Canada were living in common-law unions. The majority were under the age of 35 and had never been married.

More than half (57%) of all people in common-law unions were between the ages 20 and 35. Over 64% of women and almost 63% of men in these unions had never been married, while an additional 25% of the women and 27% of the men were divorced.

Collection of Data on Common-law Status:

For the 1981 and 1986 Censuses, data on common-law status was derived based on the "Relationship to Person 1" question. In 1991, the determination of common-law status was the result of a comparison between the response to the "Relationship to Person 1" question and that from a new, direct question on the census form. The resulting increase in the number of common-law unions is, therefore, partially due to the inability to identify an unknown number in 1986. Caution should be exercised when comparing 1991 data on common-law families with those from previous censuses.

Census Families - What Are They?

Census families are divided into those formed by couples and those headed by a lone-parent. Married couples (termed "now-married" in census publications) and common-law couples are considered families whether or not they have never-married sons or daughters living with them. Now-married and common-law couples together comprise husband-wife families.

In censuses prior to 1991, the families of now-married and common-law couples were combined as "husband-wife families". To enable comparisons between censuses, 1991 Census publications include data for husband-wife families as well as for now-married and common-law families.

A lone-parent, of any marital status, living with one or more never-married sons or daughters also constitutes a family.

Never-married sons and/or daughters are blood, step or adopted sons and daughters who have never married (regardless of age) and who are living with their parent(s). In this release, the terms "child" and "children" refer to these never-married sons and/or daughters living with their parent(s).

Catalogue 11-001E (Français 11-001F) ISSN 0827-0465

Statistics Canada

Tuesday, September 15, 1992

MOTHER TONGUE

HIGHLIGHTS

- More Canadians had a non-official language as mother tongue

- Little change in proportion of the population with English mother tongue

- Proportion of French mother tongue population declined slightly

- Considerable diversity in metropolitan areas

Mother Tongue

Mother Tongue (93-313, $40) covers official and non-official languages and provides information on mother tongue by age and sex for Canada, provinces and territories.

This product is also available on diskette. The diskette version contains data for CMAs not presented in the publication.

 Statistics **Statistique**
Canada **Canada**

Canadä

This release describes Canada's language groups, mixed language couples and language transfer to children.

More Canadians had a non-official language as mother tongue

Between 1986 and 1991, there was a significant increase in the percentage of the population who reported a non-official language as their only mother tongue – from 11.3% in 1986 to 13% in 1991. When people with more than one mother tongue were included, the proportion of the population who reported a non-official language as mother tongue in 1991 was 14.9%, up from 13.8% in 1986. This increase was due largely to the rise in the number of recent immigrants whose mother tongue was neither

Population with a Non-official Language as Mother Tongue[1]

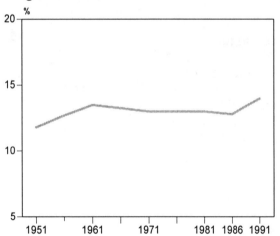

1 For 1986 and 1991, multiple responses were distributed among the language indicated using a method which makes the data approximately comparable to those of the previous censuses

English nor French. Much of the increase in non-official languages occurred in Ontario, British Columbia and Quebec where the majority of recent immigrants settled. Another factor contributing to the increase was the inclusion in the Census, for the first time, of refugee claimants and other non-permanent residents, few of whom had English or French as

mother tongue. (For further information, see the note on Data Comparability on page 183).

In 1991, the three largest mother tongue language groups other than English and French were Italian (reported by 512,000 people), Chinese (reported by 492,000) and German (reported by 476,000). Combined, these three language groups represented about one-third (36%) of all persons with a mother

> ### Mother Tongue
>
> *Mother tongue is defined as the first language a person learned at home in childhood and still understood at the time of the census. Information on mother tongue was collected from all Canadians in 1991. Additional information on knowledge of languages and language spoken at home was collected from a sample of 20% of households and starts on page 41.*

tongue other than English or French, but only 5% of Canada's total population. The next three largest language groups were much smaller – Portuguese (reported by 211,000 people), Polish (reported by 197,000) and Ukrainian (reported by 196,000).

In 1991, 29 different Aboriginal languages and families of languages were used to compile mother tongue data. The three largest Aboriginal language groups were: Cree (reported by 84,000 people), Ojibway (reported by 25,000) and Inuktitut (reported by 25,000). Incomplete enumeration of some Indian reserves resulted in under-reporting of Aboriginal language data. (For further information, see the note on Data Comparability on page 183).

The non-official language group which grew the most over the 1986-1991 period was Chinese. Between 1986 and 1991, the number of people who reported Chinese as their mother tongue increased by 183,000, or 59%. This large growth was primarily the result of immigration. Spanish, often the mother tongue of recent immigrants from Latin America, experienced the next largest increase (reported by 83,000 more people in 1991 than in 1986). Punjabi and Arabic, with increases of 65,000 and 62,000 respectively, experienced the third and fourth largest increases over the same period.

There was a substantial decline in three language groups which were more heavily represented in earlier waves of immigration: Ukrainian (decrease of 81,000 people), German (decrease of 52,000) and Italian (decrease of 42,000).

Change in Size of the 20 Largest Non-official Language Groups, 1986-1991[1]

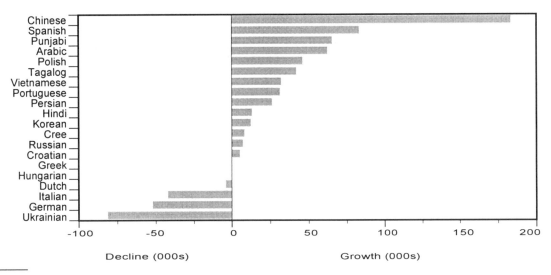

Decline (000s)   Growth (000s)

1 Includes single and multiple responses to the mother tongue

Little change in proportion of the population with English mother tongue

In 1991, 16.5 million people, or 60.5% of the population, indicated English as their only mother tongue, almost unchanged from 1986 when the proportion was 60.6%. When people with more than one mother tongue were included, the proportion of the population who reported English as mother tongue in 1991 was 62.9% down from 64.2% in 1986.

The slight decrease in the percentage of the population reporting English as mother tongue followed a long period of increases. In 1961, 58.5% of the population reported English as their mother tongue, as did 60.2% in 1971 and 61.3% in 1981. Data from Employment and Immigration Canada indicated that the trend in recent years was due largely to increased immigration to Canada of people with a mother tongue other than English.

Another contributing factor was the inclusion for the first time in the Census of non-permanent residents, relatively few of whom had English as their mother tongue (For further information on non-permanent residents see the note on Data Comparability on page 183).

Anglophones (persons with English as mother tongue) were the majority in all of the provinces and territories except Quebec. However, in 1991, the size of this majority varied substantially, from 56.1% of the population in the Northwest Territories to 98.7% in Newfoundland. Two provinces, Ontario and British Columbia, experienced a significant decrease in the relative size of their anglophone populations over the last census period. Between 1986 and 1991, the proportion of the population reporting English as their only mother tongue decreased from 76.3% to 75.1% in Ontario and from 80.9% to 79.4% in British Columbia. This decline was primarily due to immigration and the inclusion of non-permanent residents.

Population with English as Mother Tongue[1]

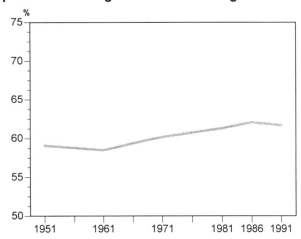

1   For 1986 and 1991, multiple responses were distributed among the language indicated using a method which makes the data approximately comparable to those of the previous censuses

The relative size of the anglophone language group in Quebec continued to decrease – 8.7% of Quebec's population reported English as their only mother tongue in 1991, compared with 8.9% in 1986. When people with more than one mother tongue were included, the proportion of the population who reported English in 1991 was 10.7%, down from 12.1% in 1986. The decrease in the proportion of anglophones between 1986 and 1991 was smaller than that which occured during the previous decade. Prior to 1986, the migration of anglophones to other provinces played a significant role in the decrease of the anglophone population in Quebec.

Single and Multiple Responses

Beginning with the 1986 Census, the census questionnaire provided respondents with the opportunity to report more than one mother tongue. In 1991, most respondents (97%) reported only one mother tongue (a single response) while about 3% reported more than one (multiple response). In 1986, some 4% of respondents reported having more than one mother tongue.

When single and multiple responses are combined, the total number of responses was greater than the total population. For example, Canada's population was 27.3 million in 1991 but there were over 28 million responses to the mother tongue question. For this reason, the percentages of the population reporting English and/or French and/or a non-official language as mother tongue add to more than 100%.

In this release when the total number (or percentage) of persons reporting a language as mother tongue is given, multiple responses are included, except where otherwise noted.

The reduction in the proportion of multiple responses (from 4% in 1986 to 3% in 1991) was partly due to two significant changes implemented by the 1991 Census affecting mainly the long form census questionnaire completed by 20% of all households. The first was to add a new question on knowledge of languages other than English or French. The second and more significant change was to group all the language questions together on the form, rather than following previous census practice of asking the mother tongue question separately. These changes, while providing more and better information on the language characteristics of the population, complicated the task of comparing 1991 Census mother tongue data with data from the 1986 and previous censuses.

Data Considerations

The 1991 Census implemented two significant changes designed to better portray the language situation in Canada. The first was to add to the long-form questionnaire (completed by a sample of 20% of households) a new question on the knowledge of language(s) other than English or French. The second, and more significant, change was to group all the language questions together on the long form, rather than follow the previous census practice of asking the mother tongue question separately from questions relating to language spoken at home and knowledge of Canada's two official languages.

The latter change was implemented following testing which showed that grouping the questions on the long questionnaire resulted in better understanding of the questions by respondents, and hence improved the accuracy of the reported information. When the mother tongue question was asked separately, respondents were more likely to report two or more languages (multiple responses). Evaluations of previous census data have shown that a significant proportion of such answers were incorrect, and that only one mother tongue should have been reported.

The 1991 Census results demonstrate clearly that when mother tongue was included as one of a series of questions on language, there were significantly fewer multiple responses – 3% of respondents provided multiple responses on the short form, where the mother tongue question was asked alone, compared with only 1.2% on the long form.

*Given these differences in response patterns, two publications on the mother tongue variable were produced. The data in the publication, **Mother Tongue** (Catalogue 93-313), are based on the combined responses as reported by all respondents, whether on the short form or the long form. These data are most suited for purposes of historical comparisons, since they are more similar to data from previous censuses than are estimates derived from the mother tongue information collected on the long-form questionnaire (i.e. based on the 20% sample of households). The second publication, **Mother Tongue: 20% Sample Data** (Catalogue 93-333), contains data based on the long-form questionnaire, and enables a more precise analysis of the mother tongue of Canadians as of June 1991.*

Population by Mother Tongue

1991 Census of Canada	% Reporting English		% Reporting French		% Reporting Non-Official Language	
	Single Response	All Responses[1]	Single Response	All Responses[1]	Single Response	All Responses[1]
Canada	60.5	62.9	23.8	24.9	13.0	14.9
Newfoundland	98.4	98.7	0.4	0.6	0.9	1.0
Prince Edward Island	93.8	94.7	4.2	4.8	1.1	1.3
Nova Scotia	93.2	94.0	3.8	4.4	2.2	2.5
New Brunswick	64.1	66.1	32.7	34.6	1.2	1.4
Quebec	8.7	10.7	81.2	83.3	7.5	8.8
Ontario	75.1	78.0	4.6	5.4	17.2	19.5
Manitoba	73.3	76.8	4.3	5.1	18.7	21.8
Saskatchewan	83.1	85.4	2.0	2.5	12.5	14.5
Alberta	81.3	83.7	2.0	2.5	14.1	16.3
British Columbia	79.4	81.6	1.4	1.8	16.8	18.9
Yukon	88.1	89.6	2.9	3.4	7.4	8.5
Northwest Territories	54.2	56.1	2.4	2.7	41.4	43.2

1986 Census of Canada	% Reporting English		% Reporting French		% Reporting Non-Official Language	
	Single Response	All Responses[1]	Single Response	All Responses[1]	Single Response	All Responses[1]
Canada	60.6	64.2	24.3	26.0	11.3	13.8
Newfoundland	98.6	99.0	0.4	0.6	0.7	0.9
Prince Edward Island	93.6	94.9	4.1	5.1	1.1	1.3
Nova Scotia	93.2	94.6	3.5	4.5	1.8	2.3
New Brunswick	63.6	67.1	31.8	35.1	1.1	1.4
Quebec	8.9	12.1	81.4	84.6	6.0	7.4
Ontario	76.3	80.3	4.7	6.0	14.9	17.9
Manitoba	71.3	77.0	4.3	5.4	18.6	23.3
Saskatchewan	80.7	84.7	2.1	2.6	13.1	16.7
Alberta	80.9	84.6	2.0	2.7	13.3	16.4
British Columbia	80.9	84.1	1.3	1.9	14.4	17.4
Yukon	88.2	90.2	2.4	2.9	7.4	9.0
Northwest Territories	53.6	57.0	2.5	3.0	40.5	43.5

1 Includes single and multiple responses to the mother tongue question.

Proportion of French mother tongue population declined slightly

There was a slight decline in the relative size of the francophone community in Quebec, primarily due to the increased number of immigrants settling in Quebec. In 1991, 81.2% of Quebec's population reported French as only mother tongue, down slightly from 81.4% in 1986. In keeping with the reduced number of multiple responses to the mother tongue question, there was a larger decline in the proportion of all those who reported French as mother tongue: from 84.6% in 1986 to 83.3% in 1991. Outside Quebec, the proportion of the population who reported French as only mother tongue declined slightly between 1986 and 1991, from 4.5% to 4.4% (5.6% reported French as mother tongue in 1986, compared to 5.2% in 1991).

Across the country, about 6.5 million people, or 23.8% of population, reported French as only mother

Population with French as Mother Tongue[1]

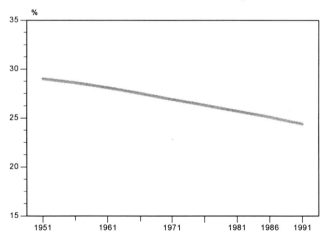

1 For 1986 and 1991, multiple responses were distributed among the language indicated using a method which makes the data approximately comparable to those of the previous censuses.

tongue in 1991, down from 24.3% in 1986. When those people who reported French and at least one other language as mother tongue were included, the size of the francophone language group was 24.9% of Canada's total population in 1991, compared with 26% in 1986. The relative size of the francophone community had been gradually declining since 1951 when 29% of the population reported French as mother tongue.

This long-term decline was primarily attributable to the low fertility of francophones since the mid-1960s and immigration to Canada of people with a mother tongue other than French.

The size of the francophone population, as a proportion of the provincial/territorial population, varied considerably across Canada. quebec had the largest proportion of its population with French as mother tongue (83.3% reporting French, 81.2% French only), followed by New Brunswick (34.6% reporting French, 32.7% French only). The francophone population was less than 6% of the population in all other provinces and territories: Ontario was highest (5.4%) and Newfoundland, lowest (less than 1%).

Population with a Non-official Language as Mother Tongue, 1991[1]

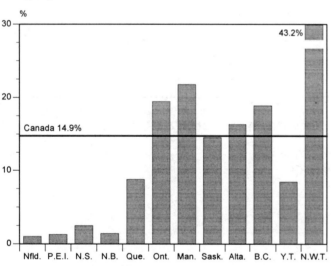

1 Includes single and multiple responses to the mother tongue question.

Canada's francophone population continued to be highly concentrated in Quebec. In 1991, as in 1986, about 85% of all francophones lived in Quebec. By comparison, only 4% of all anglophones lived in Quebec. Of the provinces and territories other than Quebec, Ontario and New Brunswick had the largest number of people reporting French as mother tongue: 547,000 in Ontario and 250,000 in New Brunswick. These two provinces accounted for three-quarters (75.7%) of all francophones outside Quebec.

Non-official languages in the provinces and territories

In 1991, the population reporting a non-official language as mother tongue was concentrated in four provinces: 49% were living in Ontario, 15% in British Columbia, 15% in Quebec and 10% in Alberta.

Of all provinces and territories, the Northwest Territories had the highest percentage of its population (43%) reporting a language other than English or French as mother tongue with the majority of this group reporting Inuktitut. Manitoba, with 22%, had the second largest proportion, followed by Ontario (20%), British Columbia (19%), Alberta (16%) and Saskatchewan (15%).

The proportion of the population reporting a non-official language as mother tongue was less than 10% in each of the other provinces and the Yukon, ranging from 9% in Quebec to 1% in Newfoundland. The smaller proportions in Newfoundland, Prince Edward Island, Nova Scotia and New Brunswick were due mainly to the tendency of immigrants to settle in other areas of the country.

The distribution of the major non-official language groups across the country tended to reflect the changing origins and destinations of different waves of immigrants. As a result, the major non-official language groups varied considerably in their concentration by province. The Italian language group was concentrated in central Canada: 63% of those reporting Italian as mother tongue in 1991 lived in Ontario and 27% lived in Quebec. Ontario was also home to 46% of the Chinese language group while an additional 31% lived in British Columbia. Over half of those reporting German as mother tongue lived in the western provinces: 15% in Manitoba, 9% in Saskatchewan, 17% in Alberta and 19% in British Columbia. Another 35% lived in Ontario.

Distribution of Non-official Language Groups, 1991[1]

	All Non-official Languages	Italian	Chinese	German	Portuguese	Polish
Canada total	**4,099,890**	**512,005**	**492,400**	**475,710**	**211,040**	**196,895**
Canada	100.0	100.0	100.0	100.0	100.0	100.0.
Newfoundland	0.1	0.0	0.2	0.1	0.1	0.1
Prince Edward Island	0.0	0.0	0.0	0.0	0.0	0.0
Nova Scotia	0.6	0.2	0.3	0.5	0.2	0.6
New Brunswick	0.2	0.1	0.2	0.3	0.1	0.1
Quebec	14.9	26.7	6.5	4.4	16.1	10.2
Ontario	48.6	63.1	46.1	34.8	70.6	62.4
Manitoba	5.9	1.1	1.9	14.7	3.6	6.7
Saskatchewan	3.5	0.2	1.3	9.1	0.2	2.3
Alberta	10.2	2.8	12.2	17.1	2.9	10.7
British Columbia	15.3	5.8	31.1	18.9	6.2	7.1
Yukon	0.1	0.0	0.0	0.1	0.0	0.0
Northwest Territories	0.6	0.0	0.0	0.1	0.0	0.0

	Ukrainian	Aboriginal Languages	Spanish	Dutch	Punjabi	Greek
Canada total	**196,160**	**192,765**	**186,255**	**138,755**	**134,685**	**129,685**
Canada	100.0	100.0	100.0	100.0	100.0	100.0
Newfoundland	0.0	1.0	0.1	0.1	0.1	0.0
Prince Edward Island	0.0	0.0	0.0	0.4	0.0	0.0
Nova Scotia	0.2	2.0	0.3	1.5	0.3	0.7
New Brunswick	0.1	0.9	0.2	0.7	0.0	0.2
Quebec	3.6	14.7	30.4	2.8	2.7	35.8
Ontario	29.2	12.3	47.2	53.6	34.9	53.4
Manitoba	20.0	18.6	2.5	3.7	2.6	1.3
Saskatchewan	14.7	16.5	1.1	1.8	0.4	0.8
Alberta	23.2	14.4	8.7	14.7	8.8	2.4
British Columbia	8.9	7.1	9.3	20.3	50.1	5.3
Yukon	0.1	0.5	0.0	0.1	0.0	0.0
Northwest Territories	0.1	11.9	0.0	0.1	0.0	0.0

1 Includes single and multiple responses to the mother tongue question.

Language diversity in our metropolitan areas

There was great variation in the linguistic composition of Canada's census metropolitan areas. Some metropolitan areas had populations which were linguistically homogeneous. St. John's, Saint John and Halifax had the highest proportion of their populations reporting English as only mother tongue: 98%, 93% and 93%, respectively. Chicoutimi-Jonquière, Trois-Rivières, and Québec had the highest proportions reporting French only: 98%, 97% and 96%, respectively.

In 1991, over half (54%) of those who reported a non-official language as mother tongue were living in Toronto, Vancouver or Montréal.

Toronto had the largest percentage (32%) of its population reporting a mother tongue other than English or French. The Italian and Chinese languages were by far the most frequently reported, each representing one-sixth (about 200,000 people) of the total non-official language population.

Vancouver had the second largest proportion of its population reporting a non-official language (27%). In Vancouver, one-third of all those who reported a non-official language as mother tongue reported Chinese.

In Montréal, 70% of the population reported French as mother tongue, 17% reported English and 17% reported a non-official language. About one-quarter of those reporting a non-official language in Montréal reported Italian – the third largest language group after French and English.

Ottawa-Hull was the census metropolitan area where the linguistic composition of the population was most similar to that of Canada as a whole: 57% of the population reported English as mother tongue, 35% reported French and 12% reported a non-official language.

Population by Mother Tongue, for Census Metropolitan Areas, 1991

	% Reporting English		% Reporting French		% Reporting Non-official Language	
	Single Response	All Responses[1]	Single Response	All Responses[1]	Single Response	All Responses[1]
Calgary	81.1	83.7	1.4	1.9	14.9	17.0
Chicoutimi-Jonquière	0.9	1.5	98.0	98.7	0.3	0.4
Edmonton	77.9	80.8	2.3	3.0	16.8	19.2
Halifax	93.1	94.1	2.7	3.3	3.1	3.6
Hamilton	79.5	82.0	1.4	1.9	16.5	18.7
Kitchener	79.4	81.9	1.3	1.7	16.8	18.9
London	84.9	86.9	1.1	1.6	11.9	13.6
Montréal	14.2	17.3	66.9	70.3	14.7	17.1
Oshawa	87.3	88.9	2.1	2.6	9.0	10.2
Ottawa-Hull	53.5	56.6	32.9	35.3	10.2	11.6
Québec	1.7	2.6	95.9	97.0	1.2	1.5
Regina	87.2	89.2	1.3	1.7	9.5	11.2
Saint John	93.3	94.4	4.4	5.3	1.2	1.4
Saskatoon	84.0	86.5	1.6	2.1	11.9	14.0
Sherbrooke	6.1	7.5	90.4	92.0	1.9	2.2
St. Catharines-Niagara	80.6	83.1	3.7	4.5	13.1	15.0
St. John's	98.1	98.4	0.3	0.4	1.3	1.5
Sudbury	59.8	64.3	27.5	30.8	8.2	9.5
Thunder Bay	80.7	83.4	2.3	2.9	14.3	16.5
Toronto	66.4	70.2	1.3	1.8	28.5	32.0
Trois-Rivières	1.2	1.9	97.3	98.1	0.6	0.8
Vancouver	71.9	74.7	1.3	1.7	23.9	26.5
Victoria	88.1	89.5	1.4	1.8	9.0	10.1
Windsor	76.0	79.8	4.7	6.2	15.4	17.9
Winnipeg	73.8	77.8	4.5	5.4	17.6	20.9

[1] Includes single and multiple responses to the mother tongue question.

Youth and seniors: differences by language groups

The proportion of children aged 0 to 14 in the various language groups varied widely. Several factors contributed to this diversity: recentness of immigration to Canada, differing levels of fertility and differences in the tendency to pass on a language as mother tongue to the next generation.

Overall, children aged 0 to 14 represented 21% of the Canadian population in 1991. They represented 23% of the English language group, 20% of the French and 12% of the non-official language group. The lower percentage of the young having a non-official language as mother tongue reflected the tendency of parents having a non-official language as mother tongue to pass English or French to their children.

Among the fifteen largest non-official language groups, the Cree language group had the highest percentage (29%) of its population in the 0 to 14 age group. Punjabi (22%) and Vietnamese (22%) were followed by Spanish (21%). These last three languages were common among more recent immigrants to Canada. The size of the child population was smallest among four language groups more heavily represented in earlier periods of immigration to Canada: Dutch (2%), Ukrainian (3%), Hungarian (4%) and Italian (6%).

Changing patterns of immigration also affected the proportion of seniors (aged 65 and over) in the various language groups. Overall, 12% of Canada's population was aged 65 and over in 1991. The English and French language groups both had 11% of their populations in this group, while 15% of the non-official language group were aged 65 and over.

The proportion of seniors in specific non-official language groups varied greatly in 1991, partly due to the waves of immigrants who had come to Canada at different times. Among the fifteen largest non-official language groups, Ukrainian was the language most frequently spoken among the senior age group (42%), followed by Hungarian (25%), German (23%), Polish (22%) and Dutch (22%). The smallest proportions of seniors occurred in three language groups which had immigrated to Canada more recently: Vietnamese (4%), Spanish (4%) and Arabic (5%).

Mother Tongue, 1991[1]

		% of the Population Aged 0 - 14
Total Population		**20.9**
Official Languages		
	English	23.2
	French	19.7
Non-Official Languages		**12.1**
	Cree	28.9
	Punjabi	22.3
	Vietnamese	22.0
	Spanish	21.4
	Arabic	19.8
	Chinese	16.1
	Portuguese	14.6
	Polish	12.5
	Greek	11.3
	Tagalog	7.6
	German	7.0
	Italian	5.9
	Hungarian	4.3
	Ukrainian	2.5
	Dutch	2.2

1   Determined using the population who reported only one mother tongue. The 15 largest non-official language groups are included in this table.

Most couples formed by partners with the same mother tongue

In 1991, there were 6.4 million husband-wife couples (people who were married or living common-law) in Canada. Of these couples, the majority of partners had the same mother tongue: 3.4 million were anglophone couples, 1.4 million were francophone couples and 800,000 were couples where both partners reported a non-official language. Anglophones and francophones were more likely to form unions with people who had the same mother tongue: 92% of anglophones had a partner reporting English as mother tongue and 91% of francophones had a partner reporting French as mother tongue. In comparison, 80% of Canada's allophones (those who reported a non-official language as mother tongue) had a partner reporting a non-official language as mother tongue.

Official language minorities (i.e. francophones outside Quebec and anglophones in Quebec) often formed unions with a partner who did not have the same mother tongue. Among anglophones in Quebec, 26% had a partner with French as only mother tongue, 68% a partner with English as only mother tongue and 6% a partner with a non-official language as only mother tongue. Among francophones in New Brunswick, 13% were living with a spouse who reported English as mother tongue, while in Ontario this figure was 36%.

Nationally, 17% of allophones had a partner who reported English as mother tongue and 2% had a partner with French as mother tongue. Among allophones in Quebec, 11% had a partner with French as only mother tongue and 6% had a partner with English as only mother tongue.

Mother Tongue, 1991[1]

		% of the population Aged 65 and over
Total Population		**11.6**
Official Languages		
	English	11.0
	French	11.0
Non-Official Languages		**15.3**
	Ukrainian	42.3
	Hungarian	25.4
	German	23.3
	Polish	22.3
	Dutch	21.7
	Italian	15.5
	Chinese	9.4
	Greek	8.5
	Tagalog	7.8
	Portuguese	6.8
	Punjabi	6.8
	Cree	6.6
	Arabic	5.3
	Spanish	3.8
	Vietnamese	3.8

1   Determined using the population who reported only one mother tongue. The 15 largest non-official language groups are included in this table.

Husband-Wife Couples: Mother Tongue of Partners of Francophones, 1991

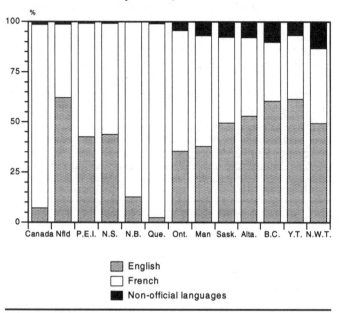

When parents have the same mother tongue

Couples where both partners had the same official language as mother tongue passed on that language to their children as the only mother tongue almost all of the time (99.7% for children of anglophone couples and 98.9% for those of francophone couples). Outside Quebec, 93% of the children of francophone couples had French as mother tongue. In Quebec, 98% of the children of anglophone couples had English as mother tongue.

Children of couples where both partners had a non-official language as mother tongue had English as the only mother tongue 33% of the time and French 1% of the time. In Quebec, 12% of the children of these couples had English as the only mother tongue and 9% French as the only mother tongue.

When parents have different mother tongues

The children of mixed language couples (where both partners reported only one mother tongue) represented 10% (551,000) of all children living in husband-wife couples. Manitoba and the Northwest Territories had the highest proportion of children living with parents from different language groups (15%), followed by the Yukon (14%) and Ontario (12%). Newfoundland (1%), Nova Scotia (6%), Prince Edward Island (6%) and Quebec (7%) all had relatively small proportions of children living with parents who had different mother tongues.

The mother tongue of children of English-French couples varied considerably by province. Children of English-French couples in Quebec had French as only mother tongue 49% of the time, English only 34% of the time and both languages 17% of the time. In Ontario, these children had English as only mother tongue 75% of the time and French only 16% of the time, while in New Brunswick 65% had English only and 26% had French only.

Mother Tongue of Children of English-French Couples, 1991

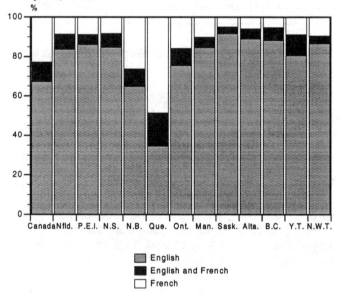

Children of couples where one of the partners had English as mother tongue and the other a non-official language learned English as mother tongue in the vast majority of cases (96%). Children of francophone and allophone partners in Quebec had French as only mother tongue 75% of the time, English 10% of the time and a non-official language as only mother tongue 6% of the time.

Mother's mother tongue most common

Other things being equal, the children of mixed-language couples were more likely to learn the language of their mother rather than that of their father. Thus, the children of English-French couples showed a greater tendency to have French as mother tongue when the wife was French than when the husband was French. For example, in Quebec, the children of francophone women and anglophone men indicated French as only mother tongue 58% of the time, English 24% of the time and both languages 18% of the time. By contrast, children of anglophone women and francophone men indicated English as only mother tongue 44% of the time, French 40% of the time and both languages 16% of the time. A similar phenomenon was found for other mixed-language couples.

Mother Tongue of Children Under 18 Years of Age Living in Husband-wife Families, 1991

Mother Tongue of Child:	Mother Tongue of Husband:	Mother Tongue of Wife:								
		English			French			Non-official Language		
		English	French	Non-Official	English	French	Non-Official	English	French	Non-Official
Canada										
English only		100	75	97	59	1	28	94	39	33
English-all responses		100	83	98	71	1	34	96	45	40
French only		0	17	0	29	99	60	0	41	1
French-all responses		0	25	0	41	99	69	0	50	2
Non-official only		0	0	1	0	0	3	4	10	59
Non-official-all responses		0	0	2	0	0	7	6	15	65
Quebec										
English only		98	44	91	24	0	7	83	14	12
English-all responses		99	60	95	42	0	12	88	19	15
French only		1	40	2	58	100	81	3	63	9
French-all responses		2	56	4	76	100	89	4	73	13
Non-official only		0	0	3	0	0	4	9	12	74
Non-official-all responses		0	0	6	0	0	8	13	19	79
Other provinces and territories										
English only		100	86	98	72	6	65	94	75	37
English-all responses		100	92	99	81	7	74	96	81	44
French only		0	8	0	19	93	23	0	11	0
French-all responses		0	14	0	28	94	32	0	17	0
Non-official only		0	0	1	0	0	3	4	7	56
Non-official-all responses		0	0	2	0	0	5	6	11	63

Catalogue 11-001E (Français 11-001F) ISSN 0827-0465

The Daily
Statistics Canada

Tuesday, December 8, 1992

IMMIGRATION AND CITIZENSHIP

HIGHLIGHTS

● Canada's immigrants: their population share remained stable

● Ontario continued to attract the majority of immigrants

● The majority of immigrants were born in Europe, but the picture is changing

● More immigrants chose to obtain citizenship

● Non-permanent residents were counted for the first time

Immigration and Citizenship

Immigration and Citizenship (93-316, $40) provides data from the 1991 Census on citizenship, period of immigration, age at immigration, and the immigrant and non-immigrant populations by place of birth. Data on non-permanent residents are also included.

The data are shown for Canada, provinces and territories. Three of the nine tables also present data for census metropolitan areas. All data are cross-classified by sex. One table provides a comparison of the 1986 and 1991 place of birth data for the immigrant population.

 Statistics Statistique
Canada Canada

Canada

This release describes where people were born – both inside and outside Canada and characteristics of Canada's immigrant population, such as when they arrived in Canada, where they lived, their age, citizenship status and place of birth.

In addition to information on the total immigrant population, Statistics Canada compiled data for the first time in 1991 on non-permanent residents of Canada. These were persons who held student or employment authorizations, Minister's permits or who were refugee claimants. Information on this segment of the population is also part of this release.

Those born in Canada stayed close to home

According to the 1991 Census, 85% of persons born in Canada who still lived here resided in their province or territory of birth. This level remained virtually unchanged since the 1971 Census.

Definitions

Immigrant Population: refers to persons who are, or have been, landed immigrants in Canada. A landed immigrant is a person who is not a Canadian citizen by birth, but who has been granted the right to live in Canada permanently by Canadian immigration authorities.

Non-immigrant Population: refers to persons who are Canadian citizens by birth.

Non-permanent Residents: refers to persons who hold a student authorization, employment authorization, Minister's permit or who are refugee claimants.

In 1991, about 90% of Canadian residents born in Quebec or Ontario still lived in their province of birth. The Yukon Territory (46%) and Saskatchewan (59%) had the lowest proportions of persons born in a province or territory in which they still lived.

The proportion of Newfoundland-born who still lived in the province was 74% in 1991. This was the same percentage as in 1986, but marks a sharp decline from 80% in 1981 to 84% in 1971.

Canada's Immigrants: their population share remained stable

According to the Census, the share of the population made up of immigrants has remained relatively stable during the past several decades. There has been, however, a substantial change over the years from where immigrants have come. Because immigrants tended to settle in certain regions, their influence was felt unevenly across the country. Overall, in 1991, 4.3 million immigrants lived in Canada. They represented 16.1% of the total population, a slight increase from the 15.6% recorded in the 1986 Census. Since the 1951 Census, immigrants represented about the same proportion – 16% – of the population.

The proportion of immigrants in the total population was highest in the first half of the century. In 1901, for example, 13% of the population were immigrants. As a result of a large influx of people into the country in the early 1900s, the immigrant share of the population jumped to 22% in 1911 and stayed at that level through 1931. During World War II, the Dominion Bureau of Statistics recorded a drop in the proportion of immigrants in the total population, to 17%. The proportion of immigrants in the population remained stable since then.

Immigrant Population

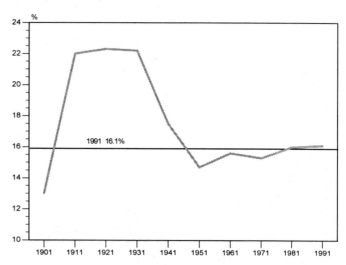

Ontario continued to attract the majority of immigrants

Over the years, immigrants tended to settle in some regions of the country more than in others. The 1991 Census found that 94% of all immigrants lived in just four provinces: Ontario, Quebec, British Columbia and Alberta. Over half of all immigrants to Canada (55%) settled in Ontario.

Immigrants represented almost 25% of the provincial populations of Ontario and British Columbia, followed by 15% in Alberta, 13% in Manitoba and 11% in the Yukon Territory. On the other hand, immigrants represented 9% of the population in Quebec, 6% in Saskatchewan and less than 5% in the Northwest Territories and in each of the four Atlantic provinces.

Immigrants chose to settle in urban areas

Immigrants were more likely than the Canadian-born population to live in large urban centres. While fewer than one-third of the total population of Canada lived in the census metropolitan areas of Toronto, Montréal or Vancouver in 1991, more than half of Canada's immigrants lived in one of these three areas. In fact, 38% or 1.5 million of the residents of the metropolitan area of Toronto were immigrants. In Vancouver, the proportion was 30% while in Montréal, 17% were immigrants.

Immigrant Population, 1991

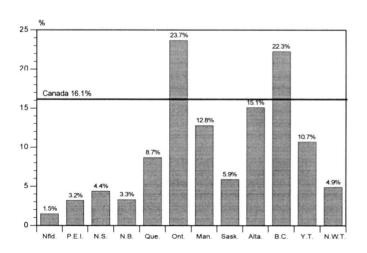

Immigrant Population in Census Metropolitan Areas, 1991

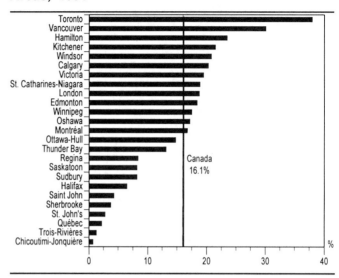

The attraction of major urban centres for immigrants was most pronounced in Quebec: although 45% of the total provincial population lived in Montréal, 88% of the province's immigrant population lived there.

In British Columbia, 66% of the immigrant population resided in Vancouver, compared with 49% of the total provincial population. A similar pattern existed in Ontario, with 62% of the immigrant population of that province living in the Toronto census metropolitan area compared with 39% of the province's total population.

Over the years, major urban centres in southern Ontario and the western provinces also attracted large numbers of immigrants. In Ontario, immigrants constituted 24% of the population in Hamilton, 22% in Kitchener, 21% in Windsor and 19% in both London and St. Catharines-Niagara. In Western Canada (other than Vancouver), Calgary and Victoria had the highest proportion of immigrants at 20% each, followed by Edmonton and Winnipeg (both at 18%) and Regina and Saskatoon (both at 8%).

On the other hand, immigrants generally made up smaller proportions of the populations of large urban areas in Quebec and the Atlantic provinces. East of Montréal, only Halifax (at 7%) had an immigrant population greater than 5%. The next largest concentration occurred in Saint John and Sherbrooke (both with 4%) and St. John's (3%).

The 1970s marked halfway point in time of arrival

Nearly half of Canada's immigrant population has lived here for more than 20 years. The proportion of immigrants was split almost evenly between those who arrived before and after the 1970s. In 1991, 48% arrived before 1971 while 24% came between 1971 and 1980 and 28% between 1981 and 1991.

The majority of immigrants were born in Europe...

Europeans still made up the largest share of immigrants living in Canada in 1991, accounting for 54% of all immigrants. This proportion declined from 62% recorded in the 1986 Census and 67% in the 1981 Census. Conversely, the percentage of the immigrant population born in Asia increased from 14% in 1981 to 18% in 1986 and to 25% in 1991. Also in 1991, 6% of all immigrants were born in the United States, 5% in the Caribbean, 5% in Central and South America, 4% in Africa and 1% in Oceania (Australia, New Zealand and the Pacific Islands).

...But the picture is changing

While the European-born were still predominant in the total 1991 immigrant population, the proportion among immigrants who had arrived since 1961 declined steadily. Immigrants born in Europe represented 90% of those immigrants who arrived before 1961. However, this proportion fell to 69% for the groups who immigrated to Canada between 1961 and 1970 to 36% for those who came during the 1971-1980 period

and to one-quarter for those who arrived between 1981 and 1991.

While the proportion of European-born immigrants declined, the share accounted for by those born in Asia and other non-European areas increased. Asian-born persons represented almost half of immigrants who came to Canada between 1981 and 1991. The European-born were the second largest group, accounting for 25% of immigrants who arrived during the same period. An additional 10% of recent immigrants were born in Central and South America, 6% in the Caribbean, 6% in Africa, 4% in the United States and 1% in Oceania (Australia, New Zealand and the Pacific Islands).

Although the proportion of Asian immigrants increased considerably among recent arrivals, Asian countries represented only three of the 10 most frequently reported places of birth for the total immigrant population. The five countries of birth reported most often by immigrants to Canada were still the United Kingdom, Italy, the United States, Poland and Germany. India was the sixth most frequently reported place of origin and was the birthplace of the greatest number of Asian immigrants. Portugal, People's Democratic Republic of China, Hong Kong and the Netherlands rounded out the top 10.

A higher proportion of older population among immigrants

The age composition of the immigrant population differed markedly from that of non-immigrants. The immigrant population was an older one because the majority of people who immigrated to Canada did so

Immigrant Population by Place of Birth and Period of Immigration

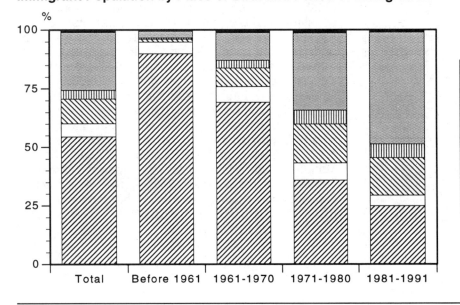
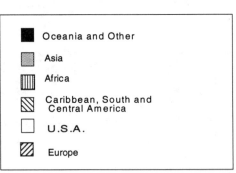

when they were young adults. Of the total immigrant population, 62% of immigrants were 20 years or older when they came to Canada compared with 11% aged 4 and under and 27% aged 5 to 19. The immigrant population was also older because children born to immigrant parents after their arrival in Canada were not counted as part of the immigrant population.

The immigrant population had both a higher proportion of older persons and a lower proportion of children than non-immigrants. In 1991, 5% of immigrants, compared with 24% of non-immigrants, were younger than 15 years. The situation was reversed at the other end of the scale with 18% of immigrants aged 65 or over, and only 10% of non-immigrants in this age group. In fact, one out of every four persons aged 65 or over in 1991 was an immigrant. The proportion of immigrants among seniors decreased slightly since the 1981 Census, when three out of every 10 persons aged 65 and over were immigrants.

In contrast, immigrants represented a smaller proportion of all persons younger than 15 years. In Canada, 4% of the population younger than age 15 were immigrants. Immigrant children aged 15 or younger represented 6% of Ontario children and 5% of children in British Columbia.

Non-immigrants and Immigrants by Age Groups, 1991

Age Groups	Non-immigrants		Immigrants	
	Number	%	Number	%
Total	22,427,745	100.0	4,342,885	100.0
0-14	5,427,645	24.2	230,825	5.3
15-24	3,380,580	15.1	402,780	9.3
25-44	7,489,570	33.4	1,590,545	36.6
45-64	3,973,650	17.7	1,352,035	31.1
65 and over	2,156,295	9.6	766,705	17.7

94% of people living in Canada are Canadian citizens

In 1991, 94% of the total population were Canadian citizens. The majority obtained their citizenship by birth while 12% were naturalized citizens. Those without Canadian citizenship represented 6% of the population in 1991. These persons were landed immigrants who were either not eligible to apply for citizenship, had chosen not to do so, or were non-permanent residents.

The Atlantic provinces had the highest proportion of Canadian citizens at 99%. The lowest proportions of people with Canadian citizenship were recorded in Ontario (91%) and British Columbia (93%).

About 2% of the total population had dual or multiple citizenship. The majority of these (57%) were Canadian citizens by naturalization who retained citizenship of the country of their birth.

More immigrants chose to obtain citizenship

Among the immigrant population, 81% of immigrants who were eligible to become Canadian citizens had done so by 1991. This proportion had increased from 79% in 1986 and 75% in 1981. Immigrants must reside in Canada for a minimum of three years before they are eligible to apply for Canadian citizenship.

Non-permanent residents counted for the first time

In addition to the total number of immigrants, the 1991 Census counted 223,410 non-permanent residents – that is, persons who held student or employment authorizations, Minister's permits or who were refugee claimants. This number represented less than 1% of the total population enumerated in the Census. (For further information, see the note on Data Comparability on page 183).

Non-permanent residents choose Ontario

Over half (56%) of all non-permanent residents enumerated in the Census lived in Ontario. Quebec had the next largest proportion (20%), followed by British Columbia (13%) and Alberta (6%). The remaining 5% lived in the other provinces and territories.

Nearly 72% of non-permanent residents lived in the three largest census metropolitan areas (Toronto, Montréal and Vancouver). Toronto had the largest concentration of non-permanent residents of any metropolitan area. In 1991, 44% of all non-permanent residents in Canada lived in Toronto, 18% in Montréal and 10% in Vancouver.

As a result, non-permanent residents represented a notable proportion of the population of these cities. Although they accounted for 0.8% of Canada's total population, the 1991 Census showed that the proportion of non-permanent residents was 2.5% in Toronto, 1.3% in Montréal and 1.4% in Vancouver.

Outside Canada's three largest cities, the distribution of non-permanent residents was diffuse. In 1991, Ottawa-Hull and Edmonton each had 3% of all non-permanent residents, Calgary and Hamilton each had 2%, and Kitchener, Winnipeg, London, Windsor and St. Catharines-Niagara each had 1%.

Non-permanent Residents, 1991

Census Metropolitain Areas	Total Population	Non-permanent Residents	% of Total Population
Canada	**26,994,045**	**223,410**	**0.8**
Toronto	3,863,110	98,105	2.5
Vancouver	1,584,120	22,345	1.4
Montréal	3,091,115	40,050	1.3
Windsor	259,290	2,220	0.9
Hamilton	593,805	4,500	0.8
Kitchener	353,110	2,680	0.8
Ottawa-Hull	912,095	7,285	0.8
Calgary	748,215	5,380	0.7
Edmonton	832,155	5,895	0.7
London	376,725	2,215	0.6
Saskatoon	207,825	1,200	0.6
Winnipeg	645,610	3,230	0.5
St. Catharines-Niagara	359,990	1,700	0.5
Victoria	283,630	1,350	0.5
Oshawa	238,030	875	0.4
Sherbrooke	136,710	475	0.3
St. John's	169,810	580	0.3
Halifax	317,630	1,060	0.3
Regina	189,445	615	0.3
Québec	637,755	1,200	0.2
Thunder Bay	122,860	240	0.2
Sudbury	156,125	210	0.1
Saint John	123,605	160	0.1
Trois-Rivières	134,890	135	0.1
Chicoutimi-Jonquière	159,600	105	0.1

The Asian-born made up largest group of non-permanent residents

Forty-four percent of enumerated non-permanent residents were born in Asia, followed by 19% in Europe, 11% in Central and South America, 9% in Africa, 8% in the United States, 7% in the Caribbean, and 2% in Oceania (Australia, New Zealand and the Pacific Islands).

The major countries of birth of non-permanent residents differed from those of recent immigrants.

For non-permanent residents, the most frequently reported birthplace was the United States, followed by the Philippines, Sri Lanka, Hong Kong and the People's Democratic Republic of China. In contrast, Hong Kong was the major country of birth of landed immigrants who came to Canada between 1981 and 1991, followed by Poland, the People's Democratic Republic of China, India and the United Kingdom. About 30% of all non-permanent residents and recent immigrants came from the top five countries.

Catalogue 11-001E (Français 11-001F) ISSN 0827-0465

The Daily

Statistics Canada

Tuesday, January 12, 1993

HOME LANGUAGE, MOTHER TONGUE, AND KNOWLEDGE OF LANGUAGES

HIGHLIGHTS

- Increased numbers of Canadians spoke a language other than English or French at home

- Little change in the proportion with English home language

- The number of people having French as home language increased, but their proportion of the total population continued to decline

- English-French bilingualism increased in almost every province

- Language shift among official language minorities increased

- In Quebec, language shifts were turning more toward French than in the past

---

Home Language and Mother Tongue
Knowledge of Languages

Home Language and Mother Tongue (93-317, $40) and *Knowledge of Languages* (93-318, $40) are based on data collected from a 20% sample of households for the 1991 Census of Canada and provide information on languages spoken most often at home, mother tongue, and knowledge of languages.

Each publication presents tables with data for Canada, provinces, territories and, in some cases, census metropolitan areas. Together, they provide a wealth of information on English, French and non-official languages in Canada.

 Statistics   Statistique
Canada   Canada

Canada

This release provides information on home language, mother tongue and knowledge of languages to add to our new portrait of Canada and Canadians.

Increased numbers of Canadians spoke a language other than English or French at home

The number of people whose home language (the language spoken most often at home) was other than English or French was 2.3 million in 1991 (8.4% of the population), compared to 1.9 million in 1986 (7.5% of the population).

The higher proportion in 1991 was due primarily to the increased number of recent immigrants whose home language was neither English nor French and to the inclusion, for the first time in the 1991 Census, of non-permanent residents. However, if non-permanent residents were excluded from the comparison, the proportion of the population reporting home language other than English or French would move from 7.5% in 1986 to 8.0% in 1991. The increase was confined to the four provinces which received the most immigrants: Ontario, British Columbia, Quebec and Alberta.

Between 1971 and 1991, the ranking of the top home languages other than English or French changed considerably. In 1971, the top three home languages were Italian (spoken by 425,000 people), German (213,000) and Ukrainian (145,000). By 1991, Chinese (430,000) had moved from fifth to first place. Italian, the home language of 288,000, dropped from first to second place, while Portuguese (153,000) rose from sixth place in 1971 to third place in 1991. Considerably fewer people had Ukrainian as home language (50,000) in 1991 and it slipped to twelfth place in ranking.

Comparison of 1971 and 1991 Census data shows that the number of people who spoke an aboriginal language as home language was essentially the same in 1971 (137,000 people) as in 1991 (138,000). It should be noted, however, that incomplete enumeration of some Indian reserves in 1991 may have resulted in under-reporting of the number of people speaking an aboriginal language at home. (For further information, see the note on Data Comparability on page 183).

Both international immigration and language shifts to English or French as the language used most often at home affect the number of people reporting home languages other than English or French. Rapid growth in a language group occurs when its members immigrate in large numbers. The rate of increase declines, however, as shifts to English or French become more common, even if immigration remains high. Finally, when immigration slows down, the number reporting a given home language declines because of little transfer from one generation to the next. In terms of home language, the Chinese, Spanish and Punjabi groups, among others, are in the growing phase, while those speaking Italian, German and Ukrainian at home are declining.

Languages other than English or French were reported less frequently as home language than as mother tongue. In 1991, the number of people with Chinese home language (430,000) was significantly smaller than the population whose mother tongue was Chinese (517,000). The contrast was much more marked for German: 134,000 with German home language compared to 491,000 with German as mother tongue.

Mother Tongue and Home Language

Mother tongue is defined as the first language a person learned at home in childhood and still understands at the time of the census. Home language means the language most often spoken at home during the period immediately preceding the census. Both concepts refer to language practices within the family, the first in childhood, the second at the time data are collected.

When people report that they most often speak a language other than their mother tongue at home, this does not necessarily mean that they never speak their mother tongue at home. They may speak it within the family, but less often than another language.

Mother Tongue and Home Language Other than English or French

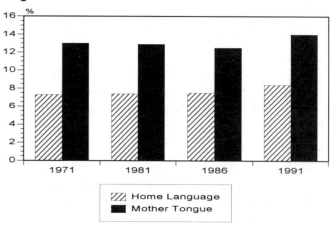

Home Language
Mother Tongue

Ten Main Home Languages Other than English or French

1971				1991		
Home Language	Number	%		Home Language	Number	%
Italian	425,230	2.0		Chinese	430,090	1.6
German	213,350	1.0		Italian	288,290	1.1
Ukrainian	144,755	0.7		Portuguese	152,530	0.6
Greek	86,830	0.4		Spanish	145,050	0.5
Chinese	77,895	0.4		German	134,460	0.5
Portuguese	74,765	0.3		Punjabi	123,775	0.5
Polish	70,960	0.3		Polish	117,150	0.4
Magyar (Hungarian)	50,675	0.2		Greek	93,160	0.3
Dutch	36,170	0.2		Arabic	82,450	0.3
Yiddish	26,330	0.1		Vietnamese	79,585	0.3

Note: In 1991, single and multiple responses were combined. See note on single and multiple responses on page 45.

Home Language, 1991

Home language		Canada		Quebec		Other Provinces and Territories	
		Number (in thousands)	%	Number (in thousands)	%	Number (in thousands)	%
Total	1991	26,994	100	6,810	100	20,184	100
	1991 a	26,771	100	6,766	100	20,004	100
	1986	25,022	100	6,455	100	18,568	100
	1981	24,083	100	6,369	100	17,714	100
	1971	21,568	100	6,028	100	15,541	100
English	1991	18,439	68.3	759	11.1	17,680	87.6
	1991 a	18,348	68.5	750	11.1	17,598	88.0
	1986	17,122	68.4	763	11.8	16,359	88.1
	1981	16,355	67.9	784	12.3	15,571	87.9
	1971	14,446	67.0	888	14.7	13,558	87.2
French	1991	6,290	23.3	5,655	83.0	635	3.1
	1991 a	6,280	23.5	5,646	83.4	634	3.2
	1986	6,032	24.1	5,364	83.1	668	3.6
	1981	5,940	24.7	5,276	82.8	664	3.7
	1971	5,546	25.7	4,870	80.8	676	4.3
Other Languages	1991	2,265	8.4	397	5.8	1,868	9.3
	1991 a	2,143	8.0	371	5.5	1,772	8.9
	1986	1,868	7.5	328	5.1	1,540	8.3
	1981	1,788	7.4	309	4.9	1,479	8.3
	1971	1,576	7.3	270	4.5	1,306	8.4

Note: Except for 1971, data were reconciled (see note on data reconciliation below) and multiple responses were equally divided between the languages reported.

1991 a   Non-permanent residents are excluded to facilitate comparison with earlier years.

Data Reconciliation

In the census, as in most large surveys, a small proportion of respondents provide inconsistent data. In almost every case, these data are corrected when the file is edited. In some cases, because of the sensitive or complex nature of the variable, the reported information is not changed and analysts are left to decide whether or not to make a correction.

For example, in the 1986 Census, of the 73,000 people in Quebec who reported French as their mother tongue and English as their home language, 26,000 stated that they could conduct a conversation in French but not in English. At the same time, elsewhere in the country, of the 16,000 people who reported English as their mother tongue and French as their home language, 6,000 stated that they could conduct a conversation in English but not in French. These inconsistent situations also occurred, but somewhat less frequently, in the 1981 Census.

Due to improved questionnaire design, the number of inconsistent cases is much smaller in the 1991 Census. Thus, in Quebec, of the 58,000 people who reported French as their mother tongue and English as their home language, only 3,000 also stated that they could conduct a conversation in French but not in English. A reduction can be observed in the total number of inconsistent situations of this type, both in Quebec and elsewhere in the country.

In order to improve the comparability of data from the last three censuses, home language was amended for this release in every inconsistent case by accepting the statement about knowledge of official languages. These corrections pertained only to English and French as home languages. After multiple responses have been distributed equally between the languages reported, the proportion represented by French as home language in Quebec is identical before and after reconciliation in 1991 (83%), because of the small number of inconsistent cases. The change is more marked in 1981 (82.5% before and 82.8% after reconciliation) and in 1986 (82.7% before, 83.1% after).

Little change in the proportion with English home language

The number of people who used English as home language rose from 17.1 million in 1986 to 18.4 million in 1991, which corresponded to a slight decrease in its proportion in the population (from 68.4% in 1986 to 68.3% in 1991). If non-permanent residents were excluded from the comparison, the proportion speaking English most often at home increased slightly (from 68.4% in 1986 to 68.5% in 1991). This

increase was smaller due to higher immigration during the most recent five-year period, than the increases observed since 1971, when a question on language most often spoken at home was first asked for the Census.

Between 1986 and 1991, Quebec experienced a slight decrease in the number of people whose home language was English (763,000 or 11.8% of the population in 1986, compared to 759,000 or 11.1% in 1991). This followed much more marked declines in the previous 15 years, when 888,000 people (14.7% of the population) reported English home language in 1971, falling to 784,000 (12.3%) in 1981 and to 763,000 (11.8%) in 1986.

In the rest of the country, the number of people with English home language continued to increase, even though the proportion declined from 88.1% in 1986 to 87.6% in 1991. This decrease, however, was due primarily to the inclusion of non-permanent residents in 1991. If they were excluded from the comparison, the 1991 proportion (88%) was only slightly below that of 1986 (88.1%).

Between 1981 and 1991, the proportion of people with English home language decreased in Ontario and British Columbia (because of high immigration to those provinces), and in Quebec. It rose or remained the same in the other provinces and territories.

English as Home Language

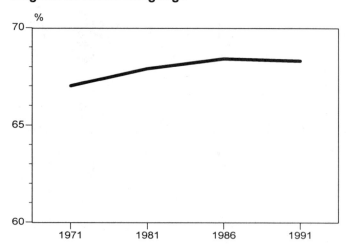

Home Language

		Total		English		French		Other Languages	
		Number (in thousands)	%	Number (in thousands)	%	Number (in thousands)	%	Number (in thousands)	%
Canada	1981	24,083	100	16,355	67.9	5,940	24.7	1,788	7.4
	1991	26,994	100	18,439	68.3	6,290	23.3	2,265	8.4
Newfoundland	1981	564	100	560	99.3	1	0.3	3	0.4
	1991	564	100	560	99.2	1	0.2	3	0.5
Prince Edward Island	1981	121	100	117	96.6	4	3.1	0	0.4
	1991	128	100	125	97.3	3	2.4	0	0.3
Nova Scotia	1981	840	100	807	96.1	24	2.9	9	1.1
	1991	891	100	858	96.3	22	2.5	11	1.2
New Brunswick	1981	689	100	468	67.9	217	31.5	5	0.7
	1991	716	100	489	68.2	223	31.2	5	0.7
Quebec	1981	6,369	100	784	12.3	5,276	82.8	309	4.9
	1991	6,810	100	759	11.1	5,655	83.0	397	5.8
Ontario	1981	8,534	100	7,311	85.7	332	3.9	891	10.4
	1991	9,977	100	8,500	85.2	318	3.2	1,159	11.6
Manitoba	1981	1,014	100	868	85.7	31	3.1	114	11.3
	1991	1,079	100	947	87.7	25	2.3	107	9.9
Saskatchewan	1981	956	100	885	92.5	10	1.1	61	6.4
	1991	976	100	921	94.4	7	0.7	48	4.9
Alberta	1981	2,214	100	2,025	91.5	29	1.3	160	7.2
	1991	2,519	100	2,305	91.5	20	0.8	194	7.7
British Columbia	1981	2,714	100	2,480	91.4	15	0.5	219	8.1
	1991	3,248	100	2,910	89.6	15	0.4	323	9.9
Yukon	1981	23	100	22	95.7	0	1.0	1	3.3
	1991	28	100	27	96.7	0	1.4	1	1.9
Northwest Territories	1981	46	100	29	63.0	1	1.4	16	35.7
	1991	57	100	38	66.8	1	1.6	18	32.0

Note: Data were reconciled and multiple responses were equally divided between the languages reported. See note on Data Reconciliation on page 44.

Single and Multiple Responses

Beginning with the 1986 Census, the questionnaire provided respondents with the opportunity to report more than one language in answer to the questions on mother tongue and language spoken most often at home. In 1991, most respondents (98.8%) reported only one mother tongue, while 1.2% reported more than one. The proportion of multiple responses was slightly higher for the question on home language (1.8%). In 1986, multiple responses were much more common for both mother tongue (3.4%) and home language (4.6%). In 1981, even though the questions stated explicitly that only one language should be given, the proportion of multiple responses (2.2% for both questions) was slightly higher than in 1991.

It would not be appropriate, except under special circumstances, to take only single responses into consideration in order to trace the evolution from 1986 to 1991 of the number or proportion in a particular language group. The size reported in 1991 would be overestimated in relation to that taken from 1986 Census data, because there were a larger proportion of single responses in 1991 than in 1986. On the other hand, if every mention of the language group under consideration (single and multiple responses) is taken together, the results of the 1991 Census in comparison to the 1986 Census would underestimate the size of the group. To be strictly accurate, both methods should be used at the same time.

To simplify the presentation of the change for home language groups, an intermediate method was used, based on equal distribution over the past three censuses, of multiple responses among the languages reported. Although it is acceptable for comparing the 1981 and 1991 censuses, it does not always ensure a high level of comparability with the 1986 Census, because of the much higher proportion of multiple responses in 1986.

The number of people having French as home language increased, but their proportion of the total population continued to decline

The population having French home language increased by 4.3%, from 6 million to 6.3 million between 1986 and 1991. However, the proportion of the population using French as home language continued to decline, from 24.1% in 1986 to 23.3% in 1991 (23.5% if non-permanent residents were excluded).

The proportion with French home language in Quebec declined from 83.1% (5.4 million) in 1986, to 83% (5.7 million) in 1991, due to the inclusion of non-permanent residents in the 1991 Census. If they were excluded from the comparison, the proportion with French as home language increased from 83.1% to 83.4%.

Outside Quebec, the population using French home language declined from 664,000 in 1981 to 635,000 in 1991, representing a drop of 4.3% over ten years. The relative size of this group decreased to 3.1% in 1991 (3.2% if non-permanent residents were excluded). The population with French as home language and the proportion it represented declined in most provinces. However, in New Brunswick, the number of people using French as home language rose from 217,000 in 1981 to 223,000 in 1991.

Large urban centres showed greater language diversity

The highest proportions of people who had home language other than English or French were found in Toronto (21%) and Vancouver (16%). In those two centres, English was the leading home language (78% and 83%, respectively), while less than 1% of the population had French as their home language. Ottawa-Hull and Sudbury were characterized by the predominance of English as home language (62% and 76%, respectively), a sizeable minority using French as home language (31% and 21%) and a relatively small proportion with home languages other than English or French (7% and 3%). French predominated as home language in Montréal (69%), a strong minority had English as home language (19%) and a significant proportion had home language other than English or French (11%).

Other metropolitan areas showed less language diversity. In four of them, all in Quebec, the proportion of people using French as home language was 92% or greater in 1991, while the proportion using English as home language was below 7%. In the other 16 metropolitan areas, 88% or more used English as home language, with the proportion using French was below 3%.

French as Home Language, Quebec

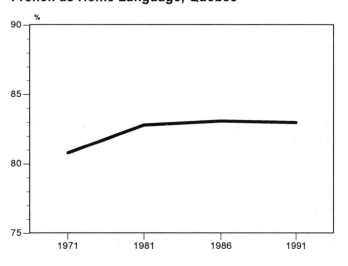

Knowledge of Languages

In the Census, knowledge of English and/or French was determined by a question about the ability to conduct a conversation in one or both official languages. A second question, asked for the first time in 1991, dealt with the ability to conduct a conversation in languages other than English or French. Respondents themselves assessed the threshold above which they reported they could conduct a conversation in a language.

Home Language by Census Metropolitan Areas, 1991

	Total		English		French		Other Languages	
	Number (in thousands)	%	Number (in thousands)	%	Number (in thousands)	%	Number (in thousands)	%
Calgary	748	100	677	90.4	4	0.5	68	9.1
Chicoutimi-Jonquière	160	100	2	1.0	158	98.8	0	0.2
Edmonton	832	100	748	89.9	7	0.9	77	9.3
Halifax	318	100	309	97.2	3	1.1	6	1.8
Hamilton	594	100	533	89.8	3	0.6	57	9.6
Kitchener	353	100	315	89.1	2	0.5	37	10.4
London	377	100	349	92.6	1	0.3	26	7.0
Montréal	3,091	100	596	19.3	2,144	69.4	351	11.3
Oshawa	238	100	226	94.8	2	1.0	10	4.2
Ottawa-Hull	912	100	569	62.4	281	30.8	62	6.8
Québec	638	100	10	1.6	623	97.6	5	0.7
Regina	189	100	182	96.2	1	0.5	6	3.3
Saint John	124	100	121	97.6	2	1.8	1	0.6
Saskatoon	208	100	197	95.0	1	0.6	9	4.4
Sherbrooke	137	100	9	6.4	126	92.3	2	1.4
St. Catharines - Niagara	360	100	333	92.4	7	1.9	21	5.8
St. John's	170	100	168	99.2	0	0.1	1	0.7
Sudbury	156	100	119	76.1	32	20.5	5	3.4
Thunder Bay	123	100	114	92.8	1	1.1	7	6.1
Toronto	3,863	100	3,021	78.2	22	0.6	820	21.2
Trois Rivières	135	100	1	1.0	133	98.6	0	0.4
Vancouver	1,584	100	1,319	83.3	7	0.4	258	16.3
Victoria	284	100	271	95.7	1	0.5	11	3.8
Windsor	259	100	229	88.2	5	1.8	26	10.1
Winnipeg	646	100	571	88.4	15	2.4	60	9.2

Note: Data were not reconciled but multiple responses were divided equally between the languages reported.

Nearly all Canadians could speak their mother tongue

In 1991, 83% of the population could conduct a conversation in English (22.5 million people), 32% in French (8.5 million) and 18% in a language other than English or French (5 million). The most frequently known non-official languages were: Italian (702,000 people or 2.6% of the population), German (685,000 or 2.5%), Chinese (557,000 or 2.1%) and Spanish (402,000 or 1.5%).

Even when another language was used more frequently at home than the mother tongue, mother tongue could nearly always still be spoken. Such was the case for those having French mother tongue (99.9% in Quebec and 96.5% in the rest of the country). Of those with mother tongue other than English or French, 96.9% reported that they could conduct a conversation in at least one non-official language, usually their mother tongue.

Other than English and French, Spanish was the most frequently acquired second language. It was estimated that some 214,000 people could speak Spanish as a second language in 1991. That figure was the difference between the number of people able to speak Spanish (402,000) and the population having Spanish as mother tongue (188,000).

Relatively few people whose mother tongue was English or French knew other languages

Of those whose mother tongue was English or French, 3.9% reported they could conduct a conversation in a non-official language. This proportion was higher among the population with English mother tongue (4.5%) than among those with French mother tongue (2.6%). This difference stems from the higher percentage of people with English mother tongue who grew up in families in which a second language (other than French) was spoken.

The rate of English-French bilingualism increased in almost every province

In 1991, 67.1% of the population reported an ability to speak English but not French (18.1 million people), 15.2% spoke French but not English (4.1 million people), 16.3% spoke both official languages (4.4 million) and 1.4% (378,000) were unable to speak either English or French. Quebec was still the province with the highest rate of bilingualism (35.4%), followed by New Brunswick (29.5%) and Ontario (11.4%).

Twenty Most Common Languages, 1991

Language	Ability To Speak	%	Mother Tongue*	%	Home Language*	%
English	22,505,420	83.4	16,454,515	61.0	18,664,635	69.1
French	8,508,955	31.5	6,623,235	24.5	6,369,360	23.6
Non-Official Languages	4,981,605	18.5	4,229,405	15.8	2,449,440	9.1
Italian	701,910	2.6	538,690	2.0	288,290	1.1
German	684,950	2.5	490,650	1.8	134,460	0.5
Chinese	557,300	2.1	516,875	1.9	430,090	1.6
Spanish	402,435	1.5	187,615	0.7	145,045	0.5
Portuguese	254,465	0.9	220,630	0.8	152,530	0.6
Ukrainian	249,535	0.9	201,315	0.7	49,995	0.2
Polish	239,580	0.9	200,395	0.7	117,150	0.4
Dutch	173,290	0.6	146,420	0.5	19,915	0.1
Punjabi	167,930	0.6	147,265	0.5	123,775	0.5
Arabic	164,380	0.6	119,255	0.4	82,450	0.3
Greek	161,325	0.6	132,980	0.5	93,160	0.3
Tagalog	136,975	0.5	115,980	0.4	75,390	0.3
Vietnamese	113,115	0.4	83,630	0.3	79,585	0.3
Hindi	111,965	0.4	40,575	0.2	26,285	0.1
Hungarian	97,410	0.4	83,915	0.3	31,175	0.1
Cree	93,825	0.3	82,070	0.3	60,855	0.2
Russian	84,055	0.3	38,030	0.1	17,165	0.1
Gujarati	54,210	0.2	42,175	0.2	29,030	0.1

*   *Includes single and multiple responses. See note on single and multiple responses on page 45.*

English-French Bilingualism Rate

	1971 %	1981 %	1986 %	1991 %
Canada	**13.4**	**15.3**	**16.2**	**16.3**
Newfoundland	1.8	2.3	2.6	3.3
Prince Edward Island	8.2	8.1	9.4	10.1
Nova Scotia	6.7	7.4	8.1	8.6
New Brunswick	21.4	26.5	29.1	29.5
Quebec	27.6	32.4	34.5	35.4
Ontario	9.3	10.8	11.7	11.4
Manitoba	8.2	7.9	8.8	9.2
Saskatchewan	5.0	4.6	4.7	5.2
Alberta	5.0	6.4	6.4	6.6
British Columbia	4.6	5.7	6.2	6.4
Yukon	6.6	7.9	8.6	9.3
Northwest Territories	6.1	6.1	6.7	6.1

While nationally the increase in bilingualism from 1986 (16.2%) to 1991 (16.3%) was very slight, a significant rise was observed in every province except Ontario. There, the rate fell from 11.7% in 1986 to 11.4% in 1991. This decrease was due to high immigration during the period and to the inclusion of non-permanent residents in the 1991 data. The decline in bilingualism among those whose mother tongue was neither English nor French (6.3% in 1991, compared to 7.1% in 1986) outweighed the combined effects of the increases which occurred in the population having English as mother tongue (7.5% in 1991, compared to 7.2% in 1986) and among those having French as mother tongue (86.7% in 1991, compared to 84.6% in 1986).

In Quebec, the rise in bilingualism was accompanied by an increase in the percentage of the population reporting the ability to speak English (from 40.2% in 1986 to 40.9% in 1991). The percent of the population with French mother tongue able to speak English rose from 29.7% in 1986 to 31.4% in 1991, and offset the decrease in the proportion able to speak English among the population having mother tongue other than English or French (67.5% in 1991, compared to 69.8% in 1986). The percent of the Quebec population who spoke French changed little between 1986 (93.5%) and 1991 (93.6%), despite the increase observed in the population having neither English nor French mother tongue (68.3% in 1991, as compared to 66.4% in 1986).

Language shift among official language minorities increased

In 1991, 6.1% of people whose mother tongue was French spoke a language (almost always English) other than French most often at home. The rate of language shift from French mother tongue was higher than in 1981 (5.1%). The increase, although slight in Quebec (1.2% in 1991, compared to 1.1% in 1981), was more pronounced outside Quebec, where the language shift from French rose from 29% in 1981 to 35% in 1991. The pattern was the same in every province. It is possible, however, that part of this increase was due to an improvement in the census language questions. (For further information, see the note on Content Considerations on page 50.)

In Newfoundland and the western provinces, the majority of the population having French as mother tongue used English more often than French at home. Outside Quebec, New Brunswick had the lowest language shift from French mother tongue (10%), followed by Ontario (37%).

In Quebec, the language shift from English mother tongue also increased, from 7% in 1981 to 10% in 1991. Language shifts from English as mother tongue to French as home language (54,000) were of similar magnitude as shifts in the opposite direction from French to English (55,000).

Rate of Language Shift by Mother Tongue

Mother Tongue		Canada	Quebec	Other Provinces and Territories
English	1981	0.8	7.3	0.5
	1991	0.7	9.8	0.4
French	1981	5.1	1.1	28.5
	1991	6.1	1.2	35.1
Other	1981	43.8	29.8	46.0
	1991	43.8	33.1	45.6

Note: The rates were calculated with reconciled data. See note on Data Reconciliation on page 44.

Language shift from languages other than English or French were less extensive in Quebec than elsewhere in the country

Nationally, the rate of language shift for the population with mother tongue other than English or French remained unchanged at 44% from 1981 to 1991. In Quebec, the rate increased to 33% in 1991 (compared to 30% in 1981), a level still well below the combined rate for the other provinces and territories (46%).

The rate of language shift varied from one language group to another depending largely on the length of time spent in Canada. Among groups in which immigration had slowed down in recent decades, language shift was often high: 87% for those with Dutch mother tongue, 76% Ukrainian mother tongue and 73% German mother tongue. Conversely,

Rate of Language Shift for French Mother Tongue, 1991

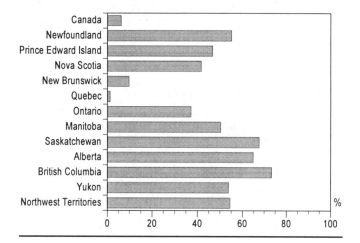

Rate of Language Shift, Main Mother Tongue Groups Other than English or French, Canada, 1991

Mother Tongue	Rate of Language Shift (%)
Italian	48.0
Chinese	18.5
German	72.7
Portuguese	32.8
Polish	40.9
Ukrainian	75.5
Spanish	26.4
Dutch	86.8
Punjabi	17.9
Greek	31.5
Arabic	33.8
Tagalog	41.8

groups experiencing high immigration usually had lower language shift: 18% for Punjabi, 19% for Chinese and 26% for Spanish.

In Quebec, language shifts were turning more toward French than in the past

In Quebec in 1991, 63% of language shifts by those having mother tongue other than English or French were directed toward English and 37% toward French. The French share was 29% in 1986 and 28% in 1981.

The French share of language shifts varied from group to group. It was over 50% in some groups whose growth, fed by immigration, began in the last 15 or 20 years; these included those whose mother tongue was one of the Creole languages (97%), Vietnamese (88%), Spanish (72%), Arabic (70%) and Portuguese (57%).

Orientation Towards English or French of the Ten Largest Mother Tongue Groups Other than English or French, Quebec, 1991

Mother Tongue	English (%)	French (%)
Italian	73	27
Spanish	28	72
Arabic	30	70
Greek	90	10
Portuguese	43	57
Chinese	79	21
Creole Languages	3	97
German	81	19
Polish	79	21
Vietnamese	12	88

Content Considerations

Changes in Data Collection: Two significant changes were made to the 1991 Census long-form questionnaire (completed by a 20% sample of households) in order to better portray the language situation in Canada. The first was the addition of a new question on knowledge of languages other than English or French. The second - and more significant - was to group all the language questions together and change the order so that questions on home language and mother tongue followed the two questions on language knowledge.

The second change was implemented following testing which showed that grouping the questions resulted in an improvement in respondents' comprehension of the questions and therefore improved accuracy in reported information. The 1991 Census results clearly show that when mother tongue is asked as one of a series of language questions, there are significantly fewer multiple responses (3% gave multiple responses when the question on mother tongue was asked alone, compared to 1.2% when the question was part of a series).

The data in this release are taken from the long- form questionnaire. A substantial decrease took place in the number and proportion of multiple responses to both the home language and mother tongue questions between 1986 and 1991, largely due to the changes described above. Although the changes provide more and better information, they make the task of comparing mother tongue and home language results from these two censuses more complex.

Exclusion of Institutional Residents: The analysis is based on data collected from a sample of 20% of households which completed the long-form questionnaire. As with the 1986 and 1981 Censuses, the data do not include institutional residents. The total number after weighting (26,994,000) is slightly smaller than the 100% data (27,297,000).

Catalogue 11-001E (Français 11-001F) ISSN 0827-0465

The Daily

Statistics Canada

Tuesday, February 23, 1993

ETHNIC ORIGIN AND OCCUPIED PRIVATE DWELLINGS

HIGHLIGHTS

- Nearly one-in-three respondents reported an ethnic background other than British or French

- Three-quarters of Quebec's population reported French only origins

- Ontario: a diversity of ethnic groups

- One-in-nine British Columbia residents were of Asian origins

- Half of all occupied dwellings in Canada were built after 1970

Ethnic Origin
Occupied Private Dwellings

Ethnic Origin (93-315, $40) presents information on ethnic ancestry from the 1991 Census for Canada, provinces and territories and, in some cases, census metropolitan areas. A list showing the ethnic origins collected in the 1991, 1986 and 1981 Censuses is included.

Occupied Private Dwellings (93-314, $40) provides data on dwelling characteristics based on a 20% sample of households from the 1991 Census. Data are shown for Canada, provinces and territories, and census metropolitan areas. Selected household variables are also presented and cross-referenced.

 Statistics   Statistique
Canada   Canada

 Canadä

This release contains information on the ethnic origins of people living in Canada and on the condition of Canada's housing stock.

WHO WE ARE

Defining ethnic origin

Ethnic origin – as defined in the Census – refers to the ethnic or cultural group(s) to which an individual's ancestors belonged; it pertains to the ancestral roots or origins of the population and not to place of birth, citizenship or nationality.

Census data show that although the share of the population made up of immigrants remained relatively stable – about 16% – during the past several decades, there was a substantial change from where the more recent immigrants had come. This, in turn, was reflected in the increasing ethnic and cultural diversity of Canada's population.

In 1991, 19.2 million people, or 71% of the population, reported only one ethnic origin, down slightly from 72% in 1986. Nearly 8 million people, or 29% of the population, reported more than one ethnic origin, indicating they were of mixed ethnic ancestry.

There was considerable regional variation in the reporting of single and multiple ethnic backgrounds. Quebec had the highest proportion of single responses, with 92% of the population reporting one ethnic origin. On the other hand, the Yukon Territory had the highest proportion of multiple responses, with nearly one-half of the population (49%) providing more than one ethnic origin.

Proportion of Single and Multiple Responses, 1991

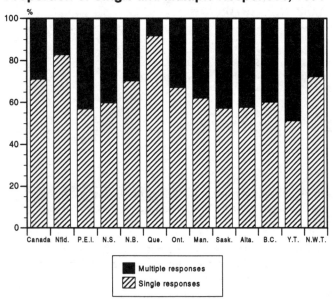

The reporting of single and multiple ethnic origins varied among ethnic groups. For example, 81% of persons reporting Irish and 79% reporting Scottish also reported other ethnic origins. This pattern of response was most common among ethnic groups originating in Northern, Western and Eastern Europe. The proportion of multiple responses for these European groups was often greater than 50% with 82% of Swedish, 78% of Norwegian, 76% of Russian, 67% of German, 63% each of Polish and Dutch and 61% of Ukrainian respondents reporting multiple origins.

On the other hand, groups reporting French and Southern European origins had a lower incidence of multiple responses. In 1991, 16% of Portuguese, 21% of Greek, 27% of French and 35% of Italian responses were multiple.

Ethnic groups with high levels of recent immigration were also more likely to report a single rather than a multiple ethnic background. For example, just 4% of Koreans, 7% of Afghans, 9% of Cambodians and 10% of Chinese reported two or more ethnic origins.

Single and Multiple Responses for Selected Ethnic Origins, 1991

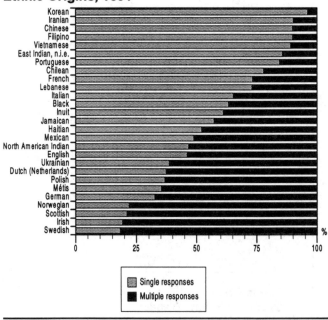

British and French still the largest ethnic groups in Canada

The first major sources of immigrants to Canada were from France, Great Britain and Ireland. According to the 1991 Census, people with British and French ethnic backgrounds were still the largest ethnic groups in Canada.

British-only origins were reported by 28% of the population in 1991 compared with 34% in 1986. This represented a decline from 8.4 million in 1986 to 7.6 million in 1991, a decline which may be accounted for by an increase in the number of persons reporting Canadian rather than British origins.

French-only origins made up 23% of the population in 1991, a decrease from 24% in 1986. The number of persons reporting French ancestry, however, increased from 6,099,095 in 1986 to 6,158,665 in 1991.

Another 4% of the population reported a combination of British and French ethnic backgrounds, while 14% reported some combination of British and/or French and other origins. These percentages were similar to those recorded in the 1986 Census.

Greater Diversity in the Canadian Mosaic

Although people with British or French backgrounds still made up the largest ethnic groups, neither group accounted for a majority of the population. In 1991, 31% of the population reported an ethnic background that did not include British or French origins. This was an increase from the 1986 Census when one-quarter of the population reported origins other than British or French.

The higher proportion of origins other than British or French in 1991 was due in part to the increased number of recent immigrants whose ethnic origins were neither British nor French and to the inclusion, for the first time in the 1991 Census, of non-permanent residents. The increase was also a result of the higher proportion of the population in 1991 reporting Canadian and Aboriginal origins.

Ethnic Origins, 1991

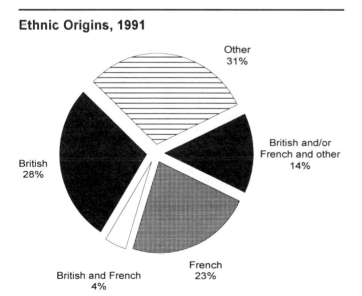

Other
31%

British and/or French and other
14%

British
28%

French
23%

British and French
4%

Defining British and French Ethnic Origins

British only origins include single responses of English, Irish, Scottish, Welsh or other British, as well as the multiple British only responses - that is, a combination of English, Irish, Scottish, Welsh or other British. French only origins include the single responses of French, Acadian, Québécois and the multiple French only responses - that is, a combination of French, Acadian or Québécois. Thus, throughout this report the terms British and French refer to these groups, unless otherwise specified.

Those reporting European ancestry traditionally comprised the largest proportion of persons having neither British nor French origins. In 1991, the population reporting a European single ethnic origin made up 15% of the total population - a proportion virtually unchanged since the 1986 Census. The three largest European single origin groups were German, Italian and Ukrainian, accounting for 3.4%, 2.8% and 1.5%, respectively, of the total population in 1991.

As a result of increasing non-European immigration to Canada in the 1970s and 1980s, there were more people reporting non-European ethnic ancestry in 1991. Those reporting Asian origins (i.e. South Asian, East and South East Asian single ethnic origins) represented 5.1% of the total population in 1991, an increase from 3.5% in 1986. The largest Asian single response groups in 1991 were Chinese (2.2% of the total population) and East Indian (1.2%).

In addition, persons of Caribbean as well as Latin/Central/South American origins comprised 0.7% of the total population in 1991, while 0.8% of the population reported a single Black ancestry. Those reporting Caribbean or Latin/Central/South American single origins increased from 80,715 persons in 1986 to 179,925 persons in 1991. Likewise, those reporting a single Black ancestry increased from 174,970 in 1986 to 224,620 in 1991.

Ethnic background varied according to region

The ethnic make-up of the population varied considerably across Canada – in large measure reflecting where immigrants have settled over time.

Atlantic Canada had strong British roots

The Atlantic provinces had the highest proportion of people of British ancestry. Newfoundland was the province with highest proportion reporting British-only origin (88%). In Prince Edward Island, 66% were of British-only ancestry, compared with 58% in Nova Scotia and 44% in New Brunswick.

Origins other than British or French, 1991

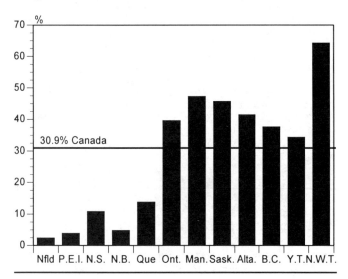

30.9% Canada

Nfld P.E.I. N.S. N.B. Que Ont. Man. Sask. Alta. B.C. Y.T. N.W.T.

People of French-only ancestry represented one-third of the population of New Brunswick in 1991. The proportion reporting French-only origins was much smaller in the other Atlantic provinces, ranging from 9% in Prince Edward Island and 6% in Nova Scotia to 2% in Newfoundland.

Of the four Atlantic provinces, Nova Scotia had the highest proportion reporting origins other than British or French: 11% compared with 5% in New Brunswick, 4% in Prince Edward Island and 3% in Newfoundland.

Persons reporting a single Black origin made up 1.2% of the Nova Scotia population and represented the fourth largest single response group in the province. In 1991, 67% of those reporting a single Black ancestry resided in the Halifax census metropolitan area.

Three-quarters of Quebec's population reported French only origins

Quebec had the highest proportion of people reporting French only origins (75%). This represented a decline from 1986 when 78% of Quebec's population reported French origins.

A number of non-British, non-French ethnic groups made Quebec their home. In 1991, 44% of persons reporting Arab single origins resided in Quebec – representing the largest Arab community in Canada. Quebec also had the largest Haitian community in Canada, with 95% of all persons in Canada reporting Haitian single origins residing in this province. Other than Ontario, Quebec had the largest communities of persons with Italian, Jewish, Greek, Portuguese, West Asian, Indo-Chinese, Latin/Central/South American, Caribbean and Black origins.

Within Quebec, the Montréal census metropolitan area had the largest concentration of ethnic groups. In fact, 85% of all provincial residents who reported origins other than French or British lived in the Montréal area. After French and British, the third largest single response group in Montréal was Italian, representing 5.4% of the population. The next largest group was Jewish (2.5%), followed by Greek (1.6%), Black (1.3%), Chinese (1.1%) and Portuguese (1.0%). Lebanese (0.9%) and Haitian (0.7%) rounded out the top ten for this urban centre. The largest Lebanese and Haitian communities in Canada were in Montréal.

Ontario: a diversity of ethnic groups

Over half of Canada's immigrant population resided in Ontario in 1991. The attraction of immigrants to Ontario was reflected in the diversity of ethnic groups living in this province. In 1991, 40% of Ontario's population reported ethnic origins other than British or French. In fact, nearly half of all people in Canada who reported origins other than British or French resided in Ontario.

Ontario was home to some of the largest ethnic communities in Canada. Over half of all persons reporting West Asian (54%), South Asian (55%), African (70%), Caribbean (63%) and Black (67%) single ethnic origins lived in Ontario.

Those of British-only ancestry made up 35% of Ontario's population, and 5% reported French-only origins. Outside Quebec, Ontario had the largest population of those reporting French ancestry.

Origins Other than British or French, Census Metropolitan Areas, 1991

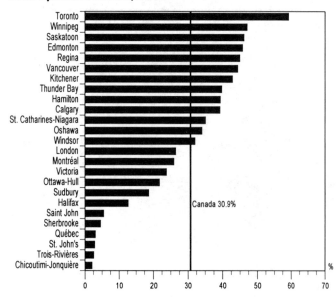

Toronto
Winnipeg
Saskatoon
Edmonton
Regina
Vancouver
Kitchener
Thunder Bay
Hamilton
Calgary
St. Catharines-Niagara
Oshawa
Windsor
London
Montréal
Victoria
Ottawa-Hull
Sudbury
Halifax
Saint John
Sherbrooke
Québec
St. John's
Trois-Rivières
Chicoutimi-Jonquière

Canada 30.9%

0   10   20   30   40   50   60   70

Toronto had the highest proportion of persons reporting origins other than British or French of any census metropolitan area. In 1991, 59% of Toronto's population reported non-British, non-French ethnic or cultural origins, up from 45% in 1986. The higher proportion in 1991 was partly due to increased numbers of recent immigrants settling in Toronto since 1986 and to the inclusion of non-permanent residents in the 1991 Census. The increase was also a result of a higher proportion of Toronto's population reporting Canadian as their ethnic origin: 7% in 1991 compared with less than 1% in 1986.

Those reporting single European ancestry made up 26% of Toronto's population, 14% were of single Asian origins and 3% reported single Black ancestry. Some of the largest ethnic or cultural communities in Canada were in Toronto. For example, the largest Italian, Portuguese, Greek, Polish, Jewish, Chinese, South Asian, Filipino, Black and Caribbean communities were in the Toronto census metropolitan area.

The Prairies reflected earlier waves of immigration

The Prairie provinces had the highest proportions of persons reporting origins other than British (excluding the Northwest Territories). The non-British, non-French group made up 47% of the population in Manitoba, 46% in Saskatchewan and 41% in Alberta.

In the three Prairie provinces, people of European ancestry represented the largest percentage of those with origins other than British: 26% in Manitoba and Saskatchewan and 21% in Alberta. In these provinces, there remained higher concentrations of ethnic groups who immigrated to Canada earlier in our history. For example, those reporting German-only ancestry made up 9% of Manitoba's population, 12% in Saskatchewan and 7% in Alberta. Similarly, Ukrainian-only origins represented 7% of Manitoba's population, 6% in Saskatchewan's and 4% of Alberta's.

Persons reporting Aboriginal origins represented a larger proportion of the population of the three Prairie provinces than elsewhere (excluding the Territories). People reporting single Aboriginal origins made up 7% of the population in both Manitoba and Saskatchewan and 3% in Alberta. In other provinces, those with single Aboriginal origins represented 1% or less of the provincial populations (except in British Columbia where they accounted for 2%).

Overall, those of British-only ancestry represented about one-quarter of the population in the three Prairie provinces. Persons of French ancestry made up 5% of Manitoba's population, and 3% in Saskatchewan and Alberta.

One-in-nine British Columbia residents was of Asian origin

In 1991, 38% of British Columbia's population reported having origins other than British or French, followed by 35% who were of British ancestry, 22% of British and/or French and other origins, and 2% of French-only origins. Those of single European ancestry were the largest of the non-British, non-French groups, accounting for 17% of the provincial population.

Persons of Asian ancestry, however, were the next largest group in the province (11% of the population), representing an increase from 8% in 1986. In 1991, 6% of British Columbia's residents reported Chinese and 3% reported East Indian as their only ethnic origin. The only other province with a larger Asian population was Ontario, where 7% of the population reported single Asian origins.

In Vancouver, those of non-British, non-French origin represented the largest proportion of the population at 44%, followed by those with British ancestry at 33%. The Vancouver cesus metropolitan area had been the focus of recent immigration to Canada from Asia – and this was reflected in the growing proportion of Asian ethnic groups. In 1991, those reporting single Asian ancestry accounted for 19% of the population, compared with 13% in 1986. After British, Chinese and East Indian were the largest single ethnic groups in Vancouver. Those reporting a Chinese single origin represented 11% of Vancouver's population, while East Indians made up 4%.

Persons with Aboriginal origins comprised the majority in the Northwest Territories

The Northwest Territories was the only province or territory where neither British nor French constituted the largest ethnic groups. Over half (51%) of the population reported single Aboriginal origins in 1991. Fully 32% of the population reported a single Inuit origin, 15% a single North American Indian origin and 4% a single Métis origin.

In the Yukon Territory, 34% of the population reported non-British, non-French ethnic origins. A further 30% reported British ancestry while 29% reported British and/or French in addition to other origins.

In 1991, 14% of the Yukon population reported single Aboriginal origins. This represented the largest single response group after British.

Increase in the number reporting Aboriginal origins

In 1991, 470,615 persons reported single Aboriginal origins. This represented an increase of 26% from 1986 (373,265). Aboriginal origins in combination with other groups were reported by 532,060 persons, an increase of 57% compared with 1986 (338,460). Of persons reporting multiple Aboriginal origins in 1991, about 10,000 gave multiple Aboriginal-only origins (that is, any combination of North American Indian, Métis or Inuit), while about 522,000 reported Aboriginal and other origins. Overall, just over one million persons in Canada reported one or more Aboriginal origins in 1991, up from nearly three-quarters of a million in 1986.

The increase in persons reporting single Aboriginal origins was highest in Newfoundland (40% or 1,500 persons), Manitoba (34% or 19,000), Quebec (33% or 16,000), Alberta (32% or 17,000) but lowest in the Northwest Territories (8% or 2,000) and New Brunswick (10% or 400). On the other hand, the growth in those reporting multiple Aboriginal origins was greatest in Quebec (128% or 41,000 persons), and the Northwest Territories (78% or 3,000) and smallest in Newfoundland (36% or 2,000) Saskatchewan (38% or 8,000), Manitoba (40% or 12,000) and British Columbia (44% or 29,000). For further information on Aboriginal origins, please see the note on page 80.

Rise in the population reporting Canadian ethnic origin

A portion of the population has always reported their ancestry as Canadian. As early as 1951, when the Census first published results on Canadian as an ethnic origin, 71,759 people reported their ethnic origin as Canadian. In 1986, 69,065 people reported a single ethnic origin of Canadian, with 43,765 additional people reporting Canadian in conjunction with other ethnic origins.

The 1991 Census recorded a substantial increase in the number of respondents who gave their ethnic ancestry as Canadian. Some 765,095 persons, or 3% of the population, reported a single origin of Canadian and 267,935 reported Canadian in conjunction with other ethnic origins. Nationally, about one million respondents, or 4% of the total population, reported Canadian ethnic ancestry (either single or multiple response).

The distribution of those reporting Canadian ethnic ancestry – both single and multiple – varied by province, with two-thirds (67%) living in Ontario. A further 12 percent resided in Alberta, 8% in British Columbia, 4% in Saskatchewan and 3% in Quebec. The remaining 6% lived in the other provinces and territories.

Most of those providing Canadian as their ethnic origin (97%) were born in Canada. Of the 3% who were born outside Canada, the United Kingdom (10,575 persons) and the United States (4,925 persons) were the most frequently reported countries of birth. Similarly, most of the respondents who gave Canadian had an English mother tongue (92%) followed by 4% with French and 4% with other language responses.

Those reporting Canadian ethnic ancestry numbered among the top 10 single response groups in every province except Quebec.

Top 10 Ethnic Groups

There was considerable regional variation in the 10 most frequently reported single ethnic origins in 1991. British was the largest single response group in each region, except in Quebec and the Northwest Territories. In Quebec, French was the most numerous group, while Aboriginal origins were the largest group in the Northwest Territories. French appeared among the top 10 groups in all provinces and territories, ranking second in the Atlantic provinces and Ontario. Similarly, Aboriginal origins were among the 10 most frequent single response groups in all provinces except Ontario.

A number of European groups also appeared among the top 10 groups across the country. For example, German and Dutch ranked among the top 10 in all provinces and territories except Quebec. Those reporting a Ukrainian single response represented a sizeable proportion in the Western provinces. Single responses of Italian and Portuguese comprised 4.9% and 1.8% respectively of Ontario's population, and 2.6% and 0.5% in Quebec.

Persons reporting Black single ancestry ranked fourth in Nova Scotia, seventh in Quebec and ninth in New Brunswick.

Groups which experienced higher levels of recent immigration were establishing communities across Canada. For example, the Chinese were the second largest ethnic group in British Columbia and sixth in both Alberta and Ontario. East Indians were the fourth largest group in British Columbia, seventh in size in Newfoundland, ninth in Ontario and tenth in both Alberta and Prince Edward Island. Persons of Filipino background ranked seventh in Manitoba.

Top 10 Single Response Ethnic Origins, 1991

Canada	Number	%	Newfoundland	Number	%
Total population	**26,994,045**	**100.0**	**Total population**	**563,940**	**100.0**
Single responses	19,199,795	71.1	Single responses	465,645	82.6
1. French(2)	6,146,605	22.8	1. British(1)	442,810	78.5
2. British(1)	5,611,050	20.8	2. French(2)	9,700	1.7
3. German	911,560	3.4	3. Aboriginal(3)	5,345	0.9
4. Canadian	765,095	2.8	4. German	1,315	0.2
5. Italian	750,055	2.8	5. Canadian	1,225	0.2
6. Chinese	586,645	2.2	6. Chinese	740	0.1
7. Aboriginal(3)	470,615	1.7	7. East Indian, n.i.e.	710	0.1
8. Ukrainian	406,645	1.5	8. Dutch(Netherlands)	440	0.1
9. Dutch(Netherlands)	358,185	1.3	9. Italian	295	0.1
10. East Indian, n.i.e.	324,840	1.2	10. Lebanese	230	0.0
Multiple responses	7,794,250	28.9	Multiple responses	98,290	17.4

Prince Edward Island	Number	%	Nova Scotia	Number	%
Total population	**128,100**	**100.0**	**Total population**	**890,950**	**100.0**
Single responses	72,930	56.9	Single responses	532,845	59.8
1. British(1)	56,405	44.0	1. British(1)	391,805	44.0
2. French(2)	11,845	9.2	2. French(2)	55,310	6.2
3. Dutch(Netherlands)	1,250	1.0	3. German	24,825	2.8
4. Canadian	795	0.6	4. Black(4)	10,825	1.2
5. German	645	0.5	5. Canadian	9,675	1.1
6. Aboriginal(3)	400	0.3	6. Dutch(Netherlands)	8,960	1.0
7. Lebanese	255	0.2	7. Aboriginal(3)	7,530	0.8
8. Polish	145	0.1	8. Italian	2,715	0.3
9. Danish	120	0.1	9. Polish	2,360	0.3
10. East Indian, n.i.e.	95	0.1	10. Lebanese	2,335	0.3
Multiple responses	55,170	43.1	Multiple responses	358,105	40.2

New Brunswick	Number	%	Quebec	Number	%
Total population	**716,495**	**100.0**	**Total population**	**6,810,300**	**100.0**
Single responses	503,820	70.3	Single responses	6,237,905	91.6
1. British(1)	236,385	33.0	1. French(2)	5,077,825	74.6
2. French(2)	235,010	32.8	2. British(1)	286,075	4.2
3. Canadian	9,325	1.3	3. Italian	174,525	2.6
4. German	4,480	0.6	4. Jewish	77,600	1.1
5. Aboriginal(3)	4,270	0.6	5. Aboriginal(3)	65,405	1.0
6. Dutch(Netherlands)	3,045	0.4	6. Greek	49,890	0.7
7. Italian	1,320	0.2	7. Black(4)	41,165	0.6
8. Chinese	1,255	0.2	8. Portuguese	37,165	0.5
9. Black(4)	1,050	0.1	9. Chinese	36,815	0.5
10. Danish	850	0.1	10. Lebanese	31,580	0.5
Multiple responses	212,675	29.7	Multiple responses	572,395	8.4

Ontario	Number	%	Manitoba	Number	%
Total population	**9,977,050**	**100.0**	**Total population**	**1,079,395**	**100.0**
Single responses	6,698,995	67.1	Single responses	669,405	62.0
1. British(1)	2,536,515	25.4	1. British(1)	183,490	17.0
2. French(2)	527,580	5.3	2. German	93,995	8.7
3. Canadian	525,240	5.3	3. Aboriginal(3)	74,340	6.9
4. Italian	486,760	4.9	4. Ukrainian	74,285	6.9
5. German	289,420	2.9	5. French(2)	53,580	5.0
6. Chinese	273,870	2.7	6. Dutch(Netherlands)	24,465	2.3
7. Dutch(Netherlands)	179,760	1.8	7. Filipino	22,045	2.0
8. Portuguese	176,300	1.8	8. Polish	21,600	2.0
9. East Indian, n.i.e.	172,960	1.7	9. Canadian	15,375	1.4
10. Polish	154,150	1.5	10. Jewish	12,265	1.1
Multiple responses	3,278,055	32.9	Multiple responses	409,985	38.0

Top 10 Single Response Ethnic Origins, 1991 - Concluded

Saskatchewan	Number	%	Alberta	Number	%
Total population	**976,035**	**100.0**	**Total population**	**2,519,185**	**100.0**
Single responses	558,675	57.2	Single responses	1,451,000	57.6
1. British(1)	160,725	16.5	1. British(1)	493,195	19.6
2. German	121,305	12.4	2. German	185,630	7.4
3. Aboriginal(3)	66,270	6.8	3. Ukrainian	104,350	4.1
4. Ukrainian	55,955	5.7	4. Canadian	92,490	3.7
5. French(2)	30,075	3.1	5. French(2)	74,615	3.0
6. Canadian	28,850	3.0	6. Chinese	71,635	2.8
7. Norwegian	13,105	1.3	7. Aboriginal(3)	68,445	2.7
8. Polish	11,770	1.2	8. Dutch(Netherlands)	54,750	2.2
9. Dutch(Netherlands)	11,285	1.2	9. Polish	32,840	1.3
10. Hungarian(Magyar)	7,920	0.8	10. East Indian, n.i.e.	32,240	1.3
Multiple responses	417,360	42.8	Multiple responses	1,068,180	42.4

British Columbia	Number	%	Yukon Territory	Number	%
Total population	**3,247,505**	**100.0**	**Total population**	**27,660**	**100.0**
Single responses	1,952,850	60.1	Single responses	14,160	51.2
1. British(1)	812,470	25.0	1. British(1)	5,300	19.2
2. Chinese	181,185	5.6	2. Aboriginal(3)	3,780	13.7
3. German	156,635	4.8	3. German	1,060	3.8
4. East Indian, n.i.e.	89,265	2.7	4. French(2)	875	3.2
5. Aboriginal(3)	74,420	2.3	5. Canadian	735	2.7
6. French(2)	68,795	2.1	6. Ukrainian	390	1.4
7. Dutch(Netherlands)	66,525	2.0	7. Dutch(Netherlands)	295	1.1
8. Canadian	60,320	1.9	8. Norwegian	180	0.7
9. Ukrainian	52,760	1.6	9. Hungarian(Magyar)	140	0.5
10. Italian	49,265	1.5	10. Italian	135	0.5
Multiple responses	1,294,650	39.9	Multiple responses	13,495	48.8

Northwest Territories	Number	%
Total population	**57,435**	**100.0**
Single responses	41,545	72.3
1. Aboriginal(3)	29,415	51.2
2. British(1)	5,885	10.2
3. French(2)	1,395	2.4
4. Canadian	1,035	1.8
5. German	885	1.5
6. Ukrainian	445	0.8
7. Dutch(Netherlands)	305	0.5
8. Chinese	270	0.5
9. Filipino	210	0.4
10. Italian	160	0.3
Multiple responses	15,890	27.7

(1) British includes the single responses of English, Irish, Scottish, Welsh and Other British, n.i.e..
(2) French includes the single responses of French, Acadian and Québécois.
(3) Aboriginal includes the single responses of Inuit, Métis and North American Indian.
(4) Black includes the single responses of Black, African Black, n.i.e. and Ghanaian.

n.i.e. = not included elsewhere

Note: These data refer to the total non-institutional population. See note on Data Comparability on page 183.

Single and Multiple Responses

A *single response* occurred when the respondent reported only one ethnic origin. For example, 750,055 persons indicated that their only ethnic origin was Italian.

A *multiple response* occurred when the respondent provided more than one ethnic origin. For example, 397,720 persons gave a response which included Italian and one or more other ethnic or cultural groups.

In 1986 and 1991, to better reflect the ethnic diversity of Canada, respondents to the Census were asked to report, where applicable, more than one ethnic origin. Some 28% did so in 1986, while in 1991, 29% reported more than one ethnic origin; of these, 17% reported having two origins, 7% gave three origins and 5% reported four or more ethnic origins.

Comparability of 1986 and 1991 Ethnic Origin Data

The ethnic origin question on the 1991 Census was similar to that asked on the last Census in 1986. In an effort to explain clearly that the purpose of the question was to measure the ancestral origins of the Canadian population, the wording of the 1991 question was changed slightly and a note was included on the questionnaire summarizing the purpose of the question. These changes should not affect the comparability of ethnic origin data between 1986 and 1991.

Nevertheless, caution must be exercised in making comparisons. Measures of ethnicity are complex, and can be affected by changes in the environment in which the questions are asked as well as by changes in respondents' understanding or views about the topic. Changes in such factors as awareness of family background or length of time since immigration can affect

responses to the question, as can confusion with other concepts such as citizenship, nationality, language or cultural identity. In the case of the 1991 Census, public attention on Aboriginal issues in the year leading up to the Census may have contributed to increased reporting of Aboriginal origins; similarly, pre-census publicity calling for the reporting of Canadian as an expression of national identity may have contributed to a substantial increase in the number of persons providing this response and a decrease in other origins, especially British.

Data on Aboriginal origins/identity

The 1991 Census question on ethnic or cultural origins provided information on the number of persons who reported North American Indian, Métis or Inuit origins, either as a single response or in combination with other origins. The Census also collected information on the number of persons who were registered Indians as defined by the Indian Act of Canada, and on their Band or First Nation affiliation.

Following the Census, a large-scale survey of a sample of persons who reported Aboriginal origins and/or who reported being registered under the Indian Act was conducted. This survey (the Aboriginal Peoples Survey) was developed in consultation with organizations representing Aboriginal peoples and was designed to provide a wide range of detailed information about employment, education, language, culture, housing and other characteristics of Aboriginal peoples.

The results of the Aboriginal Peoples Survey show that of the slightly over one million people who reported Aboriginal origins in the Census, approximately 626,000 reported that they identified with their Aboriginal origins, that is, that they considered themselves to be North American Indian, Métis or Inuit, and/or were registered under the Indian Act.

The 1991 Census question on Ethnic Origin

15. To which ethnic or cultural group(s) did this person's ancestors belong?

    Mark or specify as many as applicable

    Note

    While most people of Canada view themselves as Canadian, information about their ancestral origins has been collected since the 1901 Census to reflect the changing composition of the Canadian population and is needed to ensure that everyone, regardless of his/her ethnic or cultural background has equal opportunity to share fully in the economic, social, cultural and political life of Canada. Therefore, this question refers to the origins of this person's ancestors.

    See Guide.

Examples of other ethnic or cultural groups are: Portuguese, Greek, Indian from India, Pakistani, Filipino, Vietnamese, Japanese, Lebanese, Haitian, etc.

08	○	French
09	○	English
10	○	German
11	○	Scottish
12	○	Italian
13	○	Irish
14	○	Ukrainian
15	○	Chinese
16	○	Dutch (Netherlands)
17	○	Jewish
18	○	Polish
19	○	Black
20	○	North American Indian
21	○	Métis
22	○	Inuit/Eskimo
		Other ethnic or cultural group(s) – specify
23		[ ]
24		[ ]

WHERE WE LIVE

Half of all occupied dwellings in Canada were built after 1970

On Census day 1991, it was reported that almost one-half of all occupied dwellings in Canada had been built after 1970. The Northwest Territories had the highest proportion of newer homes, with 72% of homes built in the previous 21 years, followed by the Yukon (63%), Alberta (58%) and British Columbia (54%).

Among major urban centres, about one-in-four dwellings in the Ottawa-Hull and Vancouver census metropolitan areas were built between 1981 and 1991. In Toronto, 22% of dwellings were built during the same decade and in Montréal the proportion was 20%. Older housing stock (that is, dwellings built before 1921), represented only about 8% of all occupied dwellings across Canada. Some 20% of dwellings in Prince Edward Island were built before 1921, compared with only 3% in Alberta.

Most dwellings in good condition

Occupants of the majority of owner-occupied private dwellings in Canada reported that their dwellings required only regular maintenance or minor repairs such as replacing missing floor tiles, bricks or shingles, fixing defective steps, etc. Only 8.2% of all households reported that their dwellings needed major repairs such as replacement of defective electrical wiring or plumbing or structural repairs to walls, floors or ceilings. Among owner-occupied dwellings 7.5% were reported as requiring major repair, compared with 9% of tenant-occupied dwellings.

Among the largest census metropolitan areas, Montréal had the greatest proportion of dwellings requiring major repair (7.3%) compared with 6.9% in Toronto, 6.4% in Ottawa-Hull and 6% in Vancouver.

Of dwellings requiring major repair, Toronto had the largest proportion which were tenant-occupied (62%), compared with 59% in Montréal, 58% in Ottawa-Hull and 54% in Vancouver.

Home-owners occupied bigger dwellings

The average Canadian home in 1991 had six rooms, while the average household comprised 2.7 persons. This continued a trend to larger dwelling size at the same time that household size was decreasing. In 1986, when the average Canadian dwelling had 5.8 rooms, 2.8 persons lived in the average Canadian household. Home-owners tended to occupy bigger dwellings, with an average of seven rooms (including three bedrooms), while tenant-occupied dwellings had an average of 4.5 rooms, including two bedrooms.

Home values highest in Ontario

Home-owners in Ontario reported the highest average estimated value of dwellings ($197,967), an increase of $93,904 on the average value in 1986. British Columbia's home-owners reported the second highest values on average ($175,559), followed by those in Alberta ($114,548). This compared with 1986 values of $98,850 and $84,936, respectively. Values reported in the Census reflect the perceptions of the respondents themselves, and are not necessarily based on market-value or real estate sales.

Among the major urban centres, home-owners in the metropolitan Toronto area reported the highest estimated value on average ($280,390), an increase of $138,108 from 1986. Vancouver's dwellings ranked second in average estimated value at $244,539, followed by those in Hamilton ($192,018) and Victoria ($187,149).

Average Estimated Value of Owner-Occupied Private Dwellings*, Census Metropolitan Areas, 1991

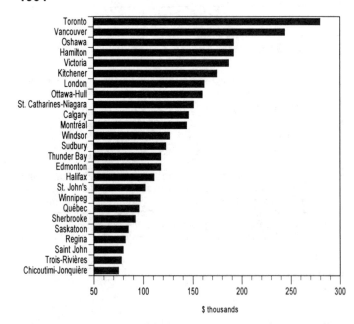

* reported for non-farm, non reserve dwellings.

Catalogue 11-001E (Français 11-001F) ISSN 0827-0465

The Daily

Statistics Canada

Tuesday, March 2, 1993

LABOUR FORCE ACTIVITY, INDUSTRY AND CLASS OF WORKER, AND OCCUPATION

HIGHLIGHTS

- Number of self-employed, particularly women, still growing

- Fewer manufacturing workers

- Managerial and Administrative Occupations increased

- More mothers in the labour force

- Seven out of ten workers employed in services

- Women's labour force participation continued to increase between 1986 and 1991

Labour Force Activity
Labour Force Activity of Women by Presence of Children
Industry and Class of Worker
Occupation

Labour Force Activity (93-324, $40) presents statistics from the 1991 Census on labour force activity, and work activity in 1990.

Labour Force Activity of Women by Presence of Children (93-325, $40) presents data from the 1991 Census on labour force activity of women with and without children at home, according to marital status and age.

Industry and Class of Worker (93-326, $40) presents detailed industry (based on the 1980 Standard Industrial Classification) and class of worker data, by sex, 1986 and 1991 Censuses.

Occupation (93-327, $40) presents detailed occupation data, by sex, (based on the 1980 Standard Occupational Classification), 1986 and 1991 Censuses.

The data in these publications are based on a 20% sample of households. Data are shown for Canada, provinces and territories.

Statistics Statistique
Canada Canada

Canada

This release contains information on labour force activity, industry and class of worker, and occupation.

Labour force and working age population growth

Canada's working age population (all people aged 15 years and over) grew by 8.5% between 1986 and 1991. Over the same period the size of the labour force – all those 15 years and over who were employed or unemployed – increased by 12%. Increasing numbers of women in the paid work force accounted for almost two-thirds (63%) of this change.

Labour Force Participation Rates

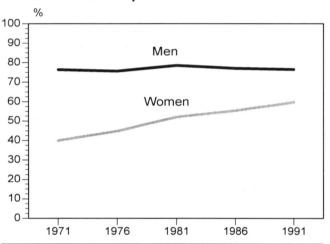

Participation in the labour force was still growing

In 1991, the labour force participation rate was 68%, up from 66% in 1986. In 1971, 58% of the population aged 15 and over participated in the labour force.

Over the past two decades, growth in the size of the labour force fluctuated, reflecting demographic and economic changes. During the 1970s, the labour force grew rapidly – by 16% over the 1971-1976 period and by 20% between 1976 and 1981 – as large numbers of baby boomers reached working age and women of all ages entered the labour force. Over the next census period, 1981-1986, the labour force grew by only 7%. This much lower rate of increase reflected the effects of the 1981-1982 recession.

One of the most significant trends in the Canadian labour market over the past twenty years was the continuing increase in the proportion of women 15 years and over who were in the labour force. In 1971, the participation rate for women was 40%. All censuses since 1971 have shown steady growth in this rate, and by 1991, the labour force participation

rate for women had reached 60%. Overall, women represented 45% of the total labour force in 1991, up from 35% in 1971.

In comparison, the participation rate for all men aged 15 years and over remained relatively stable during the two most recent census periods – from 78% in 1981 to 77% in 1986 and 77% in 1991. The 1971 Census reported a participation rate for men of 76%.

Labour Force Participation Rates, 1991

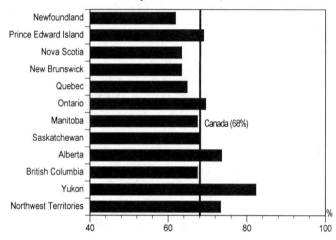

Census Data on Labour Force Activity

Labour Force: Canada's total paid labour force is composed of all people aged 15 years and over who were employed or unemployed during the week prior to Census Day (the reference week). The employed are those who hold paid jobs or who are self-employed in the paid labour market, that is, their work contributes to the production of those goods and services included in the System of National Accounts measures such as Gross Domestic Product. The employed also include those who were absent from their job during the reference week. The unemployed are those who are without a paid job, who are looking for work, who have been laid off, or who have a new job to start within the next 4 weeks.

Labour Force Participation Rate: The labour force participation rate is the percentage of the population 15 years of age and over (excluding institutional residents) who were in the labour force (employed or unemployed) during the week prior to Census Day (the reference week). For example, a participation rate of 67.9 indicates that 67.9% of the population were participating in the labour force during the reference period.

Historical Comparisons: A slightly different definition of the labour force was used in the 1971 Census than in 1991. As a result, 1991 Census labour force activity figures used in historical comparisons will differ from other 1991 Census labour force activity, industry, occupation and class of worker figures contained in the publications.

*Users should refer to the "Reference Material" section in **Labour Force Activity** (Catalogue No. 93-324) or the **1991 Census Dictionary** (92-301E) for full definitions and other remarks.*

Over the past twenty years there were large changes in the participation rates for the young and older workers in the labour force. For the youngest people in the labour force, those aged 15 to 19 years, participation increased from 42% in 1971 to 55% in 1991. During this period, the participation rate for young men increased from 47% to 56% and for young women from 37% to 54%. In the 15 to 19 year age group, the participation rates for men and women were closest.

Very substantial changes, but in the opposite direction, were evident at the other end of the age scale. Since 1971, the participation rate for those aged 60 to 64 has fallen from 51% to 40%. Almost all of this decline is due to a decrease in the participation of men – from 74% to 54%. In comparison, the already low participation rate for women in this age group dropped only slightly – from 29% in 1971 to 28% in 1991.

Across the country

Labour force participation rates varied among the provinces and territories in 1991. They were highest in the Yukon (82%), Alberta (74%), the Northwest Territories (73%) and Ontario (70%) and lowest in Newfoundland (62%), New Brunswick (63%) and Nova Scotia (63%). These highs and lows were unchanged from 1986.

In 1991, the labour force participation rates for all provinces and territories were higher than they were in 1986, with the size of the increase ranging from slightly over 1 percentage point (Ontario) to almost 4 percentage points (Northwest Territories).

Moms in the labour force

There was continued growth in the number of women with children at home, who had paid jobs or were looking for paid employment. In 1991, 68% of all women with children living at home were in the paid labour force, up from 1986 (61%) and from 1981 (52%). Since 1981, there was a significant increase in the labour force participation of married women living with their spouse, regardless of the ages of the children. The participation rate for women living with

Labour Force Participation Rate for Women with Children at Home*

	With children at home %	All children less than 6 years %	Some children less than 6 years %	All children 6 years and older %
Total marital status				
1981	52.4	50.0	44.8	54.9
1986	60.6	61.7	55.4	61.4
1991	68.4	67.2	63.9	69.8
Single				
1981	50.1	45.3	32.9	61.1
1986	54.4	51.5	37.6	62.7
1991	54.5	47.3	39.8	67.2
Married spouse absent**				
1981	62.8	60.8	51.8	65.5
1986	67.7	64.7	56.5	70.6
1991	69.2	63.1	57.3	73.4
Married spouse present***				
1981	52.1	49.4	44.6	55.0
1986	61.2	62.1	55.8	62.1
1991	70.1	69.0	65.3	71.6
Widowed				
1981	35.3	53.1	36.6	35.1
1986	33.9	57.5	46.6	33.4
1991	33.0	56.5	52.5	32.5
Divorced				
1981	68.7	64.8	45.8	71.4
1986	71.9	68.5	54.3	73.7
1991	75.9	68.0	57.2	78.2

Includes females in private households only.
** *Includes separated and common-law partner absent.*
*** *Includes common-law partner present.*

their spouse whose children were all under the age of six increased from 49% in 1981 to 69% in 1991. Over the same period, the rate for married women living with their spouse who had children both younger and older than six increased from 45% to 65%. In comparison, over the past decade, the participation rate for women without children has increased only slightly: to 54% in 1991 from 51% in 1981.

Full-time or part-time

Of those people who worked in 1990, women were much more likely to have worked mostly part-time than were men. Almost 30% of all women worked mostly part-time, compared to only 12% of all men.

However, out of all women who worked in 1990, 45% worked full-year, full-time, compared to 59% for men. Full-year, full-time workers are those people who worked mostly full-time hours (30 hours or more per week) for 49 to 52 weeks of the year.

Change in Class of Worker by Sex, 1986-1991

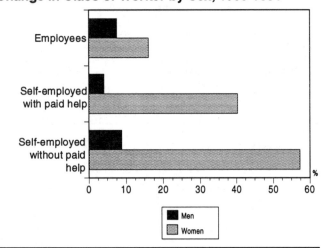

Number of people who were their own boss increased

While nine out of 10 Canadians work for someone else, the number who were self-employed continued to grow. Although their numbers remained relatively small (10% of the total labour force), the number of self-employed Canadians grew by 16% between 1986 and 1991, compared with a 10% increase in the previous five-year period. In contrast, there was an 11% increase in the number of people who were employees between 1986 and 1991.

More women employers

The number of women who were self-employed increased faster than the number of men for all types of self-employment (incorporated and unincorporated, with or without paid help). Particularly significant was the 40% growth in the number of self-employed women with paid help, (i.e., employers).

Seven of every ten workers in services

In 1991, 72% of Canada's workers were found in the service-producing industries, up from 69% in 1986 (service-producing industries are defined in the table on page 88). Despite an overall economic downturn which began in the early 1990s, the labour force of the service-producing industries grew by 16% between 1986 and 1991. This follows an 11% increase over the first half of the 1980s.

Overall, nine of the ten fastest growing Industry Divisions were service producers (there are 18 Industry Divisions in all). This growth was led by Business Service Industries, which had an increase of 36%. Of the eight individual Industry Groups that make up the Business Service Division, all grew by more than 15%. Very large increases were found in Computer and Related Services (69%), Architectural, Engineering and Other Scientific and Technical Services (35%) and Accounting and Bookkeeping Services (32%).

Census Data On Industry

Industry refers to the general nature of the business carried out in the establishment where a person worked. Industry data are available for people aged 15 and over, excluding institutional residents.

If someone was not employed in the week prior to Census Day, the information relates to the job of longest duration since January 1, 1990.

*In this release, industry data are presented for the **experienced labour force** only. The experienced labour force excludes unemployed people who had never worked or who last worked prior to January 1, 1990.*

*Industry data are presented at three levels of detail: Industry Division, Major Group and Group. In total, there are 18 Industry Divisions which are then subdivided into 75 Major Groups and 296 Groups. Readers not familiar with the classification structure should note that there are some Industry Divisions with only one Major Group, e.g. Business Service Division. Additional information on this industrial classification system is presented in **Industry and Class of Worker** (Catalogue No. 93-326).*

Experienced Labour Force by Industry Divisions

	Both Sexes			Men			Women		
	1986	1991	% Change	1986	1991	% Change	1986	1991	% Change
Experienced Labour Force	12,740,225	14,220,235	11.6	7,294,215	7,839,245	7.5	5,446,010	6,380,990	17.2
Agricultural & Rel. Serv.	512,695	521,335	1.7	365,640	343,340	-6.1	147,060	177,995	21.0
Fishing & Trapping	46,495	48,165	3.6	39,860	40,295	1.1	6,635	7,875	18.7
Logging & Forestry	112,980	106,485	-5.7	98,510	90,610	-8.0	14,470	15,875	9.7
Mining	193,340	192,030	-0.7	164,350	161,455	-1.8	28,990	30,575	5.5
Manufacturing	2,196,745	2,084,115	-5.1	1,555,085	1,466,000	-5.7	641,660	618,115	-3.7
Construction	759,165	933,425	23.0	679,820	826,195	21.5	79,345	107,230	35.1
Transportation & Storage	565,725	581,810	2.8	471,075	468,455	-0.6	94,655	113,355	19.8
Communication & Other Utility	411,880	479,185	16.3	275,215	312,300	13.5	136,665	166,880	22.1
Wholesale Trade	584,840	614,345	5.0	415,830	429,075	3.2	169,010	185,265	9.6
Retail Trade	1,606,010	1,831,350	14.0	800,705	904,850	13.0	805,305	926,500	15.0
Finance & Insurance	464,825	576,860	24.1	153,510	189,265	23.3	311,310	387,600	24.5
Real Est. Operator Insurance Agent	226,075	233,705	3.4	117,225	119,270	1.7	108,850	114,430	5.1
Business Service	588,670	802,405	36.3	322,570	439,925	36.4	266,100	362,475	36.2
Government Service	969,280	1,111,385	14.7	583,200	639,730	9.7	386,080	471,660	22.2
Educational Service	838,075	972,520	16.0	345,070	370,315	7.3	493,005	602,205	22.1
Health & Social Service	1,041,450	1,277,340	22.7	221,950	255,110	14.9	819,495	1,022,225	24.7
Accomm., Food & Beverage	806,035	909,710	12.9	326,580	374,730	14.7	479,455	534,980	11.6
Other Service	815,950	944,065	15.7	358,025	408,325	14.0	457,925	535,745	17.0
Goods-Producing[1]	3,958,585	4,042,895	2.1	3,014,530	3,050,455	1.2	944,055	992,445	5.1
Service-Producing[2]	8,781,640	10,177,340	15.9	4,279,685	4,788,790	11.9	4,501,955	5,388,545	19.7

1. *Goods Producing Industries include the following Industry Divisions: Agricultural and Related, Fishing and Trapping, Logging and Forestry, Mining, Manufacturing and Construction; as well as the Other Utility Major Group from the Communication & Other Utility Industry Division.*
2. *Service Producing Industries include the following Industry Divisions: Transportation and Storage, Wholesale Trade, Retail Trade, Finance and Insurance, Real Estate Operator and Insurance Agent, Business Service, Government Service, Educational Service, Health and Social Service, Accommodation, Food and Beverage Service, Other Services; as well as the Communication Major Group from the Communication & Other Utility Industry Division.*

Goods-producing industries showed little growth

Over the 1986-1991 period, the goods-producing labour force grew by only 2%. Of these, only Construction Industries, at 23%, and Other Utilities, at 15%, showed notable increases in their labour force between 1986 and 1991.

Manufacturing still number one, but smaller

Manufacturing Industries continued to be the largest single Industry Division, with a labour force of slightly over 2 million people in 1991. However, between 1986 and 1991, this labour force declined by 5%, a decrease at the Industry Division level second only to that of Logging and Forestry (6%). The remaining goods-producing Industry Divisions also showed low growth or declines.

Growth in Industry Sector Work Force, 1986-1991

	All Industries	Goods-Producing	Service-Producing
Canada	**11.6**	**2.1**	**15.9**
Newfoundland	9.2	3.2	12.1
Prince Edward Island	8.5	3.9	10.8
Nova Scotia	8.3	.8	11.2
New Brunswick	9.6	4.8	11.7
Quebec	11.6	5.1	14.5
Ontario	11.8	-2.6	18.9
Manitoba	4.9	-2.8	8.1
Saskatchewan	1.3	-4.6	4.5
Alberta	10.2	5.8	12.1
British Columbia	19.9	14.9	21.7
Yukon	23.8	26.9	23.1
Northwest Territories	16.7	-3.0	22.1

Across the country

Overall, these patterns of Industry Division growth and decline were similar throughout the provinces and territories, with some exceptions.

Among the five provinces which experienced a decline in Manufacturing, Ontario had the largest decrease (-12%). In contrast, British Columbia experienced an 8% increase in its Manufacturing labour force.

Manitoba and Saskatchewan were the only two provinces to show declines in Construction: in Manitoba the decline was 5% and in Saskatchewan it was 13%.

Of all the provinces and territories, Manitoba experienced the smallest increase in its Business Service Industries (15%). This relatively small increase can be compared to the more than 40% increase in Business Service Industries in Ontario, British Columbia, Yukon and Northwest Territories.

A closer look

At the more detailed Major Group level, ranking the ten largest industries by the size of their 1991 labour force again illustrates the importance of the service-producing industries. Only two of these ten Major Groups are goods-producing: Trade Contracting ranks fifth and Agricultural Industries eighth. It is worth noting that one out of every six workers was in one of the two largest Major Groups (Educational Service, and Health and Social Service).

What the jobs were

The number of workers in the Managerial and Administrative occupation category (e.g. accountants, human resource managers, and sales and advertising managers) grew faster than the number in any other broad occupational category, increasing by 30% from 1986 to 1991. The number of women in this category increased much faster than the number of men – 55% versus 18%. Other fast-growing occupation categories for both men and women included the Social Sciences, up 28% from 1986, and the Natural Sciences, Engineering and Mathematics, also up 28%. In comparison, as noted earlier, the experienced labour force grew by only 12% over the same period.

Out of the 22 broad occupation categories, the Clerical, Services, and Managerial and Administrative Occupations were the largest. Combined, these three groups accounted for 43% of Canada's experienced labour force in 1991. This was up slightly from 1986, when they represented 41%.

Industry Major Groups Ranked by Size of Labour Force, 1991

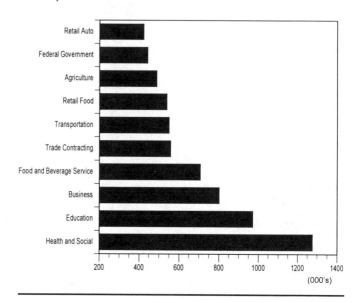

And what they weren't

Over the 1986-1991 period, the experienced labour force declined in eight broad occupational categories. The largest decreases were seen in Forestry and Logging Occupations (-9%), Processing Occupations (-8%), Product-Fabricating, Assembling and Repairing Occupations (-7%) and Farming Occupations (-7%). Occupations in each of these categories are closely associated with goods-producing industries.

Census Data on Occupations

Occupation refers to the kind of work a person was doing during the reference week, as determined by the kind of work and the description of the most important duties in the job. If someone did not have a job in the week before Census Day, the information relates to the job of longest duration since January 1, 1990.

*Occupation data in this release are presented for the **experienced labour force** only. The **experienced labour force** excludes unemployed people who had never worked or who had last worked prior to January 1, 1990.*

*Occupation data are based on the Standard Occupational Classification. This structure is composed of three levels: there are 22 Major Groups which are subdivided into 80 Minor Groups, which in turn contain a total of 514 detailed occupations. The data here are presented for Major Groups (called broad occupation categories or groups) and for detailed occupations (called "specific occupations" or referred to by name, i.e. community planner). Additional information on this occupational classification can be found in **Occupation** (Catalogue No. 93-327).*

Experienced Labour Force by Major Occupational Group

	Total			Men			Women		
	1986	1991	% Change	1986	1991	% Change	1986	1991	% Change
Experienced Labour Force	**12,740,225**	**14,220,235**	**11.6**	**7,294,215**	**7,839,245**	**7.5**	**5,446,015**	**6,380,985**	**17.2**
Managerial, administrative	1,341,970	1,739,165	29.6	919,690	1,086,150	18.1	422,280	653,015	54.6
Natural sciences, engineering	447,800	572,515	27.9	369,420	458,325	24.1	78,380	114,190	45.7
Social sciences	246,465	316,365	28.4	103,895	122,650	18.1	142,565	193,715	35.9
Teaching	543,640	626,520	15.2	207,450	224,730	8.3	336,190	401,790	19.5
Medicine and health	614,095	727,335	18.4	130,275	151,490	16.3	483,820	575,845	19.0
Religion, artistic, literary	241,890	279,195	15.4	146,100	162,665	11.3	95,785	116,535	21.7
Clerical	2,318,620	2,573,060	11.0	494,415	556,395	12.5	1,824,210	2,016,665	10.6
Sales	1,153,160	1,308,705	13.5	641,750	707,085	10.2	511,410	601,625	17.6
Services	1,617,520	1,818,375	12.4	742,615	795,030	7.1	874,905	1,023,345	17.0
Farming, horticultural	508,310	474,360	-6.7	383,970	342,310	-10.8	124,340	132,050	6.2
Fishing, trapping, forestry, mining	202,840	195,955	-3.4	191,045	180,890	-5.3	11,795	15,060	27.7
Processing	446,800	410,665	-8.1	336,980	304,495	-9.6	109,820	106,170	-3.3
Machining	280,735	266,185	-5.2	261,000	249,435	-4.4	19,730	16,750	-15.1
Product fabricating, assembling	955,155	888,985	-6.9	725,160	690,055	-4.8	229,995	198,930	-13.5
Construction	753,485	843,345	11.9	735,390	820,530	11.6	18,095	22,815	26.1
Transport equipment operating	468,830	508,565	8.5	432,435	461,760	6.8	36,385	46,805	28.6
Material handling	236,480	225,660	-4.6	182,190	173,280	-4.9	54,290	52,375	-3.5
Other(1)	362,455	445,270	22.8	290,440	351,970	21.2	72,020	93,300	29.5

(1) Includes other crafts and equipment operating occupations and occupations not elsewhere classified.

In three of the declining occupation categories – Farming, Forestry, and Mining – the number of men in the labour force decreased while the number of women increased.

The jobs of women

In 1991, the three largest occupation categories for women were Clerical, Service, and Managerial and Administrative. Together, they accounted for 58% of the experienced female labour force. Between 1986 and 1991, the proportion of the experienced female labour force in Service Occupations remained stable at about 16% while the proportion in Managerial and Administrative Occupations increased – from 8% to 10%. Over the same period, the proportion in Clerical Occupations declined from 34% to 32%.

For women, Clerical Occupations and Service Occupations ranked first and second in all provinces and territories. There was variation in the next largest occupation group: the Managerial and Administrative

Twelve Most Frequent Jobs for Women, 1991

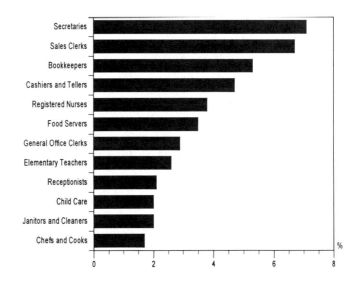

Occupations group was third in Ontario, Quebec, Yukon, and the Northwest Territories; the Sales Occupations group was third in British Columbia and Alberta; and the Medicine and Health Occupations group placed third in the other provinces.

And men

The three largest occupation groups for men remained unchanged from 1986 – Managerial and Administrative, Construction, and Service Occupations. Together, these groups accounted for 35% of the experienced male labour force. In general, male workers were more dispersed among the occupational groups than were female workers.

Among the provinces and territories, there was considerable variation in the largest occupation groups for men. In Nova Scotia, Service Occupations was the largest group, in Saskatchewan it was Farming, in Ontario, Quebec, Manitoba, Alberta and the Northwest Territories, the Managerial and Adminstrative Occupations group ranked first. Construction was the largest group in Newfoundland, Prince Edward Island, New Brunswick, British Columbia and Yukon.

Twelve Most Frequent Jobs for Men, 1991

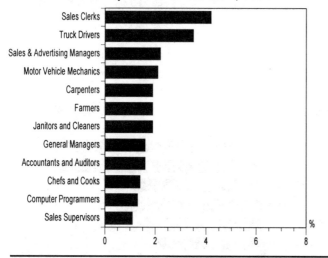

More women in management and the sciences

Additional insights into occupational trends can be obtained by looking at more detailed occupational data.

Many specific occupations showed increases in the size of their female labour force, but notable increases occurred in some occupations requiring more years of higher education. Between 1986 and 1991, the number of women economists increased by 65%, social workers by 49%, lawyers and notaries by 71%, educational and vocational counsellors by 59%, and accountants and auditors by 42%. Women also showed a large percentage increase for judges and magistrates (82%), although their numbers remained small. Among architects, engineers and community planners, women more than doubled their numbers over the 1986-1991 period, although they continued to make up a small percentage of the total number.

In 1991, the four most frequent occupations for women were the same as in 1986: secretaries and stenographers, sales clerks, bookkeepers and accounting clerks, and cashiers and tellers. Combined, these four specific occupations represented 23% of the experienced female labour force in 1991, down slightly from 25% in 1986.

High skill jobs for men

The male labour force showed dramatic increases in a number of Natural Science, Engineering and Mathematics, and Social Science occupations. During the 1986-1991 period, the number of men who were community planners increased by 68%, aerospace engineers by 58%, and systems analysts and computer programmers by 51%. The number of men who were civil engineers, architects, and welfare and community service workers also increased, but by smaller amounts: 29%, 28% and 26%, respectively.

Whereas the four most frequent occupations for women accounted for 23% of the female labour force in 1991, the top four for men accounted for only 12% of the male labour force. These occupations were: sales clerks, truck drivers, sales and advertising managers, and motor vehicle mechanics. The continuing decrease in farming occupations contributed to farmers dropping from third in 1986 to sixth in 1991.

A new female dominated profession

Between 1986 and 1991, there was a 38% increase in the number of female dispensing opticians. This increase, coupled with a 2% decline in the number of men in this occupation, resulted in more women (2,665) than men (2,090) dispensing opticians in 1991.

A similar change occurred for pharmacists over the 1981-1986 period – in 1986, women accounted for 51% of the labour force in this occupation, up from 42% in 1981. This trend continued into 1991, when almost 56% of all pharmacists were women.

Catalogue 11-001E (Français 11-001F) ISSN 0827-0465

Tuesday, March 30, 1993

ABORIGINAL DATA – AGE AND SEX

HIGHLIGHTS

The 1991 Census shows...

- Over one million reported Aboriginal origins

- Just over half with Aboriginal origins reported non-Aboriginal origins as well

- The majority of people in the Northwest Territories reported Aboriginal origins

The 1991 Aboriginal Peoples Survey shows...

- 626,000 people identified with an Aboriginal group

- Those who identified with an Aboriginal group tended to be younger than Canada's total population

- The majority who identified with an Aboriginal group lived west of Ontario

Age and Sex
Aboriginal Data

Age and Sex (94-327, $30) focuses on the Aboriginal Population in Canada. The information presented was obtained from the 1991 Census of Canada and the 1991 Aboriginal Peoples Survey (APS).

The census population consists of those persons who reported at least one Aboriginal origin (i.e., North American Indian, Métis, or Inuit ancestry) on the census long questionnaire. The census data presented show both single Aboriginal origin responses and multiple responses broken down by Aboriginal group.

The APS includes persons who identified with at least one Aboriginal group (North American Indian, Métis, Inuit, or a specific group such as Cree or Inuvialuit) or who reported registered Indian status under the *Indian Act* of Canada.

Both data sources provide age and sex distributions for Canada, provinces, territories, and census metropolitan areas.

 Statistics Statistique
Canada Canada

Following the 1991 Census, the agency conducted the first Aboriginal Peoples Survey. This release presents Aboriginal data on age, sex and geographical distribution from both the census and the survey.

The 1991 Census provides data for the approximately one million people who reported Aboriginal origins while the 1991 Aboriginal Peoples Survey provides data for those people (some 626,000) who identified with an Aboriginal group and/or who were registered Indians as defined by the **Indian Act** of Canada.

Over one million with Aboriginal ancestry

In the 1991 Census, 1,002,675 people reported having Aboriginal origins, either as their only ancestry or in combination with other origins. This is an increase of 41% from 1986 when 711,720 people reported Aboriginal origins. Demographic factors, such as changes in fertility and mortality, cannot explain an increase of this size over a five-year period. Clearly, significant numbers of people who had not previously reported an Aboriginal origin did so in 1991, most likely due to heightened awareness of Aboriginal issues arising from the extensive public discussion of these matters in the period leading up to the 1991 Census.

1991 Census Aboriginal Ancestry

The 1991 Census question on ethnic or cultural origins provided information on the number of people who reported North American Indian, Métis, or Inuit origins, either as a single response or in combination with other origins. The Aboriginal population defined through the Census includes those people who reported at least one Aboriginal origin. For further information on the historical comparability of data on ethnic origins, see the note on page 77.

The increase in reported Aboriginal ancestry varied among the provinces and territories. In Quebec, where the percentage increase was greatest, the number of people reporting Aboriginal origins rose by 70%, largely the result of an increase in the number reporting Aboriginal ancestry in combination with other origins. The Northwest Territories experienced the smallest increase (16%), although here as well, much of the increase was due to a rise in the number of people reporting Aboriginal ancestry in combination with other origins.

Overall, the proportion of Canada's population reporting Aboriginal origins increased from 2.8% in 1986 to 3.7% in 1991.

The Northwest Territories were the only province or territory where people reporting Aboriginal origins represented the majority (62%) of the population. People with Aboriginal origins accounted for almost one-quarter (23%) of the population in the Yukon, 11% in Manitoba, 10% in Saskatchewan, 6% in Alberta, and 5% in British Columbia. In each of the provinces east of Manitoba, the population with Aboriginal origins accounted for less than 3% of the total population.

Population Reporting Aboriginal Origins, 1986 and 1991 Censuses

	1986	1991	% Change
Canada	**711,720**	**1,002,675**	**41**
Newfoundland	9,555	13,110	37
Prince Edward Island	1,290	1,880	46
Nova Scotia	14,225	21,885	54
New Brunswick	9,375	12,815	37
Quebec	80,945	137,615	70
Ontario	167,375	243,550	46
Manitoba	85,235	116,200	36
Saskatchewan	77,650	96,580	24
Alberta	103,925	148,220	43
British Columbia	126,625	169,035	33
Yukon	4,995	6,390	28
Northwest Territories	30,530	35,390	16

Population Reporting Aboriginal Origins, 1991 Census

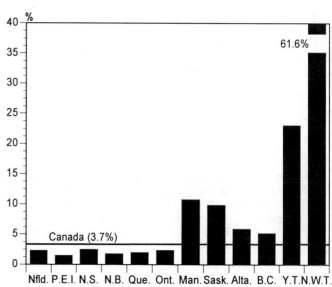

Population Reporting Aboriginal Origins, 1986 and 1991 Censuses

	Single Responses			Multiple Responses		
	1986	1991	% Change	1986	1991	% Change
Canada	**373,260**	**470,615**	**26.1**	**338,460**	**532,060**	**57.2**
Newfoundland	3,825	5,340	39.6	5,730	7,770	35.6
Prince Edward Island	410	395	–	875	1,480	69.1
Nova Scotia	5,960	7,530	26.3	8,260	14,355	73.8
New Brunswick	3,880	4,270	10.1	5,500	8,550	55.5
Quebec	49,325	65,405	32.6	31,620	72,210	128.4
Ontario	55,560	71,005	27.8	111,815	172,545	54.3
Manitoba	55,410	74,345	34.2	29,820	41,855	40.4
Saskatchewan	55,645	66,270	19.1	22,005	30,310	37.7
Alberta	51,665	68,445	32.5	52,265	79,780	52.6
British Columbia	61,130	74,420	21.7	65,495	94,620	44.5
Yukon	3,280	3,775	15.1	1,715	2,610	52.2
Northwest Territories	27,175	29,415	8.2	3,355	5,970	77.9

Just over half with Aboriginal origins also reported non-Aboriginal origins

Of those people who reported having Aboriginal ancestors, 47% reported a single Aboriginal origin while 53% reported multiple ancestries. Among those reporting multiple ancestries, the majority (98%) reported Aboriginal origins in combination with non-Aboriginal origins. The remaining 2% had multiple Aboriginal origins only, for example, North American Indian and Inuit origins.

Over the 1986-1991 period, the number of people who reported having one Aboriginal origin in combination with other origins grew faster than the number who reported a single Aboriginal origin only. In 1991, 532,060 people reported that they had Aboriginal origins in combination with other origins, up 57% from 1986. In comparison, the number of people who reported a single Aboriginal origin rose by 26% over the same period: from 373,260 in 1986 to 470,615 in 1991.

North American Indian responses more numerous

Over three-quarters (78%) of the 1,002,675 people who reported Aboriginal origins reported North American Indian ancestry. When single and multiple responses are combined, 783,980 people reported North American Indian, 212,650 reported Métis and 49,255 reported Inuit.

Some people reported a combination of different Aboriginal/non-Aboriginal origins. These combinations of responses were counted under each relevant Aboriginal group. As a result, the sum of the various

Persons Reporting North American Indian, 1991 Census

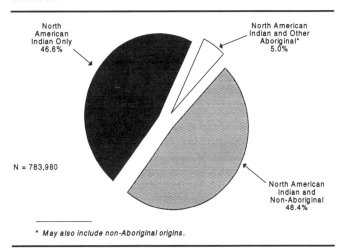

* May also include non-Aboriginal origins.

Aboriginal responses (1,045,885) was slightly greater than the total population reporting an Aboriginal ancestry (1,002,675).

Of the three Aboriginal groups, those people reporting an Inuit origin were the least likely to report having another origin: 61% of people who reported Inuit reported having Inuit origins only. Among people who reported North American Indian origins, slightly more had North American Indian origins in combination with non-Aboriginal origins (379,470 people) than had only North American Indian origins (365,375). A similar situation was recorded for people who reported Métis origins: 99,560 reported Métis and non-Aboriginal origins while 75,150 reported Métis origins only.

Persons Reporting Métis, 1991 Census

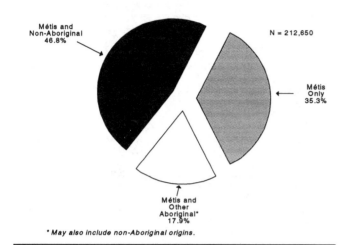

N = 212,650

Métis and Non-Aboriginal 46.8%

Métis Only 35.3%

Métis and Other Aboriginal* 17.9%

May also include non-Aboriginal origins.

Persons Reporting Inuit, 1991 Census

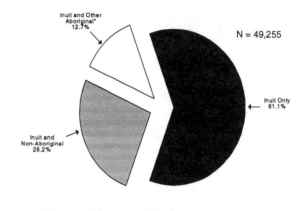

N = 49,255

Inuit and Other Aboriginal* 12.7%

Inuit Only 61.1%

Inuit and Non-Aboriginal 26.2%

May also include non-Aboriginal origins.

Indian reserves and settlements

The 1991 Census enumerated 207,470 people living on Indian reserves and settlements across the country. Of these, 188,270 people reported Aboriginal origins. A large proportion, 86%, of all those who were living on Indian reserves and settlements in 1991 reported having a single Aboriginal origin.

While the 1991 Census enumerated the majority of Indian reserves and settlements in Canada there were 78 Indian reserves and settlements (out of about 950 occupied and unoccupied territories) where enumeration was not permitted, was interrupted before it could be completed, was late or the quality of the collected data was considered inadequate. It is estimated that approximately 38,000 persons were missed on these incompletely enumerated Indian reserves and settlements. (For further information, see the note on page 77).

Among people living on Indian reserves and settlements who reported an Aboriginal origin, the majority, 94%, reported North American Indian as their only origin. Only a small proportion (4%) reported having a single Aboriginal origin (North American Indian, Métis or Inuit) in combination with a non-Aboriginal origin.

Overall, 48% (176,620 people) of all those who reported having North American Indian origins only, lived on Indian reserves and settlements. In comparison, 2% of those who reported Métis origins only, and less than 1% of those with Inuit origins only, lived on Indian reserves and settlements.

The 1991 Census also collected information on the number of persons who were registered Indians as defined by the **Indian Act** of Canada. Some 386,000 people reported being registered under this Act. This count excludes people who were living on Indian reserves and settlements where enumeration was not permitted, was interrupted, occurred too late for inclusion, or where the quality of the data collected was considered inadequate. Also excluded from this count were Registered Indians living in institutions and those who were otherwise missed by the census.

Population on Indian Reserves and Indian Settlements, 1991 Census

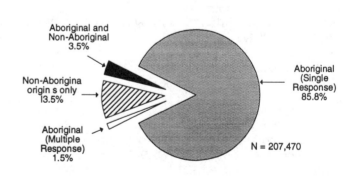

Aboriginal and Non-Aboriginal 3.5%

Non-Aboriginal origins only 13.5%

Aboriginal (Multiple Response) 1.5%

Aboriginal (Single Response) 85.8%

N = 207,470

May also include non-Aboriginal origins.

Almost all identified with one Aboriginal group

The 1991 Aboriginal Peoples Survey found that 625,710 people who reported Aboriginal origins and/or who were registered under the **Indian Act** of Canada identified with an Aboriginal group. The vast majority (99%) of these people identified with just one Aboriginal group – North American Indian, Métis or Inuit.

Seven out of ten lived west of Ontario

Approximately 69% of the population who identified with an Aboriginal group lived west of Ontario, compared to 29% of Canada's total population. The difference was most apparent in the Prairie provinces. Manitoba, Saskatchewan and Alberta were home to almost half (46%) of all people who identified with an Aboriginal group in 1991, but home to only 17% of Canada's total population. The Northwest Territories, with less than 1% of Canada's total population, accounted for almost 6% of the population who identified with an Aboriginal group.

> ### 1991 Aboriginal Peoples Survey
>
> *A large-scale survey of people who reported Aboriginal ancestry and/or who reported being registered under the **Indian Act** of Canada was conducted after the 1991 Census. This survey, the Aboriginal Peoples Survey, was developed in consultation with Aboriginal organizations and government departments. From those people who identified as North American Indian, Métis or Inuit, the survey collected information on such issues as employment, education, language, health and mobility.*
>
> *It should be noted that 181 Indian reserves and settlements (approximately 20,000 persons) and another 14 Aboriginal communities (approximately 2,000 persons) who participated in the 1991 Census did not participate in the Aboriginal Peoples Survey. (For further information on Indian reserves and settlements not surveyed by the Aboriginal Peoples Survey, see the note on page 77).*

People who identified with an Aboriginal group were much less likely to live in a major urban centre than was the Canadian population in general. Overall, 26% of those who identified with an Aboriginal group lived in the eleven census metropolitan areas included in the Aboriginal Peoples Survey. In comparison, those eleven metropolitan areas were home to almost 47% of Canada's total population.

A young population

Age distributions reveal other differences between the total Canadian population and the population who identified with an Aboriginal group. The Aboriginal Peoples Survey revealed that the population identifying with an Aboriginal group tended to be much younger than Canada's total population: 38% were under the age of 15, compared with 21% for Canada's total population. Seven per cent of the population identifying with an Aboriginal group was aged 55 years and over, compared to 20% for Canada's total population.

Population Distribution, 1991 Aboriginal Peoples Survey

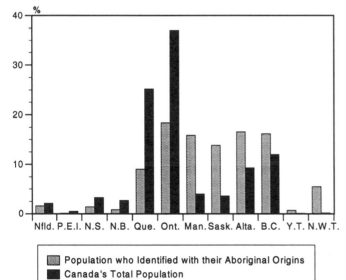

Population Distribution by Age Groups, 1991 Aboriginal Peoples Survey

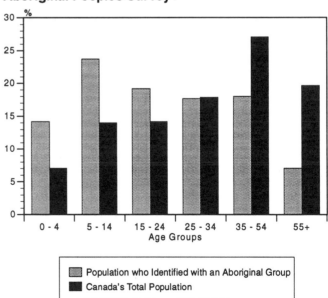

North American Indian

The Aboriginal Peoples Survey found that 460,680 people identified themselves as North American Indian. Of these, 64% lived off-reserve, while the remainder, 36%, lived on-reserve. It should be noted that 181 Indian reserves and settlements (representing approximately 20,000 people) and another 14 Aboriginal communities (representing approximately 2,000 people) who participated in the 1991 Census did not participate in the Aboriginal Peoples Survey. (For further information on Indian reserves and settlements not surveyed by the Aboriginal Peoples Survey, see note on page 77).

Geographically, the population identifying as North American Indian was concentrated in five provinces: Ontario, Manitoba, Saskatchewan, Alberta and British Columbia. Combined, these provinces were home to 84% of people who reported that they identified as North American Indian.

Population Distribution, 1991 Aboriginal Peoples Survey

	Canada's Total Population %	Population Who Identified as North American Indian %
Canada	**100.0**	**100.0**
Number	**26,994,045**	**460,680**
Newfoundland	2.1	0.8
Prince Edward Island	0.5	0.2
Nova Scotia	3.3	1.9
New Brunswick	2.7	1.1
Quebec	25.2	9.0
Ontario	37.0	22.3
Manitoba	4.0	14.4
Saskatchewan	3.6	13.0
Alberta	9.3	14.1
British Columbia	12.0	20.2
Yukon	0.1	0.9
Northwest Territories	0.2	2.1

Compared to Canada's total population, those who identified as North American Indian were 2.5 times as likely to live in Manitoba, Saskatchewan or Alberta. These provinces accounted for almost 42% of the population who identified as North American Indian, compared to just 17% of Canada's total population.

Of the eleven census metropolitan areas included in the Aboriginal Peoples Survey, Regina had the highest concentration of people who identified as North American Indian (3.9%) while Saskatoon and Winnipeg, with 3.1% identifying as North American Indian, were next.

Distribution by Age Groups, 1991 Aboriginal Peoples Survey

Age Groups	Canada's Total Population %	Population Who Identified as North American Indian %
Total	100.0	100.0
0 - 4	7.1	14.0
5 - 14	14.0	23.4
15 - 24	14.2	19.4
25 - 34	17.9	17.6
35 - 54	27.1	18.4
55 +	19.7	7.2

The Aboriginal Peoples Survey found that almost one-quarter (23%) of the population who identified as North American Indian was between the ages of 5 and 14 in 1991, compared to only 14% for the total Canadian population. Some 14% of those who identified as North American Indian were under the age of five, compared to 7% for Canada's total population.

When all age groups were compared, the biggest difference between the population identifying as North American Indian and Canada's total population occured in the over 55 age group: just 7% of the North American Indian group belonged to this age group compared to 20% of Canada's total population.

Métis

Population Distribution, 1991 Aboriginal Peoples Survey

	Canada's Total Population %	Population Who Identified as Métis %
Canada	**100.0**	**100.0**
Number	**26,994,045**	**135,265**
Newfoundland	2.1	1.5
Prince Edward Island	0.5	-
Nova Scotia	3.3	0.2
New Brunswick	2.7	0.1
Quebec	25.2	6.4
Ontario	37.0	8.9
Manitoba	4.0	24.6
Saskatchewan	3.6	20.0
Alberta	9.3	28.6
British Columbia	12.0	6.7
Yukon	0.1	0.1
Northwest Territories	0.2	2.9

Distribution by Age Groups, 1991 Aboriginal Peoples Survey

Age Groups	Canada's Total Population %	Population Who Identified as Métis %
Total	100.0	100.0
0 - 4	7.1	14.1
5 - 14	14.0	23.7
15 - 24	14.2	18.6
25 - 34	17.9	18.4
35 - 54	27.1	18.3
55 +	19.7	6.9

The Aboriginal Peoples Survey found that of the 625,710 individuals who identified with an Aboriginal group 135,265 identified as Métis.

When compared to Canada's total population, people who identified as Métis were much more likely to live in Manitoba, Saskatchewan and Alberta. Almost three-quarters (73%) of people who identified as Métis lived in these three provinces while the same can be said for only 17% of Canada's total population.

While 25% of Canada's total population lived in Quebec and another 37% in Ontario, these two provinces were home to just 6% and 9%, respectively, of the population who identified as Métis.

Compared to the population who identified as North American Indian, the population who identified as Métis was more likely to live in a major metropolitan area. While about one-quarter (24%) of the North American Indian population lived in the eleven census metropolitan areas included in the 1991 Aboriginal Peoples Survey, almost 38% of the Métis population lived in these cities. Overall, 47% of Canada's population lived in these eleven census metropolitan areas.

Of the eleven census metropolitan areas included in the Aboriginal Peoples Survey, Saskatoon had the highest concentration of people who identified as Métis (2.7%), followed by Winnipeg (2.3%), Regina (2.0%) and Edmonton (1.6%).

The age structure of the population who identified as Métis was very similar to that of the population who identified as North American Indian. A large proportion (38%) of the population who identified as Métis were under age 15 and a small proportion (7%) were over age 55. Of Canada's total population, 21% were under age 15 and 20% were aged 55 and over.

Persons Who Identified as Métis and North American Indian Living in Selected Census Metropolitan Areas, 1991 Aboriginal Peoples Survey

	Canada's Total Population Number	Métis Number	Métis %	North American Indian Number	North American Indian %
Halifax	317,630	–	–	1,135	0.4
Montréal	3,091,115	1,675	0.1	5,400	0.2
Ottawa-Hull	912,100	1,425	0.2	5,195	0.6
Toronto	3,863,105	1,430	0.1	12,920	0.3
Winnipeg	645,610	14,990	2.3	20,255	3.1
Regina	189,440	3,720	2.0	7,300	3.9
Saskatoon	207,825	5,585	2.7	6,380	3.1
Calgary	748,210	4,285	0.6	9,870	1.3
Edmonton	832,155	13,515	1.6	15,910	1.9
Vancouver	1,584,115	4,070	0.3	21,845	1.4
Victoria	283,630	345	0.1	4,130	1.5

Inuit

The Aboriginal Peoples Survey found that 36,215 people identified as Inuit.

Almost 91% of people who identified as Inuit lived in the Northwest Territories, Quebec (primarily the northern areas), Newfoundland and Labrador. In comparison, 28% of Canada's total population lived in these areas.

Population Distribution, 1991 Aboriginal Peoples Survey

	Canada's Total Population %	Population Who Identified as Inuit %
Canada	100.0	100.0
Number	26,994,045	36,215
Newfoundland	2.1	13.0
Prince Edward Island	0.5	-
Nova Scotia	3.3	0.2
New Brunswick	2.7	0.2
Quebec	25.2	19.4
Ontario	37.0	2.2
Manitoba	4.0	1.3
Saskatchewan	3.6	0.4
Alberta	9.3	3.7
British Columbia	12.0	1.4
Yukon	0.1	0.2
Northwest Territories	0.2	58.1

Distribution by Age Groups, 1991 Aboriginal Peoples Survey

Age Groups	Canada's Total Population %	Population Who Identified as Inuit %
Total	100.0	100.0
0 - 4	7.1	17.0
5 - 14	14.0	25.5
15 - 24	14.2	20.3
25 - 34	17.9	16.6
35 - 54	27.1	14.2
55 +	19.7	6.3

While the proportion of those 15 years and under for the North American Indian and Métis populations were larger than for the total Canadian population, this difference was even greater for those who identified as Inuit: almost 43% were under 15 years, compared to 37% of those who identified as North American Indian, 38% of those who identified as Métis and 21% for the total Canadian population.

Compared to the other two Aboriginal groups, a slightly smaller proportion of those who identified as Inuit were over age 55: 6% of the population who identified as Inuit versus about 7% for the populations who identified as North American Indian or Métis.

Comparability of 1986 and 1991 Ethnic Origin Data

The ethnic origin question on the 1991 Census was similar to that asked on the last Census in 1986. In an effort to explain clearly that the purpose of the question was to measure the ancestral origins of the Canadian population, the wording of the 1991 question was changed slightly and a note was included on the questionnaire summarizing the purpose of the question. These changes should not affect the comparability of ethnic origin data between 1986 and 1991.

Nevertheless, caution must be exercised in making comparisons. Measures of ethnicity are complex, and can be affected by changes in the environment in which the questions are asked as well as by changes in respondents' understanding or views about the topic. Changes in such factors as awareness of family background or length of time since immigration can affect responses to the question, as can confusion with other concepts such as citizenship, nationality, language or cultural identity. In the case of the 1991 Census, public attention on Aboriginal issues in the year leading up to the Census may have contributed to increased reporting of Aboriginal origins; similarly, pre-census publicity calling for the reporting of Canadian as an expression of national identity may have contributed to a substantial increase in the number of persons providing this response and a decrease in other origins, especially British.

Single and Multiple Responses

*A **single response** occurs when a respondent reports one ethnic origin only. For example, 365,375 persons gave North American Indian as their only origin.*

*A **multiple response** occurs when a respondent provides two or more ethnic origins. In 1991, 532,060 people gave a combination of **at least** two of the following types of responses: North American Indian, Métis, Inuit and non-Aboriginal.*

In responding to the census question on ethnic origin, some people reported a combination of Aboriginal/non-Aboriginal origins. These combinations of responses are counted under each relevant Aboriginal group. As a result, the sum of the various Aboriginal responses is greater than the total population reporting an Aboriginal ancestry.

Incompletely Enumerated Indian Reserves: 1991 Census and 1991 Aboriginal Peoples Survey:

Some 78 Indian reserves and Indian settlements were incompletely enumerated during the 1991 Census. As a result, data for 1991 are not available for those reserves and settlements. Because of these missing data, users are cautioned that for affected geographic areas, comparisons (e.g. percentage change) between 1986 and 1991 are not exact. For larger areas (Canada, provinces, territories, census metropolitan areas) the impact of the missing data is quite small.
Because the sample for the Aboriginal Peoples Survey was selected from the 1991 Census, these 78 reserves and settlements are also not included in the Aboriginal Peoples Survey. An additional 181 Indian reserves and settlements, representing some 20,000 people, were incompletely enumerated during the Aboriginal Peoples Survey because enumeration was not permitted or was interrupted before all questionnaires could be completed.

*Lists of these incompletely enumerated reserves and settlements can be found in **Age and Sex** (Catalogue No. 94-327).*

Catalogue 11-001E (Français 11-001F) ISSN 0827-0465

Tuesday, April 13, 1993

INCOME

HIGHLIGHTS

- Real family incomes increased in every province and territory during 1985-90, largely offsetting losses which occurred during the recession of the early 1980s

- Women represented 20% of the earners in the 10 highest paying occupations in 1990, up from 14% in 1985. Women also accounted for three out of four earners in the 10 lowest paying occupations

- Nearly half of all earners in the 10 highest paying occupations were general or senior managers, of whom eight out of 10 were men

- The lowest average employment income in 1990 was for child care occupations at $13,518

- After adjustment for inflation, women's average wage grew 11% between 1985 and 1990, while men's average wage grew by only 3%

Selected Income Statistics
Employment Income by Occupation

Selected Income Statistics (93-331, $40) presents information on the 1985 and 1990 total income and employment income of individuals 15 years and over by sex, age, work activity and marital status; 1985 and 1990 family and household income by structure, combination of earners, household type and size and the incidence of low income among families, unattached individuals and the population in 1985 and 1990.

Employment Income by Occupation (93-332, $40) presents information on the average employment income of the population 15 years of age and over in 1985 and 1990, and for the population working full-year, full-time by sex and detailed occupation.

Both publications provide 20% sample data from the 1991 Census for Canada, provinces and territories. Census metropolitan area data are included in *Selected Income Statistics*.

 Statistics   Statistique
Canada   Canada

This release describes some of the changes in income distributions and income levels for individuals, families, and households across the country. Because the 1991 Census was conducted half way through the year, it measured income levels for 1990. Similarly, the 1986 Census measured income for 1985.

Although more recent survey data for 1991 incomes at the national and provincial levels have been published by Statistics Canada, the national census is the only source of data which permits analysis of incomes of all kinds for smaller geographic areas (such as metropolitan areas) and for specific subgroups of the population (such as lone-parent families, recent immigrants, seniors, or persons with disabilities). Of equal importance, census data enable detailed analysis of incomes in relation to a wide range of factors such as education, occupation or language knowledge which influence income levels.

Impact of inflation

All income data in this release are presented in constant 1990 dollars. Incomes from previous censuses have been adjusted for changes in the prices of goods and services using the Consumer Price Index.

For example, the average income of a census family in 1990 was $51,300 compared with $37,800 in 1985. This is an increase of 36% before adjustment. When changes in prices are taken into account, real (constant-dollar) family income was higher by only 9% compared with 1985.

Incomes heading into the '90s

In 1990, there were 19.4 million income recipients, 49% of whom were women. The aggregate income of individuals from various sources amounted to $466 billion in 1990. The average income of men from all sources was $30,205, up 4.3% from 1985, and $17,577 for women, up 11.9%. Average total income of all income recipients was $24,001 in 1990.

The recession of the early 1980s had a significant impact on Canadian incomes. The 1986 Census showed that, on average, real incomes of individuals and families in 1985 were lower than in 1980. By 1990, average incomes of families and households had mostly recovered to, or surpassed, pre-recession levels although more recent survey data show a recession-induced decline again in 1991.

Most family incomes grew during the last half of the 1980s

Average family income was $51,342 in 1990. After accounting for a 1% decline from 1980-85, and then a 9% increase in the second part of the decade, average family income climbed 8% between 1980 and 1990. The largest percentage increase in family incomes in the last half of the 1980s occurred among female lone-parent families (about 788,000 families). After close to a 3% decline during 1980-85, their average income increased 11% during 1985-90. At $26,550, it was still only 52% of the overall average family income. Male lone-parent families (165,000) had the largest decline in average family income during 1980-85, and their 1990 average income at $40,792 was 1.3% below the 1980 peak.

By far the largest proportion of Canadians live in husband-wife census families (6.4 million). Overall, average family income ($54,667) for this group was 9% above the 1980 level, again after a decline and recovery cycle during the first and second halves of the 1980s. The incomes of husband-wife families varied substantially depending on whether the wife had employment income. The 4.2 million husband-wife families where the wife had employment income were the only families that maintained their income levels during 1980-85, and they subsequently had an increase of 9%, to an average of $61,950 in 1990. However, the average family income of the 2.2 million families where the wife had no employment had yet to recover from the 1980-85 decline in their average income. In 1990, their average family income at $40,568 was 1.4% below their 1980 level.

Census Family

A census family is a now-married couple (with or without never-married sons or daughters of either or both spouses), a couple living common-law (again with or without never-married sons or daughters of either or both partners), or a lone parent of any marital status, with at least one never-married son or daughter living in the same dwelling.

Number of Census Families and their Average Income in Constant (1990) Dollars

	Number of Census Families				
	1980	1985	1990	% change 1980-85	% change 1985-90
All Families	**6,325,315**	**6,733,845**	**7,355,730**	**6.5**	**9.2**
Husband-wife Families	5,611,495	5,880,550	6,402,090	4.8	8.9
Wife with employment income	3,101,375	3,464,815	4,221,510	11.7	21.8
Wife without employment income	2,510,125	2,415,735	2,180,575	-3.8	-9.7
Lone-parent Families	713,815	853,300	953,645	19.5	11.8
Male lone-parent	124,380	151,485	165,245	21.8	9.1
Female lone-parent	589,435	701,815	788,400	19.1	12.3
	Average Family Income				
	1980 $	1985 $	1990 $	% change 1980-85	% change 1985-90
All Families	**47,565**	**47,087**	**51,342**	**-1.0**	**9.0**
Husband-wife Families	50,124	50,068	54,667	-0.1	9.2
Wife with employment income	57,396	57,536	61,950	0.2	7.7
Wife without employment income	41,139	39,358	40,568	-4.3	3.1
Lone-parent Families	27,452	26,540	29,018	-3.3	9.3
Male lone-parent	41,333	38,903	40,792	-5.9	4.9
Female lone-parent	24,523	23,871	26,550	-2.7	11.2

Income increases varied by region

Between 1980 and 1985, average family incomes declined in the Yukon Territory and five provinces. In the other provinces and the Northwest Territories, family incomes stayed the same or had modest increases.

Family incomes subsequently increased in every province and territory between 1985 and 1990. Manitoba, Saskatchewan and Alberta experienced the smallest increase in family income – between 2% and 4% – while families in Nova Scotia and Quebec gained 7% to 8%. In all other provinces and territories, average family income increased between 10% and 14%.

When the effect of these increases is combined with the declines of the early 1980s, changes in family incomes in the provinces and territories between 1980 and 1990 varied substantially. Over the decade (1980 to 1990) the largest gains were recorded by families in the Northwest Territories (20%), Prince Edward Island (18%), Ontario (15%) and Nova Scotia (13%). The

Average Income of Census Families in Constant (1990) Dollars

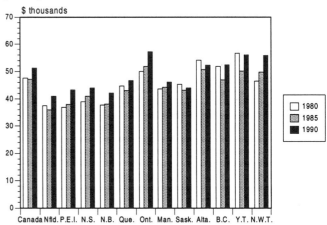

1990 family incomes in the Yukon, Alberta and Saskatchewan were still lower than the 1980 level.

Regional disparities continued to decline

Historically, family incomes have ranged widely among the provinces and territories. In 1970, the Yukon had the highest average family income and Newfoundland had the lowest: the two averages differed by 68%. By 1980, the disparity had decreased to 54% between the regions with the highest (the Yukon) and lowest (Prince Edward Island) average family incomes. In 1990, this spread between the highest (Ontario) and this lowest (Newfoundland) had decreased to 40%.

More families had higher incomes

The distribution of families by income size changed between 1985 and 1990 with more families falling into

higher income groups. The proportion of families with a total income of $80,000 or more increased to 14.6% (representing 1.1 million families) in 1990, up from 11.3% in 1985. In contrast, the proportion of families with a total income of less than $20,000 declined to 15.8% (representing 1.2 million families) in 1990 from 18.6% in 1985.

This trend occurred for all family types between 1985 and 1990. For example, among male lone-parent families, the proportion with an income of less than $20,000 decreased to 23.7% in 1990 from 27.6% in 1985 and it decreased to 47% from 52.8% for female lone-parents over the same period.

Census Families by Family Structure and Combination of Employment Income Recipients Showing Family Income Groups, 1990

Combination of employment income recipients	Number (000s)	Under $20,000	$20,000-$39,999	$40,000-$59,999	$60,000-$79,999	$80,000-$99,999	$100,000 +	Average income $
All Families	**7,356**	**15.8**	**27.2**	**26.3**	**16.1**	**7.5**	**7.2**	**51,342**
Husband-wife Families								
Husband-wife and child	899	1.9	9.6	23.4	27.1	18.2	19.7	78,372
Husband and wife	3,063	5.3	22.3	33.4	21.8	9.2	7.9	59,069
Husband and child	257	3.8	19.8	32.3	22.3	10.6	11.3	64,925
Husband only	958	13.9	39.2	29.3	9.7	3.3	4.5	44,894
Wife and child	58	7.8	28.9	32.0	17.5	8.0	5.8	52,681
Wife only	201	25.5	43.4	20.4	6.6	2.2	2.0	35,031
Child only	111	13.9	34.5	28.1	13.6	5.8	4.2	46,185
No recipient	855	42.0	40.6	11.3	3.6	1.3	1.2	27,665
Lone-parent Families								
Male								
with employment income	147	16.8	36.1	27.9	11.2	4.0	3.9	44,089
without employment income	18	80.0	15.5	3.0	0.7	0.4	0.3	14,109
Female								
Female lone-parent and child	187	14.1	41.2	28.6	10.7	3.3	2.1	41,298
Female lone-parent only	287	47.0	41.2	9.5	1.6	0.4	0.4	23,689
Child only	122	28.9	39.3	20.3	7.1	2.6	1.9	34,748
No recipient	193	90.7	7.8	1.0	0.3	0.1	0.1	11,319

Impact of number of earners on family income

Family incomes vary widely depending on the number and combination of employment income recipients in the family. In 1985, 55% of all husband-wife families reported employment income for both spouses. By 1990, this proportion had increased to 62%. Their average family income in 1990 at $63,451 was 57% higher than that for all other husband-wife families.

Husband-wife families where no family member reported employment income had an average income of $27,665, and four out of 10 had incomes under $20,000. At the other end of the spectrum were families where husbands, wives and at least one child had employment income in 1990. Their average income was $78,372, and two out of 10 had an income of at least $100,000.

In 1990, average incomes were $11,319 for female lone-parent families and $14,109 for male lone-parent families with no earners. With one earner in the family, these average incomes increased to $31,474 for female lone-parent families and to $44,089 for male lone-parent families.

Household incomes rose in major metropolitan areas

Average household income rose in almost all metropolitan areas between 1985 and 1990. The increases ranged from 1% in Regina to almost 18% in Sudbury. Saskatoon was the only metropolitan area where average household income declined slightly (-0.4%) compared to 1985. Nine areas registered increases above the national rate of 8.2% (Sudbury, Victoria, Vancouver, Kitchener, Saint John, Toronto, Hamilton, Oshawa and London).

Ranked by size of average household income, households in Toronto had the highest income ($59,450), followed by Oshawa, Ottawa-Hull and Calgary. Although these four areas were also at the top in 1985, Oshawa moved up from fourth to second highest in 1990. At the other end of the scale, the areas with the lowest average household income in 1990 were Sherbrooke ($36,611), followed by Trois-Rivières, Chicoutimi-Jonquière and Saskatoon.

Families by Income Groups and Number of Earners, 1990

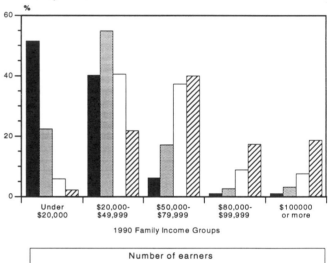
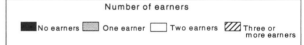

Average Household Income for Census Metropolitan Areas

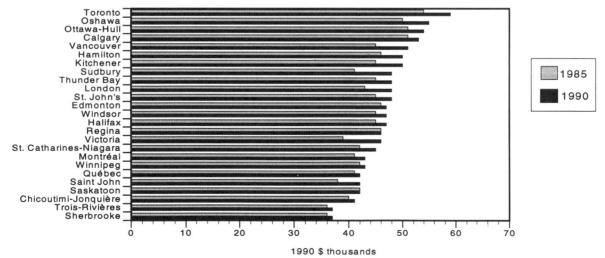

One-person households shared in the increase

Almost one-quarter (22.8%) of all households in 1990 consisted of only one person. Their average income of $23,716 was just over half of the $46,137 average for all households (which averaged 2.7 persons per household). Among metropolitan areas, increases in the average income of one-person households between 1985 and 1990 ranged from 3% in Calgary to 15% in St. Catharines-Niagara. Saskatoon was the only area where the average income of one person households declined (-1%). In 1990, average income for one-person households was lowest ($18,650) in Trois-Rivières and highest ($30,527) in Toronto.

More Canadians reported employment income

Close to 15 million Canadians reported employment income (wages and salaries, and net income from farm and non-farm self-employment) in 1990, up 2 million from 1985. Of these, 52% or 7.7 million worked full-year, full-time. About 61% of full-year, full-time workers were men, down from 65% in 1985, and 39% were women, up from 35% in 1985.

Women fared better than men

Women's average earnings increased 11% while men's increased 3% between 1985 and 1990. As a result, average employment income of women as a percentage of average employment income of men increased slightly, for full-year, full-time workers as well as for all workers. This continued the trend of increasing the ratio of female to male earnings seen since 1970.

Employment income increased in most metropolitan areas

Average employment income increased between 1985 and 1990 in 17 metropolitan areas across the country, from 0.3% in Québec City to 13% in Sudbury. Areas experiencing declines included all five Prairie metropolitan areas (Winnipeg, Regina, Saskatoon, Calgary and Edmonton), two in Quebec (Chicoutimi-Jonquière and Sherbrooke), and one in Ontario (Windsor).

Toronto, Ottawa-Hull and Oshawa metropolitan areas recorded the highest average employment incomes in 1990 while Sherbrooke and Saskatoon recorded the lowest.

For women, earnings increased in all metropolitan areas, between 15% to 20% in six areas, and by 21% in Hamilton and 23% in Oshawa. For men, average earnings fell in eight metropolitan areas, notably in all Prairie metropolitan areas. Earnings for men increased in metropolitan areas in British Columbia and the Atlantic provinces, while Windsor, Ontario, posted the largest decline (-3.6%).

Highest and lowest paying occupations

Over a quarter of a million (268,200) full-year, full-time workers were in the 10 occupations with highest earnings, while 235,500 were engaged in the 10 lowest paying occupations. (Employment income data are available for 514 occupational categories).

Average Employment Income by Work Activity in Constant (1990) Dollars

Population 15 years and over with employment income	Number			Average Employment Income		
	1985	1990	% change	1985	1990	% change
Both Sexes	13,074,460	14,905,395	14.0	23,319	24,329	4.3
Worked full-year, full-time(1)	6,580,875	7,718,780	17.3	33,337	33,714	1.1
Worked part-year or part-time	6,493,580	7,186,610	10.7	13,166	14,248	8.2
Male	7,386,820	8,105,020	9.7	28,918	29,847	3.2
Worked full-year, full-time(1)	4,249,365	4,699,895	10.6	37,972	38,648	1.8
Worked part-year or part-time	3,137,455	3,405,125	8.5	16,655	17,701	6.3
Female	5,687,640	6,800,370	19.6	16,047	17,751	10.6
Worked full-year, full-time(1)	2,331,515	3,018,885	29.5	24,890	26,033	4.6
Worked part-year or part-time	3,356,125	3,781,485	12.7	9,904	11,139	12.5

(1) Worked 49-52 weeks in the reference year, mostly full-time.

Judges and magistrates recorded the highest average earnings ($102,646) in 1990, followed by physicians and surgeons ($102,370) and dentists ($95,776). General managers and other senior officials, with an average employment income of $67,997, accounted for 48% of all persons in the top 10 occupations.

Women made strong inroads in high paying occupations

Women made up 20% of all earners in the 10 highest paying occupations. This was a significant increase from 1985 when the proportion of women in these occupations was 14%.

Between 1985 and 1990, the number of men in these occupations dropped by a percentage point, due to a decrease of 13% in male general managers and senior officials. The number of women, on the other hand, increased by 53%. This increase was spread across the 10 occupations.

While the largest relative increase occurred among osteopaths and chiropractors, the largest numeric increase occurred among general managers

and other senior officials, where the number of women rose by 44% from 17,100 in 1985 to 24,600 in 1990.

In 1985, overall earnings of women in these occupations amounted to 60.2% of men's earnings. This ratio increased to 61.2% in 1990, with average employment income of women at $48,609 compared to $79,463 for men.

In the lowest paying occupations, three out of four workers were women

In 1990, overall average earnings of full-year, full-time workers in the 10 lowest paying occupations were $15,092. The average earnings for each of the 10 occupations in this group did not vary much from the overall average. The lowest average employment income ($13,518) was for child-care occupations, while the highest at $16,600 was for livestock farm workers.

The average earnings of women ($13,673) in these occupations amounted to 72.8% of the average for men ($18,794). Nearly three-quarters of full-year, full-time workers in the 10 lowest paying occupations in 1990 were women.

Average Employment Income of Earners, in Constant (1990) Dollars

	Both Sexes		Men		Women	
	1990	% change from 1985	1990	% change from 1985	1990	% change from 1985
Canada	**24,329**	**4.3**	**29,847**	**3.2**	**17,751**	**10.6**
Sudbury	25,990	13.0	33,574	13.4	17,119	16.9
Toronto	29,133	10.0	35,451	7.0	22,082	17.9
Kitchener	24,872	9.7	31,309	7.6	17,437	17.9
London	24,961	8.1	30,942	5.9	18,499	15.6
Saint John	22,944	8.0	29,337	9.7	15,352	8.3
Hamilton	26,306	7.6	33,029	4.0	18,494	21.2
Oshawa	27,971	6.9	35,180	3.4	19,342	23.4
Victoria	23,727	6.8	29,119	4.6	17,788	14.0
Ottawa-Hull	28,248	3.8	33,870	1.7	21,954	10.1
Vancouver	26,217	3.5	32,335	2.1	19,180	8.8
Thunder Bay	25,085	3.2	31,478	0.4	17,511	15.2
St. Catharines-Niagara	23,379	2.9	30,129	0.9	15,416	15.4
St. John's	22,496	2.8	27,779	3.5	16,650	5.4
Halifax	24,155	2.1	29,866	1.0	17,603	8.0
Montréal	24,969	1.8	30,153	0.7	18,865	7.4
Trois-Rivières	23,035	0.7	28,949	1.0	15,299	6.0
Québec	24,314	0.3	29,417	-0.4	18,267	5.8
Sherbrooke	21,605	-0.2	26,340	-0.8	16,182	4.2
Winnipeg	22,773	-0.6	27,818	-3.3	17,147	7.3
Chicoutimi-Jonquière	24,576	-1.2	30,588	0.4	15,934	2.4
Edmonton	24,285	-1.2	30,022	-1.8	17,643	2.1
Windsor	25,139	-1.3	31,335	-3.6	17,690	9.4
Calgary	26,595	-1.4	33,142	-2.0	19,027	2.1
Saskatoon	22,147	-2.8	27,722	-3.6	15,961	2.2
Regina	23,794	-2.9	29,395	-3.6	17,668	0.5

Women's wages rose much faster than men's

About 13.5 million people reported wages and salaries in 1990. The number of wage earners increased three times faster in the second half of the 1980s than in the first half. Compared with an addition of only 520,000 persons between 1980 and 1985, the number of wage earners increased by 1.5 million between 1985 and 1990. In both periods, the rate of increase was much faster for women than for men. Over the past decade, the number of male wage earners increased by 10.5% while that of women increased by about 28%.

Even more noteworthy were the changes in the average wages of men and women during the period. The recession of the early 1980s was much more severe on male wage earners than on female wage earners. Between 1980 and 1985, the average wage of women grew by 3% but that of men declined by 3%. While the average wage of men grew by 3% to $29,757 between 1985 and 1990, that of women increased by 11% to $17,933. Thus, over the decade, the real wages of female wage earners increased by 14%; male wage earners, on average, were no better off in 1990 than in 1980.

Average Earnings of Full-Year, Full-Time[1] Working Men and Women in Ten Highest and Ten Lowest Paying Occupations, 1990

Occupation*	Number of Earners			Average earnings		
	Total	Men	Women	Total $	Men $	Women $
Ten highest paying occupations	**268,220**	**214,755**	**53,460**	**73,313**	**79,463**	**48,609**
Judges and magistrates	2,135	1,660	475	102,646	109,313	79,204
Physicians and surgeons	31,435	24,120	7,320	102,370	111,261	73,071
Dentists	6,775	6,015	760	95,776	99,280	67,997
Lawyers and notaries	41,180	30,755	10,430	76,966	86,108	50,012
General managers and other senior officials	129,225	104,645	24,580	67,997	74,425	40,633
Other managers and administrators mines,quarries and oil wells	3,870	2,915	950	64,893	73,281	39,151
Air pilots, navigators and flight engineers	7,490	7,110	375	64,316	66,087	31,026
Osteopaths and chiropractors	2,470	2,030	440	64,299	68,404	45,368
Management occupations, natural sciences and engineering	14,305	12,520	1,785	63,566	66,668	41,800
University teachers	29,335	22,985	6,350	62,064	65,671	49,000
Ten lowest paying occupations	**235,455**	**65,225**	**170,230**	**15,092**	**18,794**	**13,673**
Livestock farm workers	16,215	10,415	5,795	16,600	19,279	11,788
Sewing machine operators, textile and similar material	32,130	2,765	29,370	16,540	22,991	15,933
Other farming, horticultural and animal husbandry occupations	25,180	13,860	11,320	16,227	19,537	12,174
Crop farm workers	11,790	6,015	5,780	16,191	19,814	12,421
Bartenders	13,765	6,320	7,440	16,067	18,558	13,952
Lodging cleaners, except private households	7,965	1,060	6,910	15,718	19,238	15,178
Service station attendants	10,435	8,370	2,065	15,586	16,135	13,359
Housekeepers, servants and related occupations	13,825	1,145	12,680	14,479	19,210	14,053
Food and beverage serving occupations	62,350	13,845	48,505	14,100	17,822	13,037
Child-care occupations	41,800	1,440	40,365	13,518	20,987	13,252
All other occupations	**7,215,105**	**4,419,915**	**2,795,195**	**32,850**	**36,957**	**26,354**
TOTAL	**7,718,780**	**4,699,895**	**3,018,885**	**33,714**	**38,648**	**26,033**

* Although athletes were in the top ten occupations, and trapping and hat-making were in the bottom ten occupations, their very small numbers rendered their income statistics unreliable. Hence, the individuals in these three occupations were excluded from the high and low groups and included in all other occupations.

(1) Worked 49-52 weeks in 1990, mostly full-time.

Low income

Low income refers to families and unattached individuals who, in 1990, had incomes below Statistics Canada's low income cut-offs for that year. The income limits were selected on the basis that families and unattached individuals with incomes below these limits spent, on average, 56.2% or more of their income on food, shelter and clothing. Low income cut-offs are relative levels determined from income expenditure patterns for various categories of families. These limits vary by size of area of residence and by size of the family. They are not intended as measures of "poverty".

As the survey from which low income cut-offs were determined excluded the Yukon, the Northwest Territories and Indian Reserves, all estimates given in the low income section exclude those areas.

Incidence of low income declined

Between 1985 and 1990, the incidence of low income declined among unattached individuals and families in every province and metropolitan area in the country. Although the number of husband-wife families increased by 492,000 during the period, the number of low income families actually dropped by 96,000, resulting in a decline in the incidence of low income from 11.7% in 1985 to 9.3% in 1990.

Among non-husband-wife families, the incidence of low income also declined although the rate for female lone-parent families remained very high (45% in 1990 compared to 51% in 1985). Unattached individuals saw the incidence of low income declined from 41% to 36.5% in 1990.

The incidence of children living in low income situations declined for children younger than six to about 20% in 1990, a decrease of 2.1 percentage points compared to 1985. The number of children younger than 15 living in low income situations also declined by 83,000, to about one million in 1990.

At the other end of the age scale, the proportion of people aged 70 and older living below the low income cut-offs declined even more – from 26% to 21% in

Incidence of Low Income Among Economic Families, Unattached Individuals and Population

	1985 %	1990 %
Economic Families	15.9	13.2
Husband-wife families	11.7	9.3
Non-husband-wife families	39.7	35.5
Male lone-parent families	21.6	18.8
Female lone-parent families	50.6	44.7
All other non-husband-wife families	24.1	21.4
Unattached Individuals	41.3	36.5
Male	35.5	31.8
Female	46.1	40.6
Population	18.3	15.8
under 6 years	21.9	19.8
6-14 years	19.8	16.9
15-17 years	19.0	16.2
18-24 years	22.0	20.5
25-34 years	16.5	15.0
35-44 years	13.7	12.0
45-54 years	13.3	10.9
55-64 years	18.6	15.7
65-69 years	19.1	15.6
70 years and over	26.2	20.8

1990. Still, one in five seniors had an income below Statistics Canada's low income cut-offs.

Among metropolitan areas, Montréal recorded the highest low income proportion with at two out of every 10 people living below the low income cut-offs in 1990. Oshawa had the lowest proportion, with less than one out of every 10 people living below the cut-offs. The greatest inroads in reducing the proportion of people in low income situations occurred in Victoria where the rate declined from 18.5% in 1985 to 13.6% in 1990.

Composition of income continued to change

Since 1970, sources of income have changed significantly. In 1990, the contribution of employment income to total income accounted, on average, for 78 cents of every dollar of income, down from 82 cents in 1980 and 86 cents in 1970. The contribution of employment income to total income varied substantially among the provinces and territories as well in 1990, with the highest being reported in the Northwest Territories (90%), the Yukon (87%), and Alberta (81%).

Government transfer payments, such as old age pensions, unemployment insurance and family allowances, contributed 11.4 cents to the average dollar of income in 1990, having risen from less than seven cents in 1970. During this period, the population aged 65 and older (who received Old Age Security payments) increased in number and as a proportion of the total population. The share of government transfer payments in total income was highest in Newfoundland at 21% and it was lowest in the Northwest Territories at 7.5%.

Other income sources, such as investment income and retirement pensions, contributed just under 11 cents to the average dollar of income in 1990, up from 10 cents in 1980 and 7 cents in 1970. During this period, as the proportion of the elderly increased, payments from pension plans also increased. Among the provinces and territories, Saskatchewan (13.5%), British Columbia (13%) and Manitoba (11.6%) recorded the highest proportion of income from other sources, while the Northwest Territories (2.4%) and the Yukon (5.3%) recorded the lowest in 1990.

Sources of Income

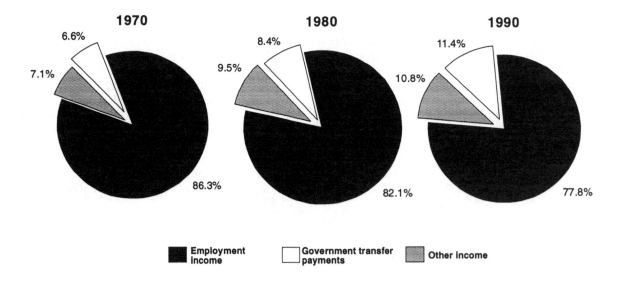

Statistics Canada - Cat. No. 96-304E

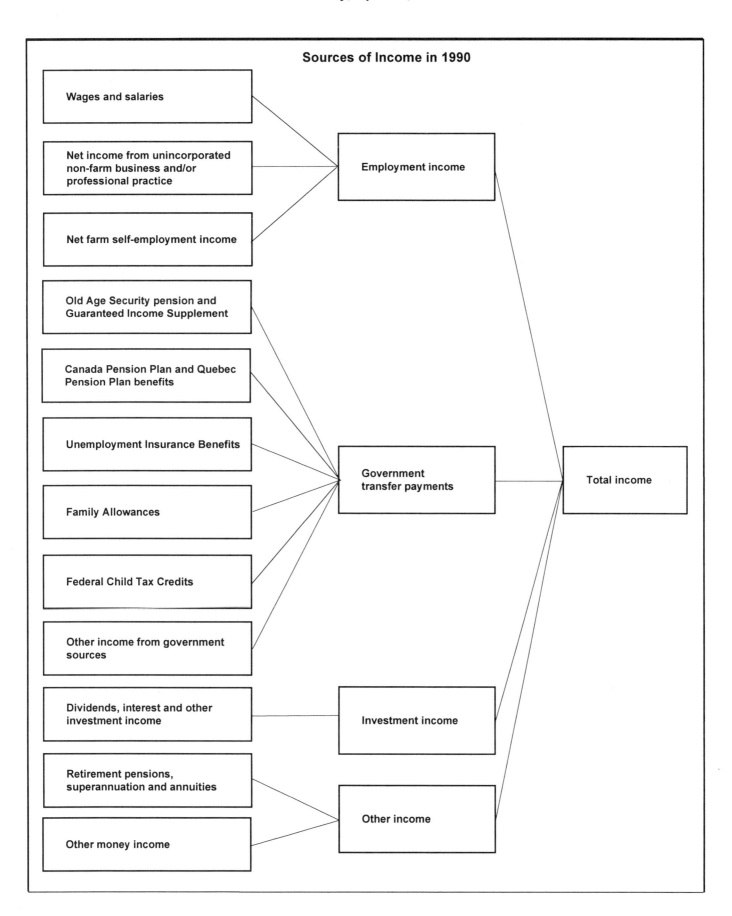

Sources of Income in 1990

Catalogue 11-001E (Français 11-001F) ISSN 0827-0465

Tuesday, May 11, 1993

EDUCATION, MOBILITY AND MIGRATION, AND SHELTER COSTS

HIGHLIGHTS

Education

- More than one in ten Canadians had a university degree in 1991

- The number of women with university degrees increased by 86%

- School attendance in 1990-91 increased for all age groups

Mobility and Migration

- Almost half of Canada's population moved between 1986 and 1991

- Only British Columbia, Ontario and the Yukon gained population as a result of interprovincial migration

- British Columbia gained the largest number of people through interprovincial migration

Shelter Costs

- 2.2 million households spent 30% or more of their household income on shelter in 1991

- Shelter costs for both renters and owners were highest in the Toronto metropolitan area

- Condominiums were an increasingly popular form of home-ownership in 1991

 Statistics Statistique
Canada Canada

Canadä

Mobility and Migration
Educational Attainment and School Attendance
Major Fields of Study of Postsecondary Graduates
Housing Costs and Other Characteristics of Canadian Households

Mobility and Migration (93-322, $40) provides a variety of tabulations on the mobility and migration patterns of Canadians for Canada, provinces and territories, and census metropolitan areas. Some of the tables cross-classify data by highest level of schooling, mother tongue, labour force activity, occupation and industry. The data are based on the 1991 Census which asked respondents to report their place of residence five years and one year ago.

Educational Attainment and School Attendance (93-328, $40) presents 1991 Census data on the educational attainment and school attendance of people aged 15 and over. Data from the 1971 and 1981 Censuses are included for comparison. Of the ten tables presented, one contains historical data dating back to 1951 and another shows school attendance figures for non-permanent residents. Other tables cross-classify data by highest level of schooling, sex, and age group and one table shows the relationship between school attendance and labour force activity for the last three decennial censuses.

Major Fields of Study of Postsecondary Graduates (93-329, $40) provides information from the 1991 Census on the major fields of study of people aged 15 and over with postsecondary qualifications. Selected data from the 1986 Census are also included. Two of the seven tables show data for Canada, provinces and territories and another table shows major fields of study for non-permanent residents.

Housing Costs and Other Characteristics of Canadian Households (93-330, $40) presents 1991 shelter cost data and 20% sample data on characteristics of private households for Canada, provinces and territories and, in selected tables, census metropolitan areas. The 12 tables present various household and dwelling characteristics such as tenure, structural type, average number of rooms and average shelter costs of private households. Some data are cross-classified by age and sex of the primary household maintainer.

This release presents information on our level and type of education, on our geographical mobility and on our housing expenditures.

MORE CANADIANS HAVE MORE EDUCATION

Canadians better educated

The number of people in Canada with more than a high school education reached a historical high in 1991: 43% of all people 15 years and over had a university degree or some other postsecondary education, compared to 36% reported by the 1981 Census. This increase in postsecondary education far out-stripped population growth: the number of people with postsecondary education grew by 38% between 1981 and 1991 while the size of the 15 and over population grew by only 14%.

Between 1981 and 1991, the number of university degree holders grew by almost one million to 2.4 million. This increase occurred at all levels of qualification: the number of people with bachelor degrees rose by 63%, with master's degrees by 78% and with earned doctorates by 49%. Overall, 11% of the 15 and over population had a university degree in 1991.

Almost half (45%) of the people with university degrees in 1991 were women, a proportion that has steadily increased since at least 1961. In fact, much of the overall increase in the number of people with university degrees was the result of proportionately more women having degrees. Between 1981 and 1991, the number of women with a university degree

grew by over half a million to 1.1 million (an increase of 86%). In comparison, the number of men in this group grew by about 428,000 to 1.3 million (an increase of 47%). Over the previous decade, 1971 to 1981, the number of women with university degrees increased by 157% and the number of men by 85%.

The number of graduates from other postsecondary institutions, which included trade schools and colleges, also rose during the latter half of the 1980s. Graduates with trade certificates increased by 15%, from 2 million in 1981 to 2.3 million in 1991, while graduates with other non-university (college) certificates rose from 1.7 million to 2.5 million, up 47%.

School attendance up

The proportion of Canada's youth and young adult population who were attending school full-time grew substantially between 1981 and 1991. While there was an overall decline in the number of people aged 15 to 19, from 2.3 million to 1.9 million, the proportion of this age group attending school full-time grew from 66% to 80% over the decade. The increase in full-time school attendance was even greater for those aged 20 to 24: in 1991, 32% were attending school full-time, up from 19% in 1981. At least part of this increase could be the result of labour market conditions, i.e., an increase in unemployment for those aged 20 to 24, an actual or perceived lack of jobs or a need for additional training.

Educational Attainment for Persons 15 Years and Over

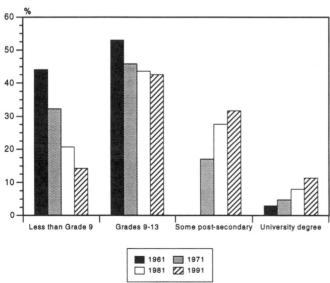

Highest Degree, Certificate or Diploma, 1991

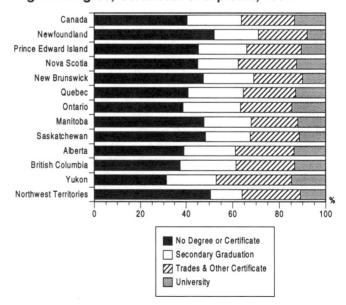

Over the decade, it became more common for people aged 20 to 24 to combine work with school. In 1991, 30% of people in this age group who were employed were also full-time students, double the rate in 1981 (15%). This increase was larger among women (from 14% in 1981 to 30% in 1991) than among men (from 17% to 29%). Among part-time students aged 20 to 24, there was almost no increase in the proportion combining work and school: in both 1991 and 1981, 10% of those with jobs were also part-time students.

What we studied

In 1991, among all postsecondary graduates (university, college and trade school), the two most popular fields of study were Engineering and Applied Science Technologies and Trades (1.8 million graduates). These fields included such diverse study areas as architectural drafting, computer programming and software, air conditioning and refrigeration, tool and die making, and Commerce, Management and Business Administration (1.7 million graduates). Combined, the two fields accounted for almost half (45%) of all people with postsecondary educational qualifications. Health Professions, Sciences and Technologies was a distant third with 885,000 graduates. The major field of study with the fewest number of graduates in 1991 was Mathematics and Physical Sciences (249,000). These rankings remained unchanged from 1986.

School Attendance Rates

Age Groups	Full-Time		Part-time	
	1981 %	1991 %	1981 %	1991 %
Total Population 15 and over	**11.7**	**11.9**	**5.8**	**5.8**
15-19	65.9	79.6	2.7	3.2
20-24	18.6	32.3	8.9	9.1
25-44	2.6	4.0	9.1	8.9
45-64	0.5	0.7	3.0	3.1
65 and over	0.2	0.2	0.6	0.5

Postsecondary Educational Qualifications, for the Population 15 Years and over

Field of Study (Major Group level)	University Graduates			Trade and Other Non-University Graduates		
	Number of Graduates		% Change 1986-1991	Number of Graduates		% Change 1986-1991
	1986	1991		1986	1991	
Total	**2,260,065**	**2,860,950**	**26.6**	**4,004,115**	**4,836,565**	**20.8**
Educational, Recreational and Counselling Services	419,760	567,755	35.3	209,925	229,400	9.3
Fine and Applied Arts	62,680	77,240	23.2	295,980	357,490	20.8
Humanities and Related Fields	304,995	340,150	11.5	101,760	127,750	25.5
Social Sciences and Related Fields	377,695	475,110	25.8	127,250	184,845	45.3
Commerce, Management and Business Administration	354,555	475,305	34.1	1,052,925	1,244,975	18.2
Agricultural and Biological Sciences/Technologies	124,895	139,410	11.6	184,650	220,475	19.4
Engineering and Applied Sciences[1]	221,285	287,300	29.8	1,481,880	1,809,130	22.1
Health Professions, Sciences and Technologies	227,525	294,360	29.4	491,340	590,130	20.1
Mathematics and Physical Sciences	158,720	199,770	25.8	44,210	49,235	11.4

(1) Engineering and Applied Sciences, Technologies and Trades for other Non-University graduates.

Statistics Canada - Cat. No. 96-304E

Major Fields of Study of Male and Female Trades and Other Non-University Certificate Holders, 1991

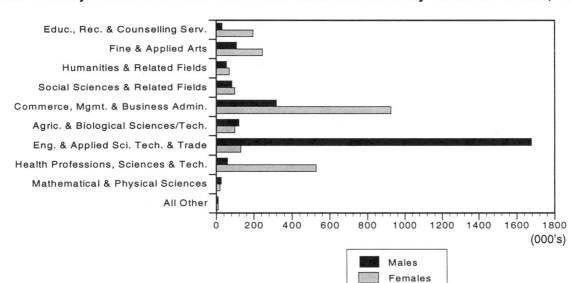

Diplomas and certificates

Among the 4.8 million people in 1991 who held diplomas and certificates from community colleges, CEGEPs, technical institutions and other institutions, Engineering and Applied Science Technologies and Trades was the most common field of study (37% had diplomas or certificates in this field). While the field continued to be dominated by men, between 1986 and 1991, the proportion of women graduates increased slightly– from 6.8% to 7.3%. Commerce, Management and Business Administration field graduates were the second largest group (26%), followed by Health Professions, Sciences and Technologies (12%).

Although it ranked seventh out of nine in total number of diploma and certificate holders in both 1986 and 1991, the Social Sciences and Related Fields experienced the fastest growth (45%) over the 1986-1991 period. Two areas of study within this field experienced especially high growth rates: Child Care and Youth Services (56%) and Police and Paralegal Technologies (54%).

Degrees and certificates

Among the 2.9 million university degree and certificate holders, there was less concentration in fields of study than there was for those with non-university diplomas and certificates: the three most common fields of study for university graduates accounted for only half of all university graduates, compared to three-quarters for all graduates from colleges, CEGEPs, and trade and technical schools. In 1991, 20% of all university graduates had studied in the Educational, Recreational and Counselling Field, 17% in Social Sciences and Related Fields and another 17% in the Commerce, Management and Business Administration field.

Between 1986 and 1991, the proportion of university graduates in the Engineering and Applied Sciences field who were women rose slightly, from 7% to 9%, while the proportion in the Commerce, Management and Business Administration field rose from 30% to 35%.

Major Fields of Study of Male and Female University Graduates, 1991

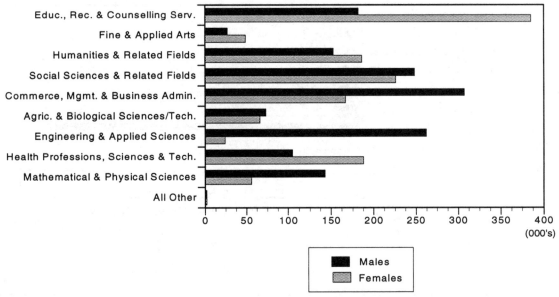

People without high school graduation

The 1991 Census found that 33% of those aged 15 and over had not completed high school, were not attending school and had not received any further training. This proportion varied substantially for different age groups and among the provinces and territories.

The proportion of the 15 and over population who had not finished high school was highest among those aged 65 and over (64%) and lowest among those in the 15 to 24 age group (15%). Contributing to the high rate among the 65 and over population is the fact that many in this group completed their formal schooling at a time when educational systems and expectations were quite different.

Foreign students

The 1991 Census found that there were 43,460 foreign students 15 years or over studying full-time and 23,610 studying part-time. The largest group (14,400) of full-time students were from Eastern Asia, which includes China, Hong Kong and Japan. The largest number of part-time students (6,115) came from South East Asia, which includes Vietnam, the Philippines and Malaysia.

Overall, male foreign students studying full-time outnumbered their female counterparts by a ratio of five to four, though this ratio varied for students from different areas of the world: among full-time students from South America, women outnumbered men by a small margin (nine to eight) while among full-time students from Africa, men outnumbered women by almost two to one.

A NATION ON THE MOVE

Migrants and movers

Traditionally, Canada's population has been very mobile: over each five-year census period since 1961, almost half the population moved from one neighbourhood, town, city, province or territory to another. In 1991, 47% of Canada's population lived in a different dwelling than they had five years earlier, up from the previous census period, 1981-1986, when 44% moved. In large part, this increase between 1986 and 1991 was due to a rise in the number of people who moved from one municipality to another.

Just around the corner

The largest group of movers (50%) changed addresses but still lived in the same municipality as they had in 1986. People who lived in a different municipality but in the same province or territory comprised the next largest group (34%). People who moved from one province or territory to another and people who had entered Canada from another country were the smallest groups of movers, each

representing about 8% of all those who moved between 1986 and 1991.

Young adults more likely to move

The most mobile group of people in Canada were those aged 25 to 29 in 1991, with seven of every 10 people in this age group reporting that they lived at a different address in 1991 than they had in 1986. From this peak, mobility declined steadily with age in a pattern similar to that of previous censuses. Of all those aged 65 and over, only one in 10 changed addresses between 1986 and 1991.

Of all the provinces and territories, the Northwest Territories had the most mobile population in 1991: almost seven out of every 10 people aged five and over had changed residence over the census period. Among the provinces, people living in British Columbia and Alberta were the most likely to move. In 1991, six out of every ten British Columbians and five out of every 10 Albertans had moved over the previous five years. The population of Newfoundland was the least mobile with only three of every 10 people moving. Generally, mobility in Canada rose from east to west, with the population of the northern areas of the country being the most mobile.

Mobility Patterns of Persons, Five Years and over

Between 1981 and 1986:

56.3% of persons
did not move

24.2% of persons
moved but remained in the same
municipality

13.5% of persons
moved to another municipality but in
the same province or territory

4.0% of persons
moved to a different province or
territory

2.0% of persons
moved to Canada from another country

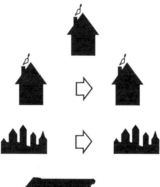
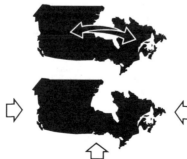

Between 1986 and 1991:

53.3% of persons
did not move

23.2% of persons
moved but remained in the same
municipality

15.9% of persons
moved to another municipality but in
the same province or territory

3.9% of persons
moved to a different province or
territory

3.7% of persons
moved to Canada from another country

British Columbia was the place to go

In 1991, almost one million people (977,000) lived in a different province or territory than they had in 1986. At the end of a census period, some provinces had lost population through interprovincial migration and some had gained. Of course, other factors, such as births, deaths and immigration, also affected provincial population trends. The level and direction of interprovincial migration were strongly influenced by provincial economic conditions.

Between 1986 and 1991, only British Columbia, Ontario and Yukon gained population through interprovincial migration. British Columbia's net gain of 126,000 people was more than two and a half times larger than Ontario's (47,000 people) while Yukon's net gain of 780 people was very small.

British Columbia attracted 238,000 migrants from across the country while only 112,000 left the province over the five-year census period. Most (67%) of the in-migrants had been living in Alberta or Ontario in 1986. Another 20% had been living in Manitoba or Saskatchewan. Alberta and Ontario were the principal destinations for people moving out of British Columbia: of the 112,000 people who left British Columbia between 1986 and 1991, 74% moved to Alberta or Ontario.

More interprovincial migrants settled in Ontario than any other province or territory (270,000) but the province also had the largest overall outflow of people to other provinces (223,000). Ontario's relatively small population gain from interprovincial migration was primarily the result of a negative population exchange with British Columbia (more people moved to British Columbia from Ontario than moved to Ontario from British Columbia).

Census Data on One-year Mobility

In 1991 the census asked respondents two questions on mobility: where they lived in 1986 and where they lived in 1990. This release presents the results from the five-year mobility question. Data are available on where respondents had lived in 1990 in Tables 1B and 2B in **Mobility and Migration**, (catalogue number 93-322).

The one-year mobility data revealed that, between 1990 and 1991:

- about 16% of Canada's population had moved;

- the largest flows were from Alberta to British Columbia (28,000 people), Ontario to British Columbia (25,000) and from Quebec to Ontario (23,000);

- Ontario experienced the largest population loss through interprovincial migration (22,000 people); and,

- British Columbia experienced the largest population gain through interprovincial migration (37,000 people).

Each of Canada's Prairie provinces experienced population losses through interprovincial migration between 1986 and 1991. Large outflows of migrants to Ontario, Alberta and British Columbia, combined with relatively small numbers of in-migrants resulted in net migration losses for Saskatchewan and Manitoba: Saskatchewan lost 60,000 people and Manitoba lost 35,000. These losses were up substantially from those of the previous five year period. Between 1986 and 1991, Alberta lost 25,000 people through interprovincial migration, about the same as over the previous five year period (28,000). Although 170,000 interprovincial migrants moved to Alberta (it was the third most popular destination after Ontario and British Columbia), large numbers of people left the province for British Columbia (93,000 people), Ontario (56,000) and Saskatchewan (15,000).

Net Interprovincial Migration

	1986-1991			1981-1986 Net Interprovincial migration	1976-1981 Net Interprovincial migration
	In-migration (1)	Out-migration (2)	Net Interprovincial migration (1-2)		
Newfoundland	20,735	34,690	-13,960	-16,550	-19,835
Prince Edward Island	8,790	9,640	-855	1,530	-10
Nova Scotia	53,265	58,140	-4,870	6,280	-8,420
New Brunswick	35,830	41,895	-6,070	-1,370	-8,510
Quebec	81,995	107,550	-25,550	-63,300	-141,725
Ontario	269,980	223,030	46,955	99,350	-78,065
Manitoba	44,050	79,310	-35,245	-1,550	-43,585
Saskatchewan	38,220	98,580	-60,350	-2,820	-5,825
Alberta	170,015	195,025	-25,015	-27,670	197,650
British Columbia	238,175	112,295	125,880	9,500	110,930
Yukon	6,460	5,685	780	-2,660	-550
Northwest Territories	9,535	11,235	-1,700	-755	-2,055

Quebec's losses from interprovincial migration declined dramatically between 1976 and 1991. Over the 1976-1981 period, the number of people who moved out of Quebec greatly exceeded the number who moved into Quebec, resulting in a net loss of 142,000 people. The next census period, 1981-1986, showed a much smaller loss (63,000 people) and over the most recent census period, 1986-1991, Quebec lost only 26,000 people. This most recent loss was due primarily to higher out-migration to Ontario and British Columbia.

Ontario continued to be the principal destination for interprovincial migrants from New Brunswick, Nova Scotia, Prince Edward Island and Newfoundland. Over the 1986-1991 period, all four provinces experienced population losses to Ontario: almost 64,000 people moved to Ontario from one of the four Atlantic provinces while only 43,000 had moved in the opposite direction.

Largest Interprovincial Migration Flow, 1986 - 1991

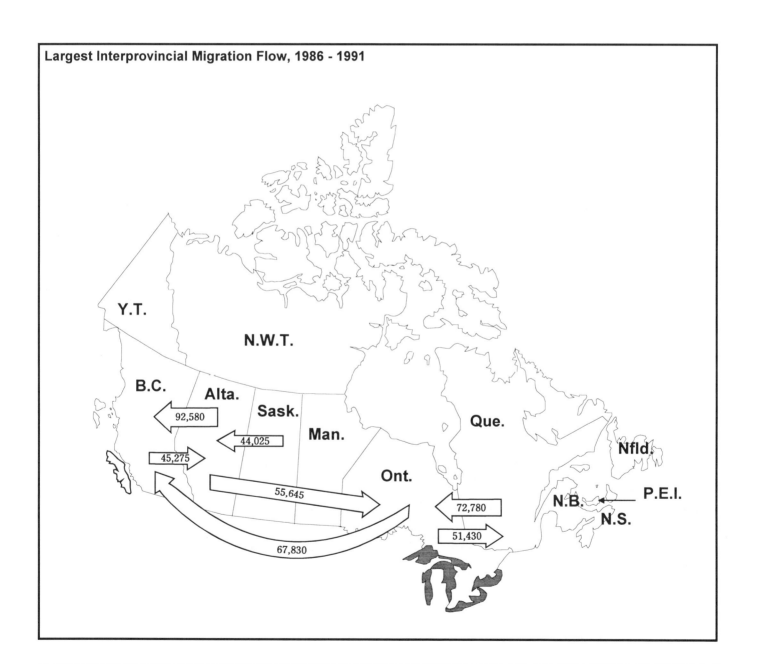

Education and unemployment influenced interprovincial movers

While just 11% of Canada's population had a university degree in 1991, 20% of all interprovincial migrants did. Overall, 68 out of every 1,000 people with a university degree had moved from one province to another between 1986 and 1991, compared to 34 out of every 1,000 people with all other levels of education.

People who were unemployed in 1991 had a higher rate of migration than did those who had jobs: 55 out of every 1,000 unemployed people had moved from one province or territory between 1986 and 1991, compared to 43 out of every 1,000 employed people.

Migration affected metropolitan areas

Some census metropolitan areas lost population through migration. Toronto, for example, lost 115,000 persons, mostly to other places within Ontario while Montréal lost 30,000 persons. Vancouver, on the other hand, gained 40,000 persons, followed by Ottawa-Hull at 25,000 persons.

THE COST OF HOUSING: OWNERS AND RENTERS

Affordability of housing

In 1991, over 2.2 million households spent 30% or more of their total household income on shelter, up 16% from 1.9 million in 1986. Renter households comprised the majority (58%) of these households while 36% were home-owning households with mortgages and 6% were home-owning households without mortgages. The proportion of income a household spent on housing was influenced by factors which included size of income, location, the type and size of dwelling, and whether the dwelling was rented, owned with a mortgage or owned free of a mortgage.

Overall, 35% of all renter households spent 30% or more of their household income on shelter costs, compared to about 25% of owner households with mortgages and only 5% of owner households without mortgages. Several factors contributed to this difference. While average shelter costs for renter households were lower than they were for owners ($546 per month versus $682 for owners), renter households also had a lower average income ($31,302) than did owner households ($55,801).

Shelter Costs

Monthly shelter costs include payments for electricity, gas, oil or other heating fuels, water and other municipal services, rent, property taxes, mortgage payments and condominium fees.

The allocation of 30% or more of a household's income to housing expenses is frequently used as a threshold for assessing housing affordability. When households, particularly low-income households, spend 30% or more of their income on shelter, this means that in some cases at least, inadequate funds are available for other essential purchases such as food, clothing, and transportation.

The 30% figure is often taken into account in setting mortgage eligibility criteria as the maximum a household should pay for property taxes and mortgage principal and interest.

Households Spending 30% or More of their Income on Shelter, 1991

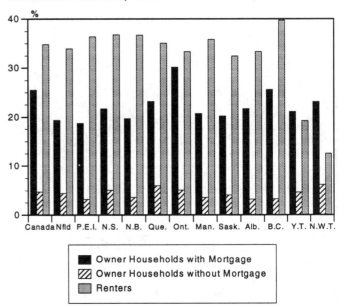

Living alone

People who lived alone were the most likely to spend more than 30% of their income on housing. Among people who lived alone and were renting, about 44% spent 30% or more of their income on housing. For people living alone who owned their home free of a mortgage, this proportion was 13% but for those with a mortgage it jumped to 51%. In large part, these relatively high proportions reflected the lower average

Home Owners Spending 30% or More of their Average Household Income on Shelter, 1991

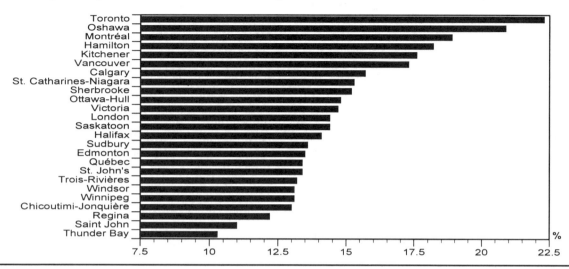

incomes of one-person households compared to the average for all households. Among renters, one-person households had an average income of $21,592, compared to $31,302 for all renters. Among home-owners, the average income for one-person households was $28,527, compared to $55,801 for all owners.

The proportion of people living alone who spent 30% or more of their income on housing was much higher in some metropolitan areas than it was in others. Among mortgage paying individuals living alone, the proportion spending 30% or more on housing peaked in Oshawa (64%) and Toronto (64%) but was only 41% in Regina. Montréal had the highest proportion (25%) of individuals who lived alone in a house they owned mortgage-free and who

spent 30% or more of their income on housing while Victoria had the lowest (7%).

Three in ten renting families spent 30% or more on shelter

Although the average monthly shelter costs of renting families tended to be lower than those of home-owning families, families who rented were much more likely to spend 30% or more of their income on shelter than were home-owning families. Overall, 29% of all one-family households living in rental accommodation spent 30% or more of their income on housing, compared to 23% of one-family households with a mortgage and only 3% of one-family households without a mortgage.

Renters Spending 30% or More of their Average Household Income on Shelter, 1991

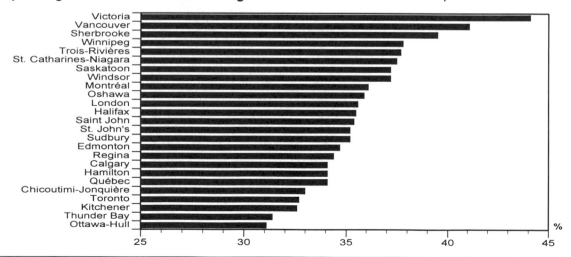

While nationally about 30% of one-family households who rented their home spent 30% or more of their income on housing, this proportion was much lower in the Northwest Territories (11%) and the Yukon (18%). These low proportions were primarily due to the higher average income of one-family households in the two territories compared to the national average. The highest proportion for one-family renter households was in British Columbia (33%).

For home-owning families with mortgages, this proportion was highest in the province of Ontario (28%) and the metropolitan area of Toronto (35%). Only very small proportions of home-owning families without mortgages spent 30% or more of their income on housing: among the provinces and territories, the highest proportion was in the Northwest Territories (5%) and among the census metropolitan areas the highest was in Montréal (5%).

Housing costs varied widely

While home-owners were building equity, they also paid more per month on housing than did renters: home-owners' average monthly shelter costs were $682 while renters paid $546. Rental accommodation had lower shelter costs since it tended to be multi-unit and smaller, and it was more likely to fall under rent-control policies.

Home-owners' monthly shelter costs were highest in the Northwest Territories ($900) and Ontario ($808)

Average Monthly Shelter Costs, 1991

	Owners $	Renters $
Canada	**682**	**546**
Newfoundland	418	459
Prince Edward Island	473	467
Nova Scotia	523	501
New Brunswick	455	428
Quebec	636	480
Ontario	808	618
Manitoba	565	455
Saskatchewan	519	422
Alberta	678	531
British Columbia	637	606
Yukon	678	550
Northwest Territories	900	524

and lowest in Newfoundland ($418), New Brunswick ($455) and Prince Edward Island ($473). Renters paid the most in Ontario ($618) and British Columbia ($606) and the least in Saskatchewan ($422) and New Brunswick ($428).

The high cost of shelter in Ontario and British Columbia reflected, in part, higher shelter costs in the major cities of these two provinces, while more expensive heating fuel and electricity contributed to the higher costs in the Northwest Territories. In Newfoundland, New Brunswick and Saskatchewan, where shelter costs for both owners and renters were relatively low, costs were affected by both economic conditions and higher proportions of mortgage-free owners.

In 1991, Toronto was the most expensive metropolitan area: on average, owners paid $1,003 and renters $703 per month for shelter. Outside Toronto, shelter costs for owners were highest in Oshawa ($944) and Ottawa-Hull ($888) and for renters in Vancouver ($665) and Oshawa ($658).

Condominiums increasingly popular

In 1991, there were 367,765 owner-occupied condominiums in Canada, up from 234,000 in 1986, an increase of 64%. Overall, condominiums represented 6% of all owner-occupied dwellings in 1991, up from 4% in 1986.

Condominium ownership was concentrated in the large metropolitan areas of Quebec, Ontario and British Columbia. Over half (64%) of all owner-occupied condominiums were in the four metropolitan areas of Toronto (104,895), Vancouver (61,205), Montréal (43,785) and Ottawa-Hull (23,465). In comparison, these four metropolitan areas accounted for 36% of all occupied dwellings.

Between 1986 and 1991, the number of condominiums in Quebec almost doubled, increasing by close to 99% (up by 30,550 units). Ontario experienced the largest increase in the actual number of condominiums (up by 42,980 units), with British Columbia a close second (up by 42,790 units).

Condominiums are an increasingly popular choice for people who live alone and for married couples without children at home. In 1991, 32% of all owner-occupied condominiums were occupied by people living alone, up from 28% in 1986. Married couples without children at home accounted for 30% of all owner-occupied condominiums in 1991, up from 27% in 1986.

Catalogue 11-001E (Français 11-001F) ISSN 0827-0465

The Daily

Statistics Canada

Tuesday, June 1, 1993

RELIGION, FAMILIES, FERTILITY AND PLACE OF WORK

HIGHLIGHTS

Religion

- Catholics remained the largest religious group in Canada

- Larger Protestant denominations continued to decline

- Eastern non-Christian religions such as Islam, Buddhist, Hindu and Sikh, as well as the number of people with no religious affiliation, grew significantly

Families

- Empty nest families increased by 40% between 1981 and 1991

- Female lone-parent families occupied higher density, smaller housing

Fertility

- Married women aged 35-39 who were childless increased from 7% in 1971 to 13% in 1991

- One in 10 single women had one or more children

- Women born outside Canada had slightly more children than women born in Canada

Place of Work

- 1.1 million members of the employed labour force worked at home

- Canadians living and working within a metropolitan area travelled 10 km on average to their place of work

Statistics Canada   Statistique Canada

Religions in Canada
Families: Social and Economic Characteristics
Fertility
Place of Work

Religions in Canada (93-319, $40) presents basic distributions of religions for Canada, provinces and territories and, in some cases, census metropolitan areas. Religion data are classified by seven major religious groups which are further classified into subgroups. The seven major groups are Catholic, Protestant, Eastern Orthodox, Jewish, Eastern non-Christian, Para-religious, and No religious affiliation. Some tables include 1981 Census data for comparison.

Families: Social and Economic Characteristics (93-320, $40) presents data on the socio-economic aspects of census families by family structure. Characteristics covering immigrant status, place of birth, highest level of schooling and labour force participation are included in three of the eight data tables. One table presents data on detailed family structure for 1981 and 1991.

Fertility (93-321, $40) provides statistics on the number of children ever born to women aged 15 and over. Data are presented for Canada, provinces and territories and, in some cases, census metropolitan areas. Some tables include 1981 Census data for comparison.

Place of Work (93-323, $40) presents statistics on the place of residence and place of work for Canada's employed labour force. The data table shows the commuting flows between census subdivisions within census metropolitan areas (CMAs) for usual places of work, as well as the number of people working at home, having no usual place of work and working outside Canada.

These publications are based on 20% sample data from the 1991 Census.

This release presents information on our religious affiliations, families, fertility, and place of work.

RELIGION

Catholic and Protestant religions continued to decline

Canada has been and continues to be predominantly Christian, with most of the population being Protestant and Catholic. For more than 100 years, Protestants outnumbered Catholics. However, by 1971, for the first time since Confederation, Catholics outnumbered Protestants. They remained the largest religious group in Canada in 1991: there were 12.3 million Catholics, up from 11.4 million in 1981. Catholics as a whole represented 46% of the Canadian population,

down slightly from 47% in 1981. Across Canada, their proportions varied considerably, from a low of 19% in British Columbia to a high of 86% in Quebec.

The Protestant denominations made up the second largest major religion in 1991, accounting for 36% of the population. This, however, was down from 41% in 1981 and 44% in 1971. Most of the decline occurred within the six largest Protestant denominations in Canada. Five of the six groups decreased in size between 1981 and 1991: Presbyterian (-22%), United Church (-18%), Anglican (-10%), Lutheran (-9%) and Baptist (-5%). The only large Protestant denomination countering this trend was Pentecostal, which increased by 29%. Jewish and Eastern Orthodox religions increased by about 7% from 1981.

Religious Affiliation

Religion	% Distribution										
	1891	1901	1911	1921	1931	1941	1951	1961	1971	1981	1991
Catholic	41.6	41.7	39.4	38.7	41.3	43.4	44.7	46.7	47.3	47.3	45.7
Roman Catholic	41.6	41.7	39.4	38.7	39.5	41.8	43.3	45.7	46.2	46.5	45.2
Ukrainian Catholic	--	--	--	--	1.8	1.6	1.4	1.0	1.1	0.8	0.5
Protestant	56.5	55.6	55.9	56.0	54.4	52.2	50.9	48.9	44.4	41.2	36.2
United Chruch(1)	--	--	--	0.1	19.5	19.2	20.5	20.1	17.5	15.6	11.5
Anglican	13.7	12.8	14.5	16.1	15.8	15.2	14.7	13.2	11.8	10.1	8.1
Presbyterian(1)	15.9	15.8	15.6	16.1	8.4	7.2	5.6	4.5	4.0	3.4	2.4
Lutheran	1.4	1.8	3.2	3.3	3.8	3.5	3.2	3.6	3.3	2.9	2.4
Baptist	6.4	5.9	5.3	4.8	4.3	4.2	3.7	3.3	3.1	2.9	2.5
Pentecostal	--	--	--	0.1	0.3	0.5	0.7	0.8	1.0	1.4	1.6
Other Protestant(2)	19.1	19.3	17.3	15.5	2.3	2.4	2.5	3.4	3.7	4.9	7.9
Eastern Orthodox	--	0.3	1.2	1.9	1.0	1.2	1.2	1.3	1.5	1.5	1.4
Jewish	0.1	0.3	1.0	1.4	1.5	1.5	1.5	1.4	1.3	1.2	1.2
No Religion(3)	--	0.1	0.4	0.2	0.2	0.2	0.4	0.5	4.3	7.3	12.4
Other(4)	1.8	1.9	2.0	1.9	1.6	1.5	1.4	1.2	1.2	1.5	3.2

(1) Between 1911 and 1931, the United Church denomination was formed through an amalgamation of the Methodists, Congregalionalists and about one-half of the Presbyterian group. For 1931 and thereafter, the figures for Presbyterian reflect the segment that did not amalgamate with the United Church.

(2) Other Protestant denominations include Methodists and Congregationalists up to 1921, and other denominations such as Adventist, Churches of Christ, Disciples and the Salvation Army. The "Other" group also includes a certain proportion of smaller Protestant denominations.

(3) In 1891, "No Religion is included in Other". In 1971, the introduction of self-enumeration methodology may have been in part a cause of the large increase in the proportion of the population reporting "No religion". However, the 1971, 1981 and 1991 figures for this group are comparable.

(4) In 1981 many of these smaller denominations were disaggregated and are counted in the "Other Protestant" category. The remainder of the "Other" group includes Eastern non-Christian religions.

Smaller religious groups grew substantially

By contrast to the larger denominations, most of the smaller Protestant denominations experienced moderate to high increases. Those which showed the greatest increase over 1981 include Spiritualist (93%), Evangelical (76%), and Christian and Missionary Alliance (75%).

Consistent with changing immigration patterns towards more Asian immigrants, Eastern non-Christian religions increased by 144% between 1981 and 1991 to 747,000 people. Among this group, the largest increases occurred for Buddhist (215%), Islam (158%), Hindu (126%) and Sikh (118%).

Religions around the world

Canada's religious composition is quite similar to that of Europe, the United States, Australia and New Zealand. However, compared to the rest of the world, there are fewer people of Eastern non-Christian religions such as Islam, Hinduism, Buddhism, para-religious groups and people with no religious affiliation. The world's population is less than one-third Christian, compared to over 80% in Europe, the United States and Canada. At the same time, 38% of the world is Eastern non-Christian (3% in Canada) and over 20% have no religious affiliation (13% in Canada).

Source : 1992 Britannica Book of the Year

Religious Composition, 1991

	Canada	Nfld.	P.E.I.	N.S.	N.B.	Que.	Ont. %	Man.	Sask.	Alta.	B.C.	Yukon	N.W.T.
Catholic	45.7	37.0	47.3	37.2	54.0	86.1	35.5	30.4	32.5	26.5	18.6	20.2	38.2
Roman Catholic	45.2	37.0	47.3	37.2	53.9	86.0	35.1	27.2	30.4	25.4	18.3	20.0	38.0
Ukrainian Catholic	0.5	--	--	--	--	0.1	0.4	3.1	2.1	1.0	0.2	0.2	0.1
Protestant	36.2	61.0	48.4	54.1	40.1	5.9	44.4	51.0	53.4	48.4	44.5	43.0	49.9
United Church	11.5	17.3	20.3	17.2	10.5	0.9	14.1	18.6	22.8	16.7	13.0	8.7	5.7
Anglican	8.1	26.2	5.2	14.4	8.5	1.4	10.6	8.7	7.2	6.9	10.1	14.8	32.0
Presbyterian	2.4	0.4	8.6	3.5	1.4	0.3	4.2	1.5	1.2	1.9	2.0	1.3	0.7
Lutheran	2.4	0.1	0.1	1.3	0.2	0.2	2.3	5.1	8.4	5.4	3.3	2.4	1.2
Baptist	2.5	0.2	4.1	11.1	11.3	0.4	2.7	1.9	1.6	2.5	2.6	3.6	1.2
Pentecostal	1.6	7.1	1.0	1.2	3.2	0.4	1.7	2.0	1.8	2.1	2.2	2.2	3.9
Other Protestant	7.9	9.8	9.0	5.5	4.9	2.2	8.8	13.2	10.5	12.9	11.4	10.2	5.2
Eastern Orthodox	1.4	0.1	0.1	0.3	0.1	1.3	1.9	1.9	2.0	1.7	0.7	0.3	0.3
Jewish	1.2	--	0.1	0.2	0.1	1.4	1.8	1.3	0.1	0.4	0.5	0.2	0.1
Eastern non-Christian	2.8	0.2	0.3	0.5	0.2	1.4	3.8	1.5	0.7	3.1	4.9	1.1	0.9
Islam	0.9	0.1	--	0.2	--	0.7	1.5	0.3	0.1	1.2	0.8	0.1	0.1
Hindu	0.6	0.1	--	0.1	0.1	0.2	1.1	0.3	0.2	0.4	0.6	0.1	0.1
Buddhist	0.6	--	--	0.2	0.1	0.5	0.7	0.5	0.2	0.8	1.1	0.1	0.1
Sikh	0.5	--	0.1	--	--	0.1	0.5	0.3	0.1	0.5	2.3	0.1	0.1
Other Eastern Non-Christian	0.1	--	0.1	0.1	0.1	--	0.1	0.1	0.1	0.1	0.2	0.7	0.4
No Religion (1)	12.7	1.7	3.8	7.7	5.5	3.9	12.6	14.0	11.3	19.9	30.7	35.2	10.7

(1) Includes Para-religious and others not elsewhere classified.

The smallest religious categories, the sects, cults and various para-religious groups grew by 109% between 1981 and 1991, to 28,160 people, representing just 0.1% of the population.

Growth in "no religion"

Prior to 1971, less than 1% of the Canadian population reported having no religious affiliation. Since that time, Canada has become increasingly secularized with more and more people reporting no religious affiliation. By 1991, 13% of the population (3.4 million people) reported no religious affiliation, a 90% increase since 1981. Included in the "no religion" category were 21,970 Agnostics and 13,510 Atheists. In British Columbia and the Yukon, about one in three people reported no religious affiliation. On the opposite side of the country, Newfoundland recorded the lowest proportion of people with no religious affiliation (2%) followed by Prince Edward Island (4%) and Quebec (4%).

Immigration contributed to changing patterns

While religious affiliation has been predominantly Christian in Canada, much of the change in religious composition can be attributed to recent immigration patterns. In 1991, the immigrant population in Canada had lower affiliation with Catholic (37%) and Protestant religions (30%) than did the Canadian-born population (47% Catholic and 38% Protestant). The immigrant population also had a much higher proportion in all other major religions than did the Canadian-born population. In particular, Eastern non-Christian religions accounted for 12% of the immigrant population compared with just under 1% of the Canadian-born population, reflecting more recent patterns of increased immigration from Eastern Asia.

Growing religions tended to have younger members

The average age of people in Canada was 34.5 in 1991. Those religious affiliations showing the largest growth between 1981 and 1991 tended to have younger members. For example, the average age among Eastern non-Christian religions was just under 30. For those people with no religious affiliation, it was 29.

The average age of almost all major religious groups increased between 1981 and 1991, with the average age of Eastern Orthodox members increasing the most – from age 35 to 38 – followed by Catholics, increasing from age 31 to 34. Para-religious groups were an exception, with their average age decreasing from 33 in 1981 to 31 in 1991. Those religious groups

Religious Composition of the Immigrant and Canadian-born Populations, 1991

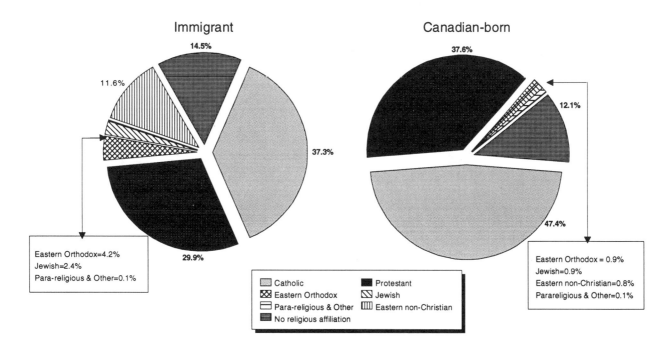

experiencing growth during the 1981-1991 period tended to have a higher proportion of young people aged 0-14 (Eastern non-Christian: 25%, no religious affiliation: 26%, para-religious: 21%), compared with religions which declined (Presbyterian: 16%, Lutheran: 17%, and Anglican: 17%).

Religious affiliation varied by ethnic origin

Ethnic origins influence religious composition. Among the six largest ethnic groups in Canada, 64% of people with British and German origin reported a Protestant affiliation in 1991, while 94% of people with French and Italian origins reported a Catholic affiliation. These ethnic groups represented 13.4 million people.

Among the 600,000 people with Chinese origins, 59% reported no religious affiliation in 1991, compared to 13% for the general population. About 51% of people who reported single Aboriginal origins were Catholic compared with 46% of the overall population.

Average Age by Major Religious Group

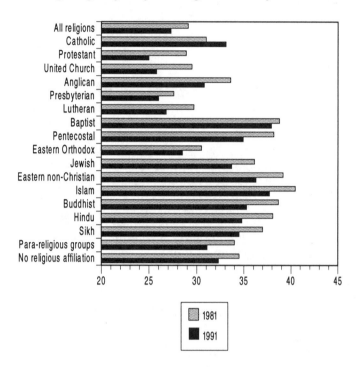

■ 1981
■ 1991

Religion by Age Groups, 1991

	Total population	Age groups				
		Less than 15	15-24	25-44	45-64	65 and over
		%				
All religions	**26,994,040**	**21**	**14**	**34**	**20**	**11**
Catholic	12,335,255	21	15	35	20	10
Protestant	9,780,715	19	13	32	21	14
United Chruch	3,093,120	19	12	32	22	16
Anglican	2,188,110	17	13	32	23	16
Presbyterian	636,295	16	11	30	24	19
Lutheran	636,205	17	12	30	25	16
Baptist	663,360	20	14	32	20	14
Pentecostal	436,435	27	17	33	16	7
Eastern Orthodox	387,390	16	15	30	25	14
Jewish	318,070	20	12	30	20	19
Eastern non-Christian	747,455	25	16	38	16	5
Islam	253,260	28	16	39	14	3
Buddhist	163,415	19	16	39	18	9
Hindu	157,010	24	16	40	17	4
Sikh	147,440	29	16	35	15	5
Para-religious	28,160	21	15	44	15	5
No religious affiliation	3,386,365	26	16	39	14	5

Religious Composition by Single Ethnic Origins, 1991

	Total	Catholic	Protestant	No religious affiliation	Other religions
			%		
Total population	**26,994,045**	**46**	**36**	**13**	**5**
British	5,611,050	21	64	14	1
French	6,146,605	94	3	3	-
German	911,560	24	64	12	-
Italian	750,055	94	4	2	-
Chinese	586,645	13	16	59	12
Aboriginal	470,615	51	34	13	2
Ukrainian	406,645	43	25	13	19

FAMILIES

In 1991, five out of six Canadians (84%) lived in families as husbands, wives, common-law spouses, lone-parents or children. Just over one-half of all families (52%) comprised a husband, wife and one or more children. However, 13% of all families had only one parent, and a further 35% of families had no children.

Childless and Empty Nest Families

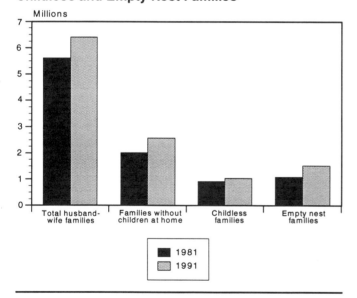

Families without children increasing

Over one million or 14% of all families were childless, that is, they had not yet had children, while another 21% were empty nest families in which the children had left home. In 21% of the childless families the wife was aged 45 or older.

While the number of families grew by 16% between 1981 and 1991, the number of empty nest families grew by a remarkable 40% in the same period, from just one million to over 1.5 million family units. This evidence of the aging of the population also saw empty nest families grow from 19% of all husband-wife families in 1981 to close to 24% in 1991.

The Northwest Territories had the lowest proportion of families without children with 12% of their families being childless and 9% empty nesters. Newfoundland also had low proportions of families with no children: 9% childless and 16% empty nest.

The highest proportions of childless families were in the Yukon Territory (16%), Quebec (16%) and British Columbia (15%). In Saskatchewan (26%) and British Columbia (25%) over one-quarter of all families were empty nest. Thus, in British Columbia, a total of 40% of all families had no children at home in 1991.

Home-owning families outnumbered renters by almost three to one

Close to three-quarters of all families lived in a dwelling they owned, while just over one-quarter lived in a dwelling they rented. Home ownership, however, varied significantly by family structure.

Female lone-parent families occupied higher density, smaller housing

Sixty percent of female lone-parent families lived in rented dwellings compared to 20% of husband-wife families with children at home and 29% of families with no children. Female lone-parent families also tended to have lower incomes and spent a larger proportion of their income on shelter than did husband-wife families. In 1990, the average income

Families Without Children at Home

		Total families	Families without children		
			Total	Empty nest	Childless
Canada	**1981**	**6,325,315**	**2,012,635**	**1,090,835**	**921,810**
	1991	**7,355,730**	**2,571,825**	**1,529,170**	**1,042,655**
Newfoundland	1981	135,130	28,820	16,970	11,860
	1991	150,715	37,435	23,660	13,770
Prince Edward Island	1981	30,285	8,315	5,025	3,290
	1991	33,900	10,240	6,655	3,580
Nova Scotia	1981	216,190	64,575	38,315	26,250
	1991	244,630	82,385	51,025	31,365
New Brunswick	1981	176,630	48,575	28,715	19,860
	1991	198,010	62,875	39,220	23,650
Quebec	1981	1,671,750	488,370	222,660	265,710
	1991	1,883,140	640,485	343,710	296,780
Ontario	1981	2,278,910	740,175	417,875	322,295
	1991	2,726,620	950,915	570,450	380,460
Manitoba	1981	262,235	89,075	54,330	34,750
	1991	285,895	101,910	64,930	36,980
Saskatchewan	1981	245,740	83,995	56,095	27,895
	1991	257,575	94,290	67,510	26,775
Alberta	1981	565,615	185,640	91,780	93,855
	1991	667,915	229,370	135,860	93,510
British Columbia	1981	727,685	271,520	157,845	113,685
	1991	887,505	357,030	223,865	133,155
Yukon	1981	5,675	1,760	580	1,175
	1991	7,105	2,295	1,170	1,135
Northwest Territories	1981	9,485	1,805	635	1,180
	1991	12,725	2,595	1,105	1,490

Economic Characteristics of Families, Selected Census Families in Private Households, 1991

		Family structure		
	All families	Husband-wife families	Lone-parent families	
			Male	Female
Number (000s)	6,512	5,774	111	628
Owned dwelling (000s)	4,562	4,255	64	243
With mortgage (000s)	2,491	2,336	34	121
Average monthly shelter payments ($)	1,053	1,061	968	919
Without mortgage (000s)	2,071	1,919	30	122
Average monthly shelter payments ($)	292	293	277	285
Rented dwelling (000s)	1,754	1,333	44	378
Average monthly shelter payments ($)	580	596	579	525
Family income ($)	52,240	55,173	42,953	26,906

for female lone-parent families was $26,900, while husband-wife families had an average income of $55,200.

About 56% of female lone-parent families who rented spent 30% or more of their income on shelter, compared with husband-wife families with children (22%) and without children (21%).

While the majority of Canadian families lived in single-detached dwellings, female lone-parent families were more likely to live in higher density housing than husband-wife families. For example, 9% of female lone-parent families lived in apartment buildings with five or more stories compared to 3% of husband-wife families with children.

A larger proportion of female lone-parent families lived in dwellings in need of major repairs (12% compared to 8% for husband-wife families with children and 7% for husband-wife families with no children).

Among families with children, female lone-parent families were more likely to occupy smaller dwellings.

Overall, female lone-parent families generally paid a greater proportion of their income for shelter but occupied higher density, smaller and poorer quality housing than other families.

Female lone-parents had lower educational attainment

In 1991, slightly more female lone-parents (17%) had attained less than a grade nine education than

> ### Diversity in families
>
> *Husband-wife families represented 87% of all families in 1991. Among all families, however, those headed by legally married couples declined from 83% in 1981 to 77% (5.7 million families) in 1991. Partially offsetting this decline was an increase in families headed by common-law couples, from 6% in 1981 to 10% (720,000 families) in 1991.*
>
> *Lone-parent families continued to increase in number and proportion, accounting for 13% of all families in 1991, up from 11% in 1981.*

husbands (15%) and wives (13%) in husband-wife families. Also, female lone-parents were less likely to have a university education (16% compared with 19% of wives and 22% of husbands).

Labour force participation

Approximately 60% of female lone-parents were in the labour force in 1991. Of those who were not, 40% had at least one child who was. By comparison, just over 63% of wives and close to 80% of husbands in husband-wife families were in the labour force.

Just over one-half of all husband-wife families had two persons in the labour force while 20% had one, 14% had three or more, and close to 15% had none.

Census Families, 1991

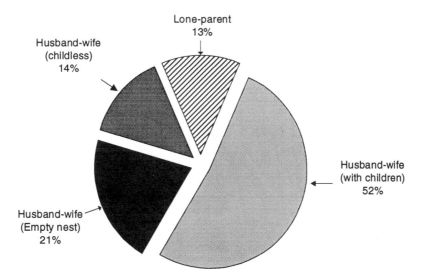

Total census families = 7,355,730

FERTILITY

Women in Canada continued to delay childbearing

The proportion of women who were or had been married but had not yet had children increased in Canada during the past two decades. In 1991, 38% of these women aged 25-29 had yet to bear children, compared with 21% in 1971. Among women aged 35-39, the corresponding percentage rose from 7% to 13%. This increase among the latter age group likely reflects a growth in the level of childlessness in Canada, as it is relatively uncommon for women to have their first child beyond the age of 39.

Several alternate indexes are used in examining fertility patterns. The analysis in this release is based on the definition traditionally used in the census. According to this definition, fertility is the number of children ever born alive to women aged 15 and older. The census definition includes children. Step-children are excluded in this fertility measure. Unless otherwise stated, the census fertility data presented in this report include children ever born to women who have ever been married (currently, or previously married), aged 15-44. This group of women was chosen to allow comparison with previous censuses.

Although it is not used in the present context, the total fertility rate (TFR) is an alternate indicator commonly used in other Statistics Canada releases, particularly those from the Canadian Centre for Health Information. The TFR is the number of children a women would have during her lifetime if she were to experience the childbearing patterns of a specific period.

Married Women* Who had Never had Children by Selected Age Groups

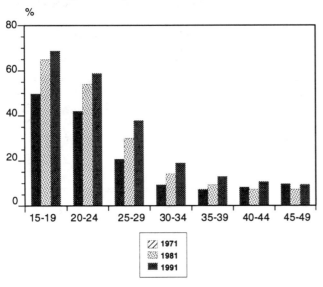

%

1971
1981
1991

---

* *Married women includes women presently married as well as those who have been married.*

One in 10 single women had at least one child

The 1991 Census collected, for the first time, fertility information from women who had never been married and who were not in common-law relationships – that is, single women. The average number of children born per 1,000 single women aged 15-44 was 145, compared to 1,622 per 1,000 for married women, and 873 per 1,000 for women living common law.

Among single women in 1991, 10% had borne at least one child. This percentage varied from a low of 8% in Ontario to considerably higher levels in Saskatchewan (14%), the Yukon (18%) and the Northwest Territories (30%).

Single Women Aged 15-44 Who had Borne One or More Children, 1991

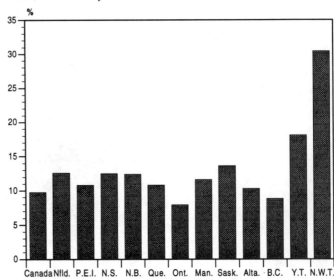

%

The average number of children born to married women declined

In 1991, the average number of children ever born to women aged 15-44 who were or had been married, was 1,628 per 1,000. This was down from 1,781 in 1981. During the same period, this average also declined for married women aged 35-44, from 2,562 to 2,029.

Between 1981 and 1991, Newfoundland experienced the largest decline, from 2,371 to 1,930 children per 1,000 married women. This was followed closely by New Brunswick, from 2,050 to 1,733. The smallest decline occurred in Alberta, from 1,746 to 1,715.

Children Ever Born per 1,000 Married Women* Aged 15-44 by the Mother's Mother Tongue

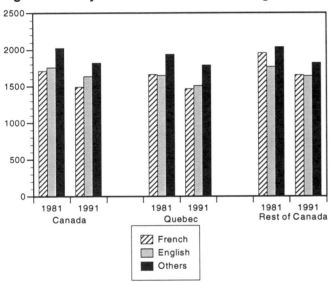

* Married women includes women presently married as well as those who have been married.

Mother tongue and fertility

At the national level in 1991, the number of children ever born to women with English mother tongue (1,636 per 1,000) was higher than the number for women with French mother tongue (1,494). The difference in the national rates, however, was more a reflection of regional differences than of differences between the two official language groups. In Quebec, the difference in the number of children born to women of French and English mother tongue was small (1,465 compared with 1,511 per 1,000 respectively) and elsewhere in Canada even less (1,652 compared to 1,640). While the rates declined for women of both English and French mother tongue

between 1981 and 1991 (inside and outside Quebec), the decline was more rapid among women of French mother tongue than among those who spoke English.

Labour force participation and education influenced fertility

Labour force participation and higher levels of education have both been linked with lower levels of fertility in Canada. For example, women who had worked recently in the paid labour force had lower fertility than those who had not. Among married women aged 25-44 who had worked since January 1990, the average number of children born per 1,000 women was 1,627. Among women who had not worked since that date, the average was higher at 2,236. Correspondingly, this average varied from a low of 1,327 for women with a university degree to a high of 2,461 for those with less than Grade 9 education.

Over the 1981-1991 period, there was little indication that there had been a convergence in the fertility of women in and outside the paid labour force (with the difference remaining at 37% in both the 1981 and 1991 Censuses). However, among women of different education levels, there had been a slight convergence in fertility. For example, in comparing the fertility of women with a university degree and those with less than Grade 9, the difference in 1991 was 85%, down from 127% in 1981.

Children Ever Born per 1,000 Married Women* Aged 25-44 by Work Experience

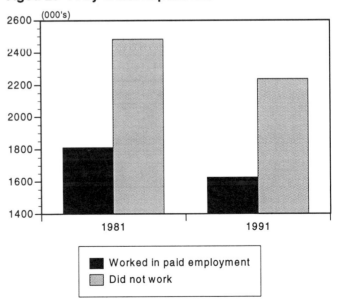

* Married women includes women presently married as well as those who have been married.

Immigrant women had slightly more children

The average number of children for immigrant women was slightly higher than among women born in Canada. While this average declined among immigrant women from 1,880 in 1981 to 1,755 in 1991, among Canadian-born women the decline was even more pronounced, from 1,759 to 1,599. Immigrant women averaged 10% more children in 1991 than women born in Canada.

Among immigrant women in Canada, those from Central America had the highest average number of children (2,268 per 1,000). They were followed closely by immigrant women born in West Asia and the Middle East (2,004) and Southern Europe (2,001). Immigrant women born in Eastern Europe (1,477) and East Asia (1,518) had the lowest averages in 1991, and they experienced the largest decline in fertility since 1981.

Fertility varied by ethnicity

Among the 10 largest ethnic groups (based on single responses) those with the lowest average number of children were women of Chinese (1,495) and French (1,505) ancestry. This average was slightly higher among women of Ukrainian (1,515), Italian (1,644), British (1,662) and Dutch (1,934) origins. Of the 10 largest groups, women of Aboriginal ancestry had the highest number of children (2,592 per 1,000 women).

Over the 1981-1991 period, women of Italian and Chinese origins exhibited the largest declines in the number of children (at 16% and 13% respectively). Although Aboriginal women also experienced a large decline (13%), their average continued to remain significantly higher than among any other major ethnic group in Canada.

Childlessness (as measured by the percentage of women who were or had been married, aged 35-44 and who had not borne any children) was the highest among Ukrainians (16%) and lowest among women of Aboriginal ancestry (5%), followed by women of East Indian origin (7%).

Children Ever Born per 1,000 Married Women* Aged 15-44 by Country of Birth

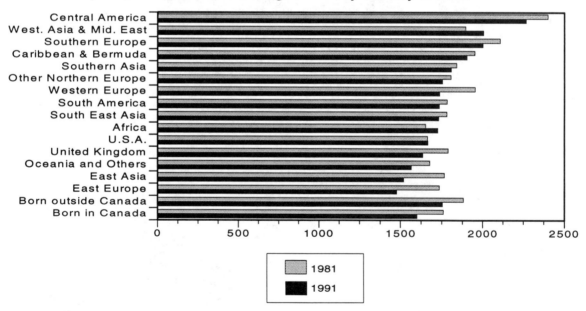

*   *Married women includes women presently married as well as those who have been married.*

PLACE OF WORK

In 1991, 90% of employed Canadians left their homes to work at another location, while 1.1 million (8%) worked at home; 152,000 (1%) reported having no usual place of work (such as construction workers), and another 46,000 (0.4%) reported working outside the country.

Close to 1.1 million of the employed labour force worked at home

In 1991, 8% (1,078,880 people) of the employed labour force worked at home. Saskatchewan recorded the highest percentage (22%) of people working at home. The western provinces in general showed the highest percentage of people working at home, with a large number of respondents indicating that they lived and worked on a farm. Nationally, 26% of Canadians who worked at home, worked and lived on a farm.

> Working at home can be measured in different ways. The place of work question asked in the 1991 Census does not measure "telework".
>
> The telework phenomenon was investigated by Statistics Canada's **"Survey of Work Arrangements"**. This survey, a supplement to the November 1991 Labour Force Survey, gathered comprehensive data on the work routines of paid workers only. Just over **600,000** employees reported working some or all of their scheduled hours at home.

Employed Labour Force by Place of Work, 1991

| | Total | | Place of work | | | | | | | |
| | | | Usual place of work | | Work at home | | No usual place of work | | Work outside Canada | |
	No.	%	No.	%	No.	%	No.	%	No.	%
Canada	13,005,505	100	11,729,265	90.2	1,078,880	8.3	151,530	1.2	45,830	0.4
Newfoundland	192,890	100	172,940	89.7	17,030	8.8	2,035	1.1	880	0.5
Prince Edward Island	59,070	100	51,485	87.2	6,230	10.5	1,155	2.0	195	0.3
Nova Scotia	390,785	100	357,500	91.5	25,405	6.5	6,070	1.6	1,810	0.5
New Brunswick	300,965	100	276,295	91.8	19,910	6.6	3,145	1.0	1,610	0.5
Quebec	3,110,795	100	2,858,670	91.9	219,180	7.0	24,085	0.8	8,855	0.3
Ontario	5,041,935	100	4,629,250	91.8	343,720	6.8	49,140	1.0	19,835	0.4
Manitoba	521,490	100	451,105	86.5	62,690	12.0	6,250	1.2	1,445	0.3
Saskatchewan	470,475	100	359,000	76.3	105,335	22.4	5,150	1.1	990	0.2
Alberta	1,308,795	100	1,136,250	86.8	149,070	11.4	19,695	1.5	3,780	0.3
British Columbia	1,568,780	100	1,400,130	89.2	127,740	8.1	34,530	2.2	6,385	0.4
Yukon	15,040	100	13,495	89.7	1,390	9.2	135	0.9	20	0.1
Northwest Territories	24,475	100	23,140	94.5	1,175	4.8	135	0.6	20	0.1

Average Distance* Between Place of Residence and Place of Work of the Employed Labour Force, 1991

	Lived in CMA Worked in CMA	Lived outside CMA Worked in CMA	Lived in CMA Worked outside CMA
		Distance in kilometres	
All Census Metropolitan Areas	**10**	**50**	**59**
St. John's	6	58	59
Halifax	8	60	77
Saint John	10	71	61
Chicoutimi-Jonquière	7	62	77
Québec	8	62	61
Sherbrooke	5	39	34
Trois-Rivières	6	47	30
Montréal	10	48	59
Ottawa-Hull	10	54	43
Oshawa	7	43	84
Toronto	12	52	86
Hamilton	7	38	70
St. Catharines-Niagara	7	46	35
Kitchener	6	35	29
London	6	49	36
Windsor	7	34	23
Sudbury	10	57	65
Thunder Bay	7	37	126
Winnipeg	9	47	58
Regina	5	63	88
Saskatoon	6	81	89
Calgary	9	59	75
Edmonton	10	67	85
Vancouver	10	51	82
Victoria	7	58	70

* based on commuters travelling 200 km or less

Close to 46,000 Canadians worked outside Canada

Close to 46,000 people reported working outside the country in 1991. Of these, 15,000 lived and worked outside the country (such as diplomats, Canadian Armed Forces personnel) when the census was conducted. Another 31,000 lived in Canada but worked outside of the country.

Going that "extra mile" to get to work

For people living and working within a census metropolitan area, the average one-way commute distance was 10 km.

Those who commuted into metropolitan areas to work in 1991, travelled an average of 50 km (one way). However, the travel distance varied significantly among metropolitan areas. Those who commuted to the metropolitan areas of Saskatoon (81 km) and Saint John (71 km) travelled over twice the distance as people who commuted to Kitchener (35 km) or Windsor (34 km). Those commuting into the metropolitan areas of Chicoutimi-Jonquière, Québec, Regina and Edmonton travelled over 60 km on average.

For people living within a metropolitan area and working outside of it, the average one-way commute distance was 59 km.

Place of work

Place of work information was collected from respondents 15 years of age and older (excluding institutional residents) who had worked since January 1, 1990. The information refers to the job held in the week prior to enumeration. However, if a person had not worked in that week, but had worked since January 1, 1990, the information refers to the job held longest during that period.

Census
of
Agriculture

Catalogue 11-001E (Français 11-001F) ISSN 0827-0465

The Daily

Statistics Canada

Thursday, June 4, 1992

SOIL CONTROL METHODS, FIELD CROP ACREAGE, GROSS FARM RECEIPTS AND LIVESTOCK

HIGHLIGHTS

- The 1991 Census of Agriculture recorded 280,043 census farms, down 4.5% from 1986

- Family-operated farms accounted for 98% of census farms in 1991, compared to 99% in 1986

- The number of four-wheel drive tractors increased by one-third in Canada between 1986 and 1991

- A steady upward trend from 1970 to 1985 in the use of commercial fertilizer and herbicides reversed with the 1991 Census

- Conservation tillage and "no till" practices were used on one-third of Canadian land prepared for seeding

- The number of farms using computers to manage the farm business quadrupled from 2.6% in 1986 to 11% in 1991

Census Overview of Canadian Agriculture: 1971-1991

The *Census Overview of Canadian Agriculture: 1971-1991* (93-348, $49) publication compares data from the 1971 to 1991 Censuses of Agriculture at the Canada and provincial levels. One set of tables provides basic counts, totals, averages and percentage changes and distributions for a large number of variables. A second set of tables presents size class distributions for selected crop, livestock, receipts and farm-type variables.

 Statistics Statistique
Canada Canada

 Canada

Fewer and larger farms in 1991

The 1991 Census of Agriculture recorded 280,043 census farms, a 4.5% decrease from the 293,089 census farms in 1986. This continued a 50-year down-trend from 1941 when the number of census farms peaked at 732,832.

As the overall number of farms decreased, the number of larger farms (gross receipts of $50,000 or more in constant 1990 dollars) increased 6% from 111,414 in 1986 to 118,365 in 1991. However, the number of larger farms decreased in three provinces: Prince Edward Island (-4%), New Brunswick (-4%) and Ontario (-1%).

Since 1986, the overall number of census farms increased in only two provinces – British Columbia (1%) and Newfoundland (11%). In contrast, the number of farms decreased at a rate slower than the national average in Saskatchewan (-4%), and Alberta (-1%).

All other provinces reported decreases greater than the national average. Prince Edward Island reported the largest decrease in census farms (-17%), continuing the double-digit downward trend between censuses that began in 1961.

Census Farm

A Census Farm is an agricultural holding that produces an agricultural product intended for sale. This broad definition is used to obtain an inventory of all the agricultural products and resources in Canada.

Census Farms and Farms with Gross Receipts of $50,000 or More

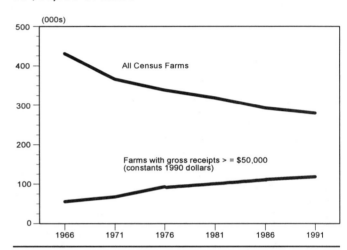

Census Farms and Farms with Gross Receipts of $50,000 or More

	All census farms			Gross Receipts > =$50,000		
	Number in 1986	Number in 1991	% change since 1986	Number in 1986	Number in 1991	% change since 1986
Canada	**293,089**	**280,043**	**-4.5**	**111,414**	**118,365**	**6.2**
Newfoundland	651	725	11.4	159	193	21.4
Prince Edward Island	2,833	2,361	-16.7	1,117	1,072	-4.0
Nova Scotia	4,283	3,980	-7.1	1,107	1,172	5.9
New Brunswick	3,554	3,252	-8.5	1,091	1,052	-3.6
Quebec	41,448	38,076	-8.1	18,574	19,008	2.3
Ontario	72,713	68,633	-5.6	27,338	26,996	-1.3
Manitoba	27,336	25,706	-6.0	11,449	11,676	2.0
Saskatchewan	63,431	60,840	-4.1	25,316	28,509	12.6
Alberta	57,777	57,245	-0.9	21,357	24,269	13.6
British Columbia	19,063	19,225	0.9	3,906	4,418	13.1

Statistics Canada - Cat. No. 96-304E

Improved land continued to increase

In 1991, the total area of land in crops in Canada was 83 million acres. This was up slightly from 1986, and continued two decades of an upward trend.

Saskatchewan had the largest share of land in crops (33 million acres or 40% of the Canada total) in 1991.

The area of summerfallow in Canada continued to decline in 1991. Acreage decreased 7% since 1986, down to 19.5 million acres in 1991.

Saskatchewan had the largest share of summerfallow acreage (14 million acres or 72% of the Canada total) in 1991.

Since 1971, the total area of improved pasture in Canada has remained relatively constant at about 10 million acres. In 1986, however, improved pasture acreage dropped to less than 9 million acres. The total area of improved pasture moved back to its former level in 1991.

Alberta had the largest share of Canada's improved pasture (4.3 million acres, 42%) in 1991, followed by Saskatchewan (2.7 million acres, 26%).

Area in Crops, Summerfallow, and Improved Pasture

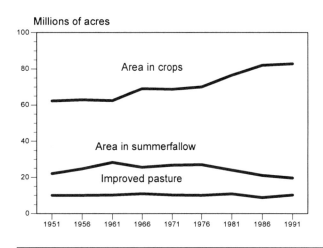

Area in Crops, Summerfallow, and Improved Pasture (acres)

	Area in crops		Area in summerfallow		Improved pasture		Total Improved land	
	1986	1991	1986	1991	1986	1991	1986	1991
Canada	**81,992,625**	**82,799,535**	**21,001,527**	**19,573,092**	**8,795,013**	**10,233,180**	**111,789,165**	**112,605,807**
Newfoundland	12,049	15,503	951	359	9,444	11,382	22,444	27,244
Prince Edward Island	386,715	380,796	6,541	2,464	55,899	47,636	449,155	430,896
Nova Scotia	270,609	262,503	9,663	2,930	89,542	75,918	369,814	341,351
New Brunswick	319,940	302,079	10,599	3,833	67,222	61,896	397,761	367,808
Quebec	4,310,496	4,048,706	78,586	36,355	744,115	669,468	5,133,197	4,754,529
Ontario	8,544,820	8,430,414	198,517	157,301	1,065,731	964,235	9,809,068	9,551,950
Manitoba	11,167,521	11,764,813	1,258,294	733,899	679,402	843,348	13,105,217	13,342,060
Saskatchewan	32,928,799	33,257,706	13,981,843	14,116,713	2,171,380	2,658,002	49,082,022	50,032,421
Alberta	22,641,092	22,961,142	5,255,965	4,377,212	3,402,183	4,305,760	31,299,240	31,644,114
British Columbia	1,410,584	1,375,873	200,568	142,026	510,095	595,535	2,121,247	2,113,434

Number of four-wheel drive tractors increased

Since 1986, the number of four-wheel drive tractors in Canada increased by one-third, while the number of two-wheel drive tractors dropped by 3%.

In 1991, half of the four-wheel drive tractors were in the 100 horsepower or over category. More than three-quarters of the two-wheel drive tractors were in the less than 100 horsepower category.

At the provincial level, the number of four-wheel drive tractors in Newfoundland more than doubled, the largest increase for any province.

The largest proportion of four-wheel drive tractors (to total tractors) in 1991 was reported in Newfoundland (31%), followed by Nova Scotia (22%) and Quebec (20%). Ontario had the single largest number of tractors (185,000) in 1991.

Farms using more round balers

In 1991, one-third of the balers in use in Canada were large round balers, compared to only one-fifth in 1986.

Change in the Number of Four-Wheel Drive Tractors, 1986-1991

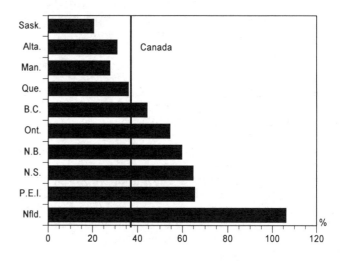

Number of Two- and Four-Wheel Drive Tractors

	Two-wheel drive tractors			Four-wheel drive tractors			Four-wheel drive tractors Province (%)	
	1986	1991	% change	1986	1991	% change	1986	1991
Canada	648,648	626,865	-3.4	79,426	107,284	35.1	10.9	14.6
Newfoundland	565	580	2.7	128	264	106.3	18.5	31.3
Prince Edward Island	5,674	5,083	-10.4	391	647	65.5	6.4	11.3
Nova Scotia	6,663	6,076	-8.8	1,067	1,758	64.8	13.8	22.4
New Brunswick	6,294	5,831	-7.4	811	1,296	59.8	11.4	18.2
Quebec	81,936	76,650	-6.5	14,154	19,243	36.0	14.7	20.1
Ontario	172,905	162,728	-5.9	14,260	22,033	54.5	6.0	11.9
Manitoba	66,876	64,490	-3.6	7,069	9,033	27.8	9.6	12.3
Saskatchewan	148,427	146,592	-1.2	18,607	22,446	20.6	11.1	13.3
Alberta	131,341	130,796	-0.4	19,138	25,076	31.0	12.7	16.1
British Columbia	27,967	28,039	0.3	3,801	5,488	44.4	12.0	16.4

Use of commercial fertilizer and herbicides decreased

A steady upward trend from 1970 to 1985 in the use of commercial fertilizer and herbicides (both in the number of farms reporting and the land areas covered), reversed with the 1991 Census.

The percentage of census farms in Canada using commercial fertilizer declined from 66% in 1985 to 59% in 1990. At the same time, 37% of Canadian census farms reported using manure on more than 5 million acres of land. Over 60% of this land was in Eastern Canada.

In 1990, Prince Edward Island had the highest percentage (71%) of farms using commercial fertilizer, whereas only 45% of British Columbia's farms reported fertilizer use.

The proportion of cropland fertilized declined from 70% in 1985 to 64% in 1990, still significantly higher than the 25% fertilized in 1970.

Area Applied With Commercial Fertilizer

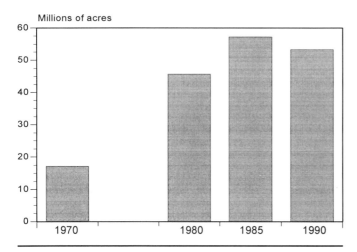

Newfoundland had the largest percentage (87%) of area in crops being fertilized in 1990, compared to only 57% in Saskatchewan.

In 1990, 49% of Canadian census farms used herbicides, a significant drop from the 59% in 1985.

In 1990, Saskatchewan had the highest percentage (68%) of farms using herbicides, in comparison to Newfoundland where 16% of farms reported using herbicides.

The total area of crops and summerfallow treated with herbicides dropped to 52% in 1990, down slightly from 55% in 1985. Nevertheless, the 1990 figure is still more than double the 22% treated with herbicides in 1970.

Area Applied With Herbicides

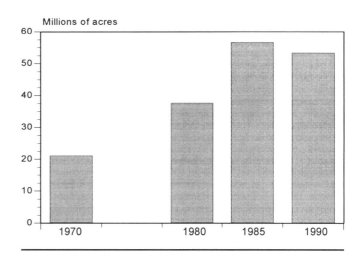

Manitoba had the highest percentage (65%) of area in crops and summerfallow treated with herbicides in 1990. Newfoundland had the lowest at 9%.

Family-operated farms still predominated

In 1991, family-operated farms accounted for 98% of all census farms in Canada, compared to 99% in 1986. Non-family corporations represented just over 1% of all farms in 1991, while the remainder were institutional farms, community pastures and Hutterite colonies.

One-quarter of census farms produced most of output

In 1991, one-quarter of census farms generated three-quarters of gross farm receipts. This situation has remained relatively unchanged over the past three censuses.

Provincially, the component of gross farm receipts generated by the top 25% of farms varied greatly. In Newfoundland and British Columbia, the top 25% of

Gross Farm Receipts for Top 25% of Farms

Year	% of Gross Farm Receipts
1966	68.7
1971	71.8
1981	74.2
1986	74.0
1991	75.5

Acres Applied With Fertilizer and Herbicides

	Commercial fertilizer				Herbicides			
	1970	1980	1985	1990	1970	1980	1985	1990
Canada	**17,121,551**	**45,727,345**	**57,199,888**	**53,280,448**	**21,179,650**	**37,610,448**	**56,708,354**	**53,371,080**
Newfoundland	5,684	10,906	11,755	13,427	912	1,234	1,660	1,414
Prince Edward Island	138,657	265,494	279,964	252,336	106,608	202,104	211,455	182,322
Nova Scotia	94,271	218,779	210,145	203,287	38,467	51,553	61,145	55,310
New Brunswick	91,879	187,792	207,688	193,079	72,659	99,334	113,171	98,495
Quebec	1,159,810	2,731,505	2,938,659	2,462,953	410,316	990,475	1,337,461	1,394,491
Ontario	3,095,117	6,261,213	6,402,812	5,617,813	2,758,119	4,753,376	4,981,059	4,426,851
Manitoba	2,930,926	7,898,613	9,208,072	9,114,074	4,193,858	6,246,626	8,859,638	8,063,498
Saskatchewan	3,701,960	13,654,683	20,077,392	18,914,810	8,007,853	13,204,633	25,788,378	24,823,839
Alberta	5,583,003	13,603,578	16,938,768	15,690,907	5,454,426	11,761,734	15,005,557	14,012,340
British Columbia	320,244	894,782	924,633	817,762	136,432	299,379	348,830	312,520

farms generated over 90% of provincial farm receipts, while in Saskatchewan, these farms generated 62%. Quebec and Manitoba (along with Saskatchewan) were below the national average at 72%.

Crop rotation most common soil erosion control method

Crop rotation (using clovers, alfalfa, etc.) was employed by 37% of Canadian census farms to control soil erosion in 1990.

In Prince Edward Island, 64% of farms practiced crop rotation compared to 17% of British Columbia farms.

To control soil erosion, 18% of Ontario farms used winter cover crops, 15% of Alberta farms used grassed waterways and Saskatchewan farms used strip-cropping (20%) and contour cultivation (17%). The most frequently reported "other practice" was conservation tillage.

Methods Used for Controlling Soil Erosion, 1990

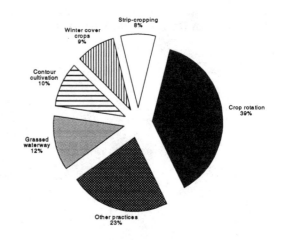

Census Farms Reporting Soil Erosion Control Practices, 1990

	Crop rotation	Winter cover crops	Grassed waterways	Strip-cropping	Contour cultivation	Other practices
Canada	37	9	11	8	9	22
Newfoundland	24	4	3	1	5	8
Prince Edward Island	64	8	10	4	9	14
Nova Scotia	28	10	7	2	6	6
New Brunswick	35	8	7	4	7	7
Quebec	42	3	3	2	3	7
Ontario	54	18	14	4	6	18
Manitoba	32	6	11	4	12	34
Saskatchewan	21	6	12	20	17	34
Alberta	38	6	15	8	10	26
British Columbia	17	8	7	1	4	9

The Daily, June 4, 1992

Conservation and "no till" practices used

In 1991, one-quarter of the land seeded in Canada (17.5 million acres) was prepared using conservation tillage. "No till" seeding was used on an additional 7% of land.

Conservation tillage and "no till" seeding was most prevalent in the Prairie provinces. Saskatchewan accounted for the largest proportion of conservation tillage and "no till" seeding, with these methods being used on 36% of land prepared for seeding.

Soil salinity

In 1991, for the first time, the Census of Agriculture asked farm operators questions about soil salinity.

Measures to control soil salinity were most prevalent in the Prairie provinces. In Saskatchewan, 24% of census farms reported using some measure to control soil salinity, compared with 15% of Manitoba farms and 11% of farms in Alberta.

Share of Seeded Land According to Tillage Method, 1991

	Conventional tillage	Conservation tillage	No tillage
Canada	**68.9**	**24.4**	**6.7**
Newfoundland	84.1	7.7	8.2
Prince Edward Island	91.2	7.9	0.9
Nova Scotia	88.3	7.8	3.8
New Brunswick	85.3	12.5	2.2
Quebec	85.2	12.3	2.5
Ontario	78.2	17.8	4.0
Manitoba	66.3	28.7	5.0
Saskatchewan	63.9	25.7	10.4
Alberta	72.6	24.3	3.1
British Columbia	83.5	11.9	4.6

Canadian farms use shelterbelts

The 1991 Census reported that, 13% of all Canadian farms (36 thousand) had soil conservation shelterbelts (windbreaks).

The total length of shelterbelts was 84 thousand kilometres or 2.3 kilometres per reporting farm. If planted in a row, these trees would circle the equator twice.

The Prairie provinces reported the most shelterbelts in Canada. In Saskatchewan, 18% of farms reported 34 thousand kilometres of shelterbelts for an average length per reporting farm of 3.2 kilometres. In 1991, 21% of Manitoba farms and 16% of Alberta farms reported having shelterbelts.

Vegetable crop acreage increased

Total vegetable acreage increased by 15 thousand acres (5%) between 1986 and 1991. Acreage increased for 14 vegetable crops and declined for eight.

In 1991, sweet corn (29%), green peas (16%) and tomatoes (10%) accounted for 55% of the vegetable crop acreage. Between 1986 and 1991, sweet corn acreage increased 8%, and green peas 43% (the largest increase of any vegetable crop), but tomatoes decreased 20%.

Some smaller crops showed the largest changes in acreage between 1986 and 1991. Rhubarb, broccoli and lettuce increased over 20%, but asparagus, brussels sprouts and cucumbers declined by more than 20%.

Sweet corn acreage increased in all provinces although it is primarily grown in Ontario and Quebec which have 57% and 31%, of the Canadian sweet corn acreage.

Green peas increased in all provinces with significant acreages, except in New Brunswick where acreage fell marginally (-2%) between 1986 and 1991.

The Ontario decline in tomato acreage (down 7,000 acres, -20%) accounted for the overall decline, due to the fact that Ontario has 89% of the tomato acreage in Canada. Tomato acreage in Quebec (9% of the acreage in Canada) also declined by more than 20%.

Vegetable Crop Acreage, 1986-1991

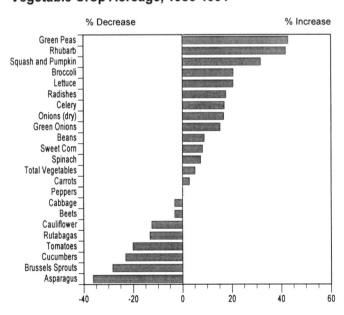

Vegetable Acreage[1]

	1986	1991	% change
Canada	**288,058**	**302,936**	**5.2**
Newfoundland	970	1,199	23.6
Prince Edward Island	2,773	3,059	10.3
Nova Scotia	8,916	9,462	6.1
New Brunswick	8,079	7,145	-11.6
Quebec	81,060	90,378	11.5
Ontario	154,046	154,493	0.3
Manitoba	3,400	4,174	22.8
Saskatchewan	1,213	1,044	-13.9
Alberta	8,895	11,536	29.7
British Columbia	18,702	20,447	9.3

1 Canada total may not equal sum of provinces due to rounding.

Acres Used for Vegetable Crops, 1991

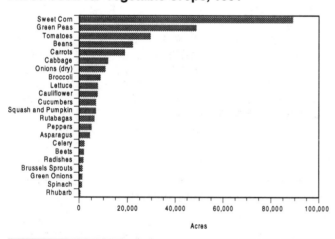

Tree fruit area down slightly

In 1991, tree fruit area in Canada was 113,000 acres, 2% less than in 1986.

Ontario, British Columbia, Quebec and Nova Scotia accounted for 98% of the tree fruit area in Canada. Except for Quebec, all these provinces experienced slight declines in tree fruit area between 1986 and 1991.

Apples remained the predominant tree fruit grown in Canada. Apples accounted for three-quarters of the area devoted to tree fruits, increasing slightly by 1% to 86,000 acres in 1991.

Peaches ranked second in terms of area in 1991 at 11,000, a 10% decrease from 1986.

Sour cherries registered the largest percentage decline in tree fruit area, down 19% from 1986 to 2,600 acres.

Area Used for Tree Fruit, 1991

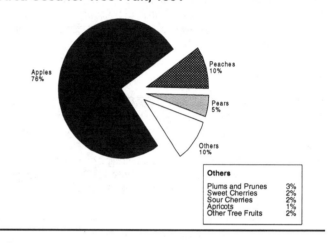

Small fruit acreage increased

Between 1986 and 1991, small fruit acreage in Canada increased by 13,000 acres (13%), to 110,000 acres.

The top three were blueberries (57% of total small fruit area), strawberries (16%) and grapes (14%).

Grapes (-40%) and strawberries (-14%) showed the only decreases in small fruit acreage between 1986 and 1991.

From 1986 to 1991, cranberry area in Canada increased 71% to roughly 3,400 acres. British Columbia had 84% of Canada's cranberry acreage.

Area Used for Small Fruit, 1991

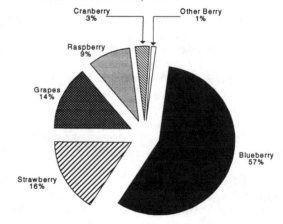

Prince Edward Island still grew most potatoes

In 1991, Canada grew 302,000 acres of potatoes, up 10% from 1986.

Ontario, with 37% of the Canadian population in 1991, reported only 12% of the total area planted in potatoes. In comparison, Prince Edward Island, with only 0.5% of the population, reported 26% of the total acreage.

Potato Acreage

	1951	1971	1991
Canada	**287,561**	**269,599**	**302,435**
Newfoundland	2,505	1,194	667
Prince Edward Island	29,607	46,752	77,809
Nova Scotia	11,331	3,487	4,386
New Brunswick	38,123	59,421	50,621
Quebec	92,024	47,535	43,280
Ontario	54,894	40,055	35,070
Manitoba	15,846	32,678	49,478
Saskatchewan	15,709	3,255	4,461
Alberta	17,730	26,139	28,339
British Columbia	9,792	9,083	8,324

From 1971 to 1991, Prince Edward Island's share of the total area planted in potatoes increased from 17% to 26%. Nova Scotia, Manitoba and Saskatchewan also reported increases, while all other provinces showed decreases.

In 1991, less than 300 farms (6% of farms with potatoes) accounted for almost half of the potatoes grown in Canada. Twenty-eight per cent (83) of these large farms were in Prince Edward Island, 24% (73) in Manitoba, 13% (39) in New Brunswick and 12% (36) in Ontario.

Area of field crops remained constant

Canada's area of field crops in 1991 was just over 82 million acres, a 0.9% increase from 1986.

Wheat remained the number one field crop accounting for 35 million acres, or 43% of total field crop area. Spring wheat made up 84% of total wheat area, followed by durum (at 14%) and winter wheat (at 2%).

Tame hay was the largest field crop after wheat, with 17% of field crop area (14.2 million acres). Alberta had the largest provincial share of hay (30% of all land in hay) with 4.2 million acres. Ontario, Saskatchewan and Quebec ranked second, third and fourth, with just over 2 million acres each.

Sunflowers showed the largest increase (189%) between 1986 and 1991, to a level of 206,049 acres. Manitoba accounted for nine-tenths of the total Canadian area of sunflowers.

Soybean area was up in the two major producing provinces. Ontario, with the largest area of soybeans (1.4 million acres) increased 50% from 1986. Quebec's area of soybeans increased almost six-fold between 1986 and 1991, to 62,445 acres.

Tobacco area declined by 5% between 1986 and 1991, to 74,000 acres. Ontario, with 90% of tobacco area, registered the only provincial increase, up 3% to 67,000 acres.

Share of Potato Acreage Among the Provinces

	1951	1971	1991
Canada	**100.0**	**100.0**	**100.0**
Newfoundland	0.9	0.4	0.2
Prince Edward Island	10.3	17.3	25.7
Nova Scotia	3.9	1.3	1.5
New Brunswick	13.3	22.0	16.7
Quebec	32.0	17.6	14.3
Ontario	19.1	14.9	11.6
Manitoba	5.5	12.1	16.4
Saskatchewan	5.5	1.2	1.5
Alberta	6.2	9.7	·9.4
British Columbia	3.4	3.4	2.8

Area Used for Field Crops, 1991

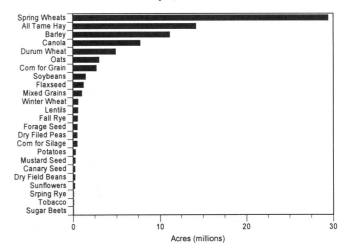

Change in Field Crop Acreage, 1986-1991

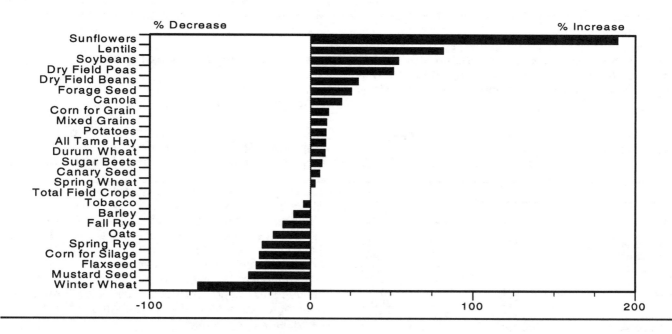

Computer use on farms quadrupled since 1986

The number of farms using computers to manage the farm business quadrupled from 2.6% in 1986 to 11% in 1991.

Farms with receipts of $500,000 or more were most likely to use a computer to manage their business. In 1991, 43% of these farms reported using a computer, up from 19% in 1986.

Among the provinces, British Columbia had the highest proportion (14%) of farms using computers.

Cattle, pig and sheep herds increased

In 1991, numbers of sheep showed the largest increase of any livestock category, up one-third since 1986 to almost 936,000 head.

The number of beef cows reached 3.8 million, an 18% increase from 1986. Alberta's share of the Canadian beef cow herd was 43%, and Saskatchewan had 23%.

In addition to beef cows and sheep, the numbers of goats, rabbits and pigs also increased between 1986 and 1991.

Farm Computer Use

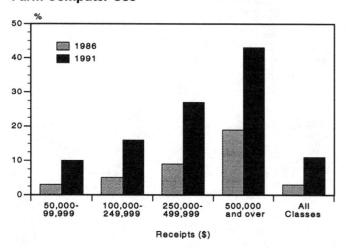

Livestock Numbers, 1991

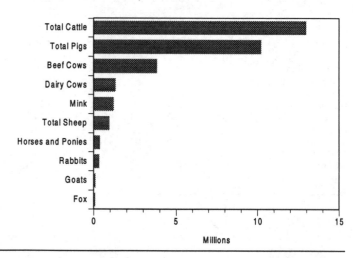

Statistics Canada - Cat. No. 96-304E

The number of fox, at 60,000, showed the largest drop of all livestock categories since 1986, down 47%.

Between 1986 and 1991, decreases were also registered in numbers of mink, horses and ponies, and dairy cows.

Change in Livestock Numbers, 1986-1991

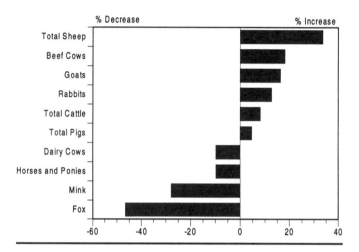

Fewer dairy cows on Canadian farms

In 1991, there were 1.3 million dairy cows in Canada, a 10% decrease since 1986.

From 1986 to 1991, the number of farms with dairy cows dropped by 22% to 40,000.

The average dairy farm had 34 dairy cows in 1991 compared to 29 cows in 1986 and only 16 cows in 1971. In 1991, nearly half of the dairy cows were in herds of fewer than 50.

Number of Dairy Cows

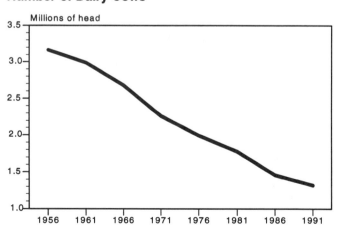

Provincial Share of Dairy Cows, 1991

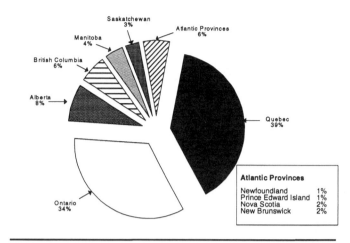

Number of pigs a record high

In 1991, 10.2 million pigs were reported on farms in Canada, a slight increase over 1986.

At the same time, the number of farms reporting pigs dropped to a record low of 30,000 in 1991, down 76% since 1971. In 1991, 8% of farms accounted for half the pigs in Canada. Of these larger farms, 40% were in Quebec, 23% in Ontario and 17% in Alberta.

Number of Pigs

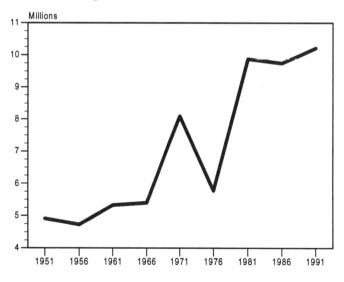

In 1991, Quebec accounted for 28% of the number of pigs, yet had only 12% of the farms reporting pigs. In contrast, Ontario accounted for the same number of pigs, but had nearly three times as many farms reporting pigs.

Between 1986 and 1991, hog production shifted from Eastern to Western Canada. In 1991, Eastern hog producers lost 5% of total hog production (just over 0.5 million) to Western producers.

Provincial Share of Pigs

	1986	1991
Canada	**100**	**100**
East	**65.8**	**60.4**
Newfoundland	0.2	0.2
Prince Edward Island	1.2	1.0
Nova Scotia	1.4	1.3
New Brunswick	1.0	0.7
Quebec	30.0	28.5
Ontario	32.0	28.6
West	**34.2**	**39.6**
Manitoba	11.0	12.6
Saskatchewan	6.1	7.9
Alberta	14.9	16.9
British Columbia	2.2	2.2

Expenses

Total farm business operating expenses in constant 1990 dollars increased marginally (3%) from 1985.

In 1990, interest expenses were $2.4 billion or 12% of total farm business expenses in Canada. The average amount of interest paid per reporting farm was $13,700.

At the national level, 15% of farms with receipts of $50,000 or more were debt-free and reported no interest expenses. For farms with receipts of less than $50,000, however, 55% were without interest expenses in 1990.

In the Atlantic provinces, interest expenses accounted for less than 10% of total farm expenses, with Newfoundland the lowest at just over 5%. Saskatchewan reported the highest share of interest to total farm expenses (15%).

Livestock expenses (feed, supplements, livestock, poultry, and veterinary expenses) were the largest component (30%) of total expenses at the national level. This proportion varied among provinces, from a low in Saskatchewan (13%) to a high in Newfoundland (52%.)

Share of Farm Expenses, 1990

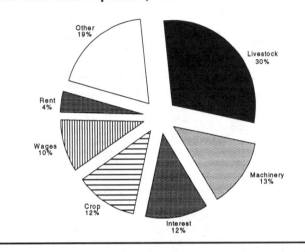

Crop expenses (fertilizer, lime, herbicides, insecticides, fungicides, seed and seedlings) made up 12% of all farm expenses in 1990.

Wages and salaries ($2 billion) accounted for 10% of farm expenses in Canada. Half of all wages and salaries were paid to family members.

Interest Expenses as a Percentage of Total Expenses, 1990

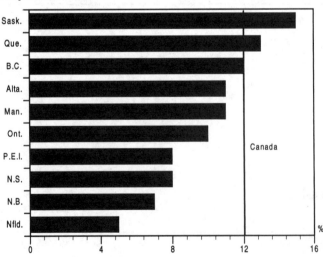

Total Expenses, 1990

	Canada		Newfoundland		Prince Edward Island		Nova Scotia		New Brunswick		Quebec	
	($'000)	% of total expenses	($'000)	% of total expenses	($'000)	% of total expenses	($'000)	% of total expenses	($'000)	% of total expenses	($'000)	% of total expenses
Total Expenses	**20,311,554**	**100**	**60,809**	**100**	**209,699**	**100**	**300,957**	**100**	**250,600**	**100**	**3,101,855**	**100**
Rent	767,911	4	241	0	6,714	3	2,824	1	2,544	1	33,178	1
Wages	2,039,667	10	10,330	17	33,244	16	55,462	18	44,981	18	357,221	12
Interest	2,373,734	12	3,190	5	17,064	8	23,532	8	18,585	7	391,976	13
Machinery	2,729,776	13	3,234	5	25,448	12	26,809	9	28,759	11	306,424	10
Crop	2,486,984	12	2,045	3	37,779	18	19,367	6	30,853	12	272,037	9
Livestock	6,088,997	30	31,682	52	52,867	25	109,735	36	76,600	31	1,128,559	36
Other	3,824,485	19	10,087	17	36,583	17	63,228	21	48,278	6	612,460	20

	Ontario		Manitoba		Saskatchewan		Alberta		British Columbia	
	($'000)	% of total expenses	($'000)	% of total expenses	($'000)	% of total expenses	($'000)	% of total expenses	($'000)	% of total expenses
Total Expenses	**5,462,588**	**100**	**1,816,781**	**100**	**3,327,847**	**100**	**4,653,484**	**100**	**1,126,932**	**100**
Rent	164,235	3	94,788	5	244,740	7	193,582	4	25,063	2
Wages	665,354	12	130,644	7	209,292	6	303,857	7	229,282	20
Interest	572,873	10	200,909	11	487,673	15	517,105	11	140,828	12
Machinery	536,593	10	310,404	17	735,614	22	641,715	14	114,775	10
Crop	603,870	11	362,695	20	544,234	16	534,930	11	79,173	7
Livestock	1,779,670	33	410,813	23	446,395	13	1,712,842	37	339,833	30
Other	1,139,993	21	306,528	17	659,899	20	749,453	16	197,978	18

Catalogue 11-001E (Français 11-001F) ISSN 0827-0465

Statistics Canada

Tuesday, November 17, 1992

1991 CENSUS OF AGRICULTURE-POPULATION DATABASE

HIGHLIGHTS

- In 1991, Canada's farm population was 867,265 — 3.2% of the total population

- 390,870 farm operators managed Canada's 280,040 farms

- 63% of Canada's farms were managed by one operator in 1991, 32% had two operators, and the remaining 4% had three or more operators

- 26% of Canadian farm operators were women

- 14% of sole operators resided off their farm

- The top four languages reported as mother tongue by farm operators were English (68%), French (15%), German (6%) and Ukrainian (3%)

I✦I Statistics   Statistique
Canada   Canada

Canadä

New data on Canadian farm operators

In 1991, for the first time, respondents could cite more than one person as farm operator[1] on the Census of Agriculture questionnaire. This change responded to requests made during client consultations across Canada, and it will help measure women's contribution to Canadian agriculture.

This new information produces a more complete picture of the men and women who make the day-to-day decisions on Canadian farms. As well, it offers insights into how farms managed by one operator compare with those managed by two or more operators.

This release offers the first look at new data on the age, sex, marital status and mother tongue of Canadian farm operators and farm population. As well, the release examines relationships between farm operator characteristics and farm variables such as days of off-farm work and residence status.

These data offer a profile of management resources in Canadian agriculture. Coupled with the second Agriculture-Population database – which outlines education levels and areas of study, and incomes by sources and occupations – the 1991 Census provides a comprehensive portrait of Canadian agriculture.

Previous Censuses of Agriculture identified only one operator per farm, while in 1991, data on up to three farm operators per holding were captured and tabulated.

In 1991, second and third operators, not previously represented on the Census of Agriculture, were younger and made up a larger component of women than those reported as first operators.

Because of these differences, the farm operator and farm population data presented in this release should not be compared to data published from previous censuses. However, more information on data comparability is available by contacting the Census of Agriculture or your nearest Statistics Canada Regional Reference Centre.

---

1   A farm operator is a person responsible for the day-to-day decisions made in the agricultural operation of the farm holding.

Most Canadian farms managed by one farm operator

In 1991, of the 280,040 farms in Canada, 63% were operated by one operator. On these 176,935 farms, 94% of operators were male and 6% were female. Prince Edward Island and Manitoba reported the lowest percentages of female sole operators at 4%. British Columbia had the highest percentage of female sole operators, at 13%.

Two operator farms accounted for one-third of Canadian farms in 1991. Of these 90,630 farms, 87% were managed by one male and one female operator, 13% by two male operators, and less than 1% by two female operators.

Farms with three or more operators[2] were the minority in Canada in 1991, accounting for 4% of all farms. Combinations of male and female operators (for example, two males and one female, or one male and two females) represented three-quarters of these multi-operator farms. Farms managed by three males accounted for 24%, and less than 1% were managed by three female operators.

---

2   For farms that reported more than three farm operators, data on only the first three were captured and tabulated.

Number of Operators per Farm, 1991

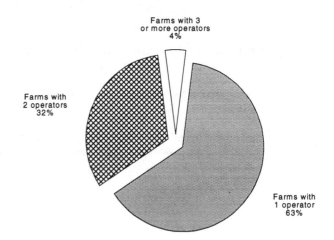

Farms with 3 or more operators 4%

Farms with 2 operators 32%

Farms with 1 operator 63%

Farms with One or More Operator, 1991

	Total farms		Farms with 1 operator		Farms with 2 operators		Farms with 3 or more operators	
	Number	%	Number	%	Number	%	Number	%
Canada	280,040	100	176,935	63	90,630	32	12,480	4
Newfoundland	725	100	565	78	140	19	20	3
Prince Edward Island	2,360	100	1,685	71	565	24	115	5
Nova Scotia	3,980	100	2,900	73	945	24	135	3
New Brunswick	3,250	100	2,380	73	740	23	125	4
Quebec	38,075	100	24,530	64	11,500	30	2,050	5
Ontario	68,635	100	39,020	57	25,925	38	3,680	5
Manitoba	25,705	100	17,200	67	7,450	29	1,055	4
Saskatchewan	60,840	100	43,900	72	15,005	25	1,935	3
Alberta	57,245	100	34,565	60	20,145	35	2,530	4
British Columbia	19,225	100	10,180	53	8,210	43	830	4

Farms with One or More Operator by Sex, 1991

	Farms with 1 operator		Farms with 2 operators			Farms with 3 or more operators		
	Male	Female	2 Males	2 Females	1 Male and 1 Female	3 Males	3 Females	Male/ Female combinations
				%				
Canada	94.0	6.0	13.0	0.4	86.6	24.2	0.2	75.6
Newfoundland	92.9	7.1	22.2	--	77.8	25.0	--	75.0
Prince Edward Island	96.1	3.9	40.2	0.9	58.9	43.5	--	56.5
Nova Scotia	91.7	8.3	21.6	1.1	77.4	33.3	--	66.7
New Brunswick	94.7	5.3	26.8	0.7	72.5	32.0	--	68.0
Quebec	93.5	6.5	14.9	0.4	84.7	22.5	--	77.5
Ontario	93.0	7.0	12.2	0.5	87.3	19.8	0.1	80.0
Manitoba	96.1	3.9	15.8	0.4	83.8	29.9	--	70.1
Saskatchewan	95.5	4.5	15.0	0.2	84.8	30.7	0.3	69.1
Alberta	94.9	5.1	11.5	0.4	88.1	26.1	0.2	73.7
British Columbia	86.6	13.4	6.0	0.7	93.4	14.5	0.6	84.9

-- *Amount too small to be expressed.*

Canada's farm population 3.2% of the total population in 1991

A total of 867,265 people, 3.2% of Canada's population, resided on farms. The highest proportion of farm to total population was reported in Saskatchewan (16.2%). Newfoundland had the lowest proportion (0.4%). Ontario had the largest farm population[1] at 226,750.

In 1991, the rural farm population[2] was 13.1% of the total rural population in Canada. Again, Saskatchewan had the largest share of its rural population on farms (41.5%).

One-quarter of Canadian farm operators in 1991 were female

At the time of the 1991 Census of Agriculture, 390,870 operators were managing Canada's 280,040 farms. Of these operators, 100,320 were female – one-quarter of the total.

British Columbia reported the highest percentage of female operators in 1991 (35%); Prince Edward Island reported the lowest (15%).

Women were best represented on two-operator farms, on which they accounted for 44% of operators. On farms with three or more operators, females accounted for 30% of operators. The lowest representation of women was on farms with one operator – 6% of sole operators were female.

---

1   Farm population is all persons who are members of a farm
    operator's household, living on a farm in a rural or urban area.
2   Rural farm population is all persons who are members of a farm
    operator's household, living on a farm in a rural area.

Farm Population as a Percentage of Total Population, 1991

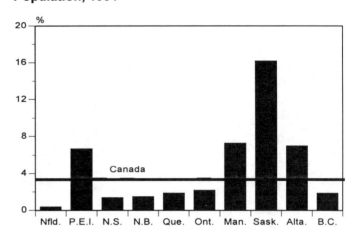

Female Farm Operators, 1991

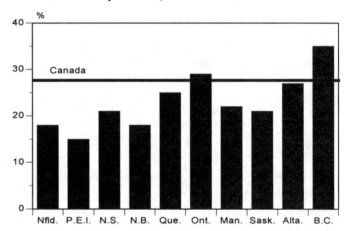

Total Farm Population and Rural Farm Population, 1991

	Total farm population		Rural farm population		
	Number of persons	% of total population	Number of persons	% of rural population	% of total population
Canada	**867,265**	**3.2**	**830,425**	**13.1**	**3.1**
Newfoundland	2,045	0.4	1,645	0.6	0.3
Prince Edward Island	8,670	6.7	8,570	11.0	6.6
Nova Scotia	12,785	1.4	12,455	3.0	1.4
New Brunswick	10,970	1.5	10,625	2.8	1.5
Quebec	128,370	1.9	122,685	7.9	1.8
Ontario	226,750	2.2	220,330	12.0	2.2
Manitoba	79,610	7.3	78,000	25.6	7.1
Saskatchewan	159,725	16.2	151,630	41.5	15.3
Alberta	177,190	7.0	171,860	33.4	6.8
British Columbia	61,135	1.9	52,625	8.2	1.6

Farm Operators by Sex and Number of Operators per Farm, 1991

	Total farms		Farms with 1 operator		Farms with 2 operators		Farms with 3 or more operators	
	Male	Female	Male	Female	Male	Female	Male	Female
					%			
Canada	**74**	**26**	**94**	**6**	**56**	**44**	**70**	**30**
Newfoundland	82	18	93	7	62	38	67	33
Prince Edward Island	85	15	96	4	69	30	79	21
Nova Scotia	79	21	92	8	60	40	74	26
New Brunswick	82	18	95	5	63	37	75	25
Quebec	75	25	93	7	57	43	70	29
Ontario	71	29	93	7	56	44	69	31
Manitoba	78	22	96	4	57	43	73	27
Saskatchewan	79	21	96	4	56	44	72	28
Alberta	73	27	95	5	55	45	71	29
British Columbia	65	35	87	13	52	47	64	36

Female farm operators more likely to share farm management responsibilities

In 1991, most female farm operators in Canada were in fact co-operators of their farm businesses: 79% on farms with two operators and 11% on farms with three or more operators. The remaining 10% reported being the sole operator of their farm business. However, the proportion of women who were sole operators varied among provinces, ranging from 24% in Newfoundland to 8% in Manitoba and Alberta.

Male farm operators were more likely to be sole operators. Nationally, 57% of all male farm operators were sole operators in 1991. An additional 34% were on farms with two operators, and 9% were on farms with three or more operators.

Proportion of Farms Managed by One or More Operator, 1991

	Male Number of farm operators			Female Number of farm operators		
	1	2	3 or more	1	2	3 or more
			%			
Canada	**57**	**34**	**9**	**10**	**79**	**11**
Newfoundland	71	23	5	24	64	12
Prince Edward Island	61	29	10	14	72	15
Nova Scotia	65	28	7	22	68	10
New Brunswick	65	27	8	17	71	12
Quebec	57	33	11	12	74	14
Ontario	50	40	10	9	79	12
Manitoba	61	31	8	8	81	10
Saskatchewan	67	27	6	12	79	9
Alberta	54	37	9	8	82	10
British Columbia	46	45	8	14	78	9

Female farm operators younger than their male counterparts

Of Canada's 390,870 farm operators, 48% were between the ages of 35 and 54 in 1991. Operators aged 55 or over constituted the next largest group with 32% of all operators, while those under 35 accounted for only 20%.

This ranking held for both male and female farm operators; however, female farm operators were, on average, younger than their male counterparts. In 1991, 21% of Canada's female farm operators were under 35, compared with 19% of male operators.

The 35 to 54 age group accounted for 52% of female and 47% of male farm operators. The 55 and over age category accounted for 26% of female and 34% of male operators.

Quebec had the largest proportion of operators in the under 35 age category (25%). Thirty-one per cent of the province's female farm operators were in this age group, almost double the proportion for British Columbia and Prince Edward Island at 16% each.

Saskatchewan had the highest proportion of farm operators in the 55 and over age group in 1991 (35%). Thirty-seven per cent were male and 30% female operators.

In 1991, the average age of Canadian farm operators was 47.5. For males, the average was 48.0; for females, it was 46.0.

Quebec had the youngest farm operators, with an average age of 41.7 for females and 45.2 for males. The overall average in Quebec was 44.3.

British Columbia reported the oldest average age for farm operators, 47.2 for females, and 49.8 for males. The overall average for British Columbia farm operators was 48.9 years.

Average Age of Farm Operators, 1991

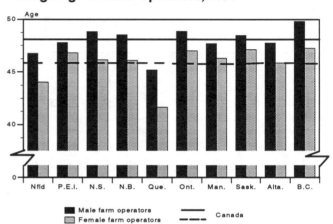

Farm Operators, 1991

	Total operators			Male operators			Female operators		
	Less than 35	35 to 54	55 and over	Less than 35	35 to 54	55 and over	Less than 35	35 to 54	55 and over
						%			
Canada	**20**	**48**	**32**	**19**	**47**	**34**	**21**	**52**	**26**
Newfoundland	15	59	26	14	58	27	21	62	18
Prince Edward Island	20	47	33	21	45	34	16	58	26
Nova Scotia	17	51	33	17	49	35	18	58	24
New Brunswick	16	52	31	16	52	33	19	56	24
Quebec	25	52	22	23	52	25	31	54	15
Ontario	18	48	34	18	46	36	19	52	29
Manitoba	21	47	32	21	45	34	21	52	28
Saskatchewan	20	45	35	20	43	37	20	49	30
Alberta	20	48	32	20	46	34	22	52	26
British Columbia	14	51	34	14	49	37	16	56	28

About one-third of farm operators work off the farm

Most of Canada's farm operators (63%) reported no off-farm employment during 1990.

The next largest group of farm operators (21%) reported working 190 days or more off the farm. This was true for 18% of female and 22% of male operators.

Male farm operators worked more days on average at their off-farm jobs. Male operators in Canada who worked off-farm averaged 72 days off the farm in 1990, compared with 63 days for female operators.

Prince Edward Island and Saskatchewan reported exceptions to this national trend: female farm operators in these provinces worked more days off the farm on average than did their male counterparts. In Prince Edward Island, female farm operators worked an average of 61 days off the farm in 1990, compared with 58 days for male operators. In Saskatchewan, female farm operators reported 63 days of off-farm work on average, while males reported 58 days.

In Manitoba, male and female farm operators worked on average virtually the same number of days off the farm; 63 days for males, 62 days for females.

Off-farm employment varied depending on the number of operators in the farm business. On farms with one operator, 63% of operators worked exclusively on the farm in 1990. Female sole

Average Days of Off-Farm Work for Farm Operators, 1990

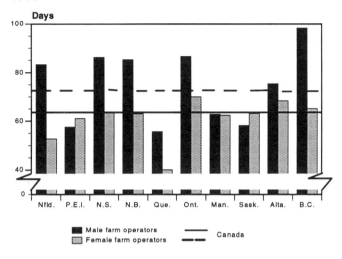

operators were more likely to work only on the farm – 68% compared with 62% of male sole operators.

On farms with two operators, 61% of operators reported no off-farm work during 1990 – 62% of female and 60% of male operators.

Operators on farms with three or more operators were least likely to work off the farm: 73% reported no off-farm work during 1990, with little difference between male and female operators.

Farm Operators Who Worked Off the Farm, 1990

Days of off – farm work	Total		Male		Female	
	Number	%	Number	%	Number	%
Number of days	**245,865**	**63**	**181,790**	**63**	**64,075**	**64**
one or more days	**145,000**	**37**	**108,760**	**37**	**36,245**	**36**
1-19	6,140	4	4,395	4	1,745	5
20-59	13,150	9	9,305	9	3,845	11
60-189	45,055	31	32,175	30	12,880	36
190 and over	80,655	56	62,885	58	17,775	49

Quebec had the highest proportion of operators without off-farm work in 1990. On Quebec farms with a sole operator, 69% of operators reported no days of off-farm work – 75% of female and 69% of male sole operators. On farms with two operators, over 77% of operators had no off-farm work. Farms run by three or more operators in Quebec had a substantially higher percentage of operators without off-farm work, at 84%.

The group with Canada's highest rate (52%) for off-farm work was males on two-operator farms in British Columbia. This was the only group with a rate of more than 50%.

In 1991, most Canadian farm operators were married

In 1991, 82% of Canadian farm operators were married, 11% were single, 4% were divorced or separated, and 3% were widowed.

More female farm operators were married – 87% compared with 81% for males.

For female farm operators, the next largest category was widowed at 6%, followed by single (4%) and divorced or separated (3%).

For male operators, the single category ranked second at 13%, followed by divorced or separated (4%) and widowed (2%).

Marital status also varied depending on the number of operators on the farm. On one-operator farms, 79% of male operators were married and 13% were single in 1991. By contrast, less than half (42%) of female sole operators were married. More female sole operators were widowed than single – 34% compared with 10%.

The highest proportion of married farm operators in 1991 was found on two-operator farms (91%). Ninety-four per cent were females and 89% males.

The lowest proportion of married male farm operators was found on farms with three or more operators, at 64%, compared with 81% of females and 69% overall. These farms also had the largest proportion of male farm operators who were single (33%), compared with 11% of females and 27% overall.

Marital Status of Farm Operators by Number of Operators per Farm, 1991

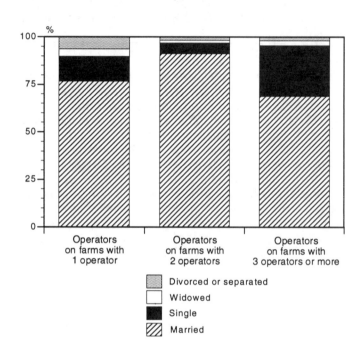

Marital Status of Farm Operators, 1991

Canada	Total operators		Male operators		Female operators	
	Number	%	Number	%	Number	%
Total	390,870	100	290,550	100	100,320	100
Married	322,405	82	234,895	81	87,510	87
Single	43,135	11	39,005	13	4,130	4
Divorced or separated	15,140	4	12,275	4	2,865	3
Widowed	10,190	3	4,375	2	5,815	6

Ninety per cent of farm operators in Canada resided on their farms

In 1991, the highest percentage of operators living on their farms occurred for two-operator farms (93%), followed by farms with three or more operators (90%). On farms with one operator, 86% of operators reported living on the farm.

Newfoundland had the lowest percentage of operators living on the farm in 1991, at 74%. Prince Edward Island and British Columbia had the highest percentage, at 94%.

Farm Operators Who Resided on their Farms, 1991

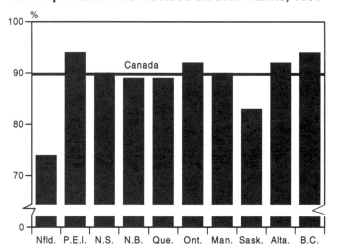

Farm Operators Who Resided on their Farms by Number of Operators per Farm, 1991

	% of operators residing on the farm			
	Total	Farms with 1 operator	Farms with 2 operator	Farms with 3 or more operators
			%	
Canada	**90**	**86**	**93**	**90**
Newfoundland	74	72	80	75
Prince Edward Island	94	95	94	91
Nova Scotia	90	89	92	88
New Brunswick	89	90	90	81
Quebec	89	86	93	87
Ontario	92	91	94	91
Manitoba	90	87	93	93
Saskatchewan	83	78	89	89
Alberta	92	88	94	93
British Columbia	94	92	95	92

Language profile of Canadian farm operators differed from the general population

Over two-thirds (68%) of Canadian farm operators reported English as their mother tongue in 1991. French was the mother tongue of the second largest group of operators (15%). German and Ukrainian ranked next.

This profile differed from that of the general Canadian population. Farm operators were more likely to speak English as their mother tongue than was the general population (68% versus 60%), and less likely to speak French (15% versus 24%). In the general population, English and French were followed by Italian and Chinese.

Manitoba was the only province that had the same top four mother tongues for the general population and for farm operators.

The percentage of operators with English as their mother tongue was highest in Newfoundland (99%), Prince Edward Island (92%) and Nova Scotia (91%). Quebec reported the lowest percentage (7%).

Mother Tongue, 1991

Farm population

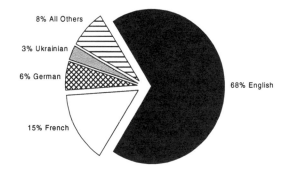

General population

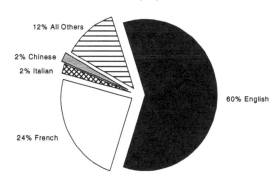

In Quebec, 90% of operators reported French as their mother tongue. New Brunswick ranked second for French with 18% of operators. British Columbia was the only province in which French was not in the top four mother tongues for farm operators.

Mother Tongue of Farm Operators, 1991

	First		Second		Third		Fourth		Remainder	
	Mother Tongue	%	Mother Tongue	%	Mother Tongue	%	Mother Tongue	%	Mother Tongue	%
Can.	**English**	**68**	**French**	**15**	**German**	**6**	**Ukrainian**	**3**	**All Others**	**8**
Nfld.	English	99	French	1	–		–		–	
P.E.I.	English	92	Dutch	3	French	2	German	1	All others	2
N.S.	English	91	Dutch	4	French	2	German	1	All others	2
N.B.	English	77	French	18	German	2	Dutch	2	All others	1
Que.	French	90	English	7	German	1	English & French	1	All others	1
Ont.	English	79	Dutch	5	German	5	French	4	All others	7
Man.	English	68	German	13	Ukrainian	7	French	5	All others	7
Sask.	English	80	German	6	Ukrainian	5	French	3	All others	6
Alta.	English	80	German	6	Ukrainian	5	French	3	All others	6
B.C.	English	74	German	8	Dutch	4	Punjabi	2	All others	12

Statistics Canada - Cat. No. 96-304E

Catalogue 11-001E (Français 11-001F) ISSN 0827-0465

Tuesday, November 16, 1993

CHARACTERISTICS OF FARM OPERATORS

HIGHLIGHTS

- For 38% of Canada's 390,725 farm operators, farming was their secondary occupation – their main occupation was non-agricultural

- Between the 1986 and 1991, the percentage of primary farmers declined, from 68% to 65%

- Two-thirds of male farm operators were primary farmers compared to fewer than half of female farm operators

- With an average 11.1 years of schooling, farm operators showed an increased level of education

- Primary farmers reported an average $124,935 in gross farm receipts compared to an average $47,676 for secondary farmers

I✦I Statistics Statistique
Canada   Canada

Canada

THE CANADIAN FARMER – A NEW LOOK

Who is running Canada's farms?

In the 1991 Census of Agriculture, about 62% of farm operators reported their principal occupation was agricultural, usually farmer/farm manager. For the other 38%, farming was a secondary occupation, part-time occupation or hobby, and their principal occupation was non-agricultural.

This release from the 1991 Census of Agriculture-Population linkage database provides an in-depth look at Canadian farm operators, and compares them with the general labour force, based on occupation and sex.

The analysis is in two parts. Part 1 focuses on all 390,725 farm operators (up to three per farm) reported

Occupations of Farm Operators, 1991

	Number	% of total
Farm operators with an agricultural occupation (primary farmers)		
Farmer / farm manager	201,635	83.6
Other agricultural occupations	39,665	16.4
Total	**241,305**	**100.0**
Farm operators with a non-agricultural occupation (secondary farmers)		
Construction trades	15,855	10.6
Managers and administrators	12,530	8.4
Sales	11,890	8.0
Clerical	11,855	7.9
Motor transport operators	10,385	7.0
Bookkeepers / account recording	9,555	6.4
Teachers	8,630	5.8
Medical and health	7,775	5.2
Mechanics and repairers	5,955	4.0
Other non-agricultural occupations	54,980	36.8
Total	**149,415**	**100.0**
All farm operators	**390,725**	**100.0**

> ### *Principal Occupation*
>
> *Like other Canadians, farm operators reported their principal occupation for the week prior to Census day on the Census of Population questionnaire. Respondents were requested to report only one occupation.*
>
> *Those operators who reported an agricultural principal occupation are referred to as* **primary farmers**. *Those operators reporting a non-agricultural occupation are denoted as* **secondary farmers**.

Farm Operators, 1991

	Total	Male	Female
	Number	%	
Canada	**390,725**	**74.2**	**25.8**
Nfld.	900	81.1	18.9
P.E.I.	3,130	85.3	14.5
N.S.	5,165	79.0	21.1
N.B.	4,235	81.8	18.2
Que.	53,300	75.2	24.8
Ont.	100,865	71.3	28.7
Man.	34,780	77.4	22.6
Sask.	78,015	79.1	20.9
Alta.	81,380	73.2	26.8
B.C.	28,955	65.3	34.7

in the 1991 Census of Agriculture. This is a significant change, because censuses of agriculture prior to 1991 allowed only one operator to be reported per farm.

Part 2 provides a historical perspective. However, second and subsequent operators from the 1991 Census of Agriculture were omitted. Only the first operator listed for each farm on the 1991 Census of Agriculture (278,095) can be compared with single operators listed in 1986 (293,090).

PART 1: FARM OPERATOR PROFILES, 1991 – ALL FARM OPERATORS

Changes to the 1991 Census of Agriculture: A more complete profile of the people who manage farms

By reporting up to three operators per farm in the 1991 Census of Agriculture, respondents have provided a more complete account of who is involved in Canadian agriculture. This allows us to examine the characteristics of all 390,725 farm operators, but it limits us to a profile for 1991; previous censuses of agriculture recorded only one operator per farm.

Of the 390,725 operators identified in the 1991 Census of Agriculture, 149,415 (38%) were secondary farmers. For these operators, farming was a secondary occupation, perhaps a part-time endeavour or a hobby. Farmers also drove trucks, taught school, worked at construction or practiced medicine, virtually every occupation.

The rest of Canada's farm operators, 241,305 or 62%, were primary farmers - usually farmers or farm managers.

Farm Operators Reporting an Agricultural Occupation, 1991

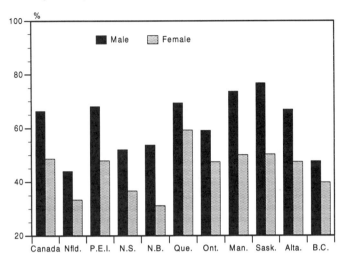

About two-thirds of male farm operators in Canada were primary farmers in 1991, compared to fewer than half of females

At the national level, 66% of male operators were primary farmers, as were 49% of women. Over half of male operators in all provinces except Newfoundland (44%) and British Columbia (48%) were primary farmers in 1991. In most provinces, female farm operators were more likely to be secondary farmers. Exceptions were Manitoba and Saskatchewan, where half of female farm operators were primary farmers, and Quebec where 59% were primary farmers.

Saskatchewan (77%), Manitoba (74%) and Quebec (69%) were the provinces with the largest concentration of male farm operators as primary farmers.

> *Most female farm operators ran a farm with someone else in 1991 (90% at the national level). Typically, these women operated farms with their husbands. They often also held full- or part-time jobs away from the farm and reported farm work as their secondary occupation. In many cases, their husbands reported managing the farm as a principal occupation.*

Female secondary farmers associated with larger farms than male secondary farmers

Not surprisingly, average gross farm receipts, farm area and farm capital were all higher for primary farmers than secondary farmers. Of primary farmers, males consistently reported higher average values than females for gross farm receipts, farm area and farm capital.

Interestingly, however, for secondary farmers, females were associated with farms which had higher average gross farm receipts, farm areas (except in British Columbia) and farm capital.

Many female secondary farmers actually ran the farm with their husbands and held off-farm jobs. In these cases, the male operators were often primary farmers while their wives were secondary farmers. Therefore, female secondary farmers were generally associated with larger operations (in size, gross farm receipts and farm capital) than male secondary farmers. Where female primary farmers operated farms on their own, they were typically smaller than farms run by male primary farmers.

Secondary farmers operate different types of farms than primary farmers

Certain types of farms were likely to be run by secondary farmers. These include maple (80%), horse (72%), goat (65%), hay (65%) and sheep (62%) farms.

1990 Gross Farm Receipts for Primary and Secondary Farmers

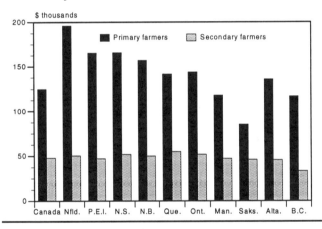

1990 Gross Farm Receipts for Primary and Secondary Farmers

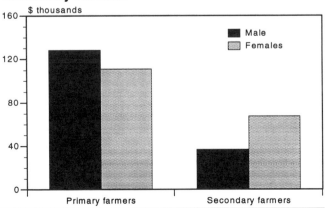

Types of farms more likely to be managed by primary farmers were mushroom (89%), tobacco (88%), dairy (86%) and pig (73%) farms.

Types of Farms of Primary and Secondary Farmers, 1991

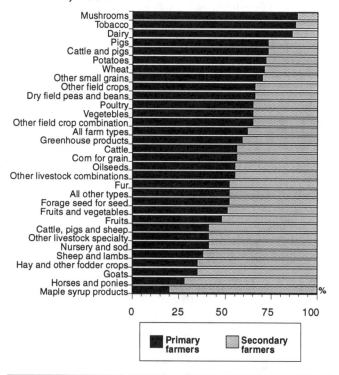

Primary farmers worked more weeks per year and hours per week

Canadian primary farmers worked more weeks in 1990 (47 weeks per year vs. 44) and more hours for the week prior to Census Day (57 hours per week vs. 41) than secondary farmers. The averages for the general working population were lower than either: 41 weeks per year and 33 hours per week.

In all cases, male operators reported an equal or greater number of weeks per year and hours per week than females. However, these figures included only farm work or paid work, and did not include volunteer work, housework, maintenance or home repairs.

Average Weeks Worked per Year, 1990

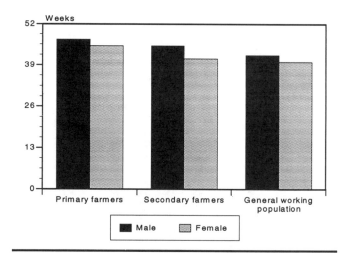

Average Hours Worked per Week, 1990

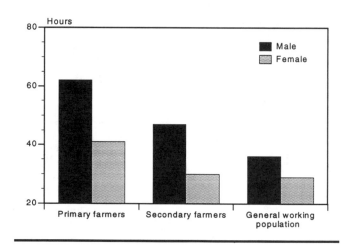

Female farm operators more highly educated than their male counterparts

Education levels of farm operators varied with sex and occupation. Generally, female operators had a higher average number of years of schooling than males. Nationally, female farm operators averaged 12.0 years of schooling, compared to 11.1 years for male operators. This compared to 13.0 years of schooling for females and 12.8 years for males among the general working population.

A higher proportion of women farm operators than men had university level education (17% compared to 12%) in 1991. This held true for both primary and secondary farmers in all provinces, except in Newfoundland and New Brunswick for primary farmers. In the general working population, 26% of women and 25% of men attained university level education. The highest level of university education attainment was among female primary farmers in Prince Edward Island (36%).

Years of Schooling, 1991

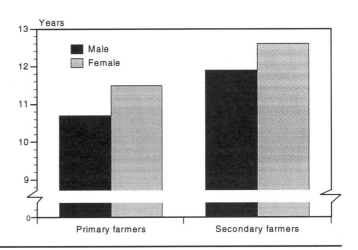

Educational Attainment, 1991

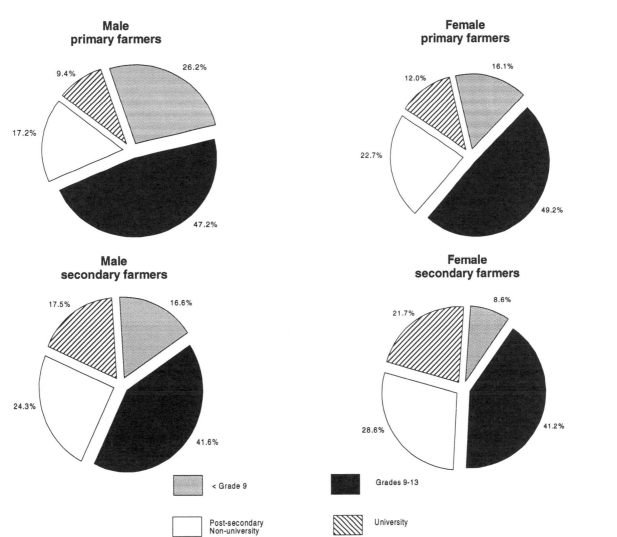

Most male primary farmers in Nova Scotia, Ontario, Saskatchewan and British Columbia were 55 years and over

The largest age category of farm operators at the national level and in the provinces was the 35 to 54 age group, regardless of occupation or gender (48% of all operators at the national level). Exceptions were male primary farmers in Nova Scotia, Ontario, Saskatchewan and British Columbia. In these provinces, the largest proportion of operators were 55 years or older.

In general, a larger proportion of secondary farmers tended to be either younger (less than 35 years) or older than primary farmers (55 years and over).

On average, secondary farmers were younger than primary farmers (45 years vs. 49 years at the national level) in 1991.

Quebec was the exception with primary farmers being slightly younger on average than secondary farmers (44 vs. 45 years). Quebec also had the lowest overall average age in 1991, at 44 years.

In addition occupation, the age of farm operators also varied by sex. Female operators averaged 46 years of age in Canada in 1991, compared to 48 years for males. Female operators were older than males on average only in Prince Edward Island (49 vs. 48 years).

At the national level, operators listed first on the questionnaire were older (49 years) than those listed

second (45 years). Third-listed farm operators were the youngest, with an average age of 34 years. This situation held true at the national level regardless of sex or occupation.

> *Age differences were observed for farm operators based on the sequence in which they were reported on the Census of Agriculture questionnaire.*

Average Age of Farm Operators, 1991

	Total	First-listed	Second-listed	Third-listed
			Years	
Male				
Total	48	49	42	31
Primary farmers	49	50	43	32
Secondary farmers	45	46	42	30
Female				
Total	46	50	45	43
Primary farmers	48	52	47	46
Secondary farmers	44	49	43	39
All operators				
Total	47	49	45	34
Primary farmers	49	51	46	35
Secondary farmers	45	46	43	34

Primary and Secondary Farmers by Age Groups, 1991

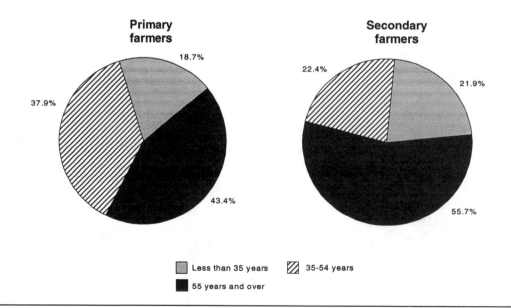

Primary farmers: 18.7%, 37.9%, 43.4%

Secondary farmers: 22.4%, 21.9%, 55.7%

Less than 35 years 35-54 years
55 years and over

Thirty per cent of British Columbia operators born outside Canada

Results of the 1991 Census indicated that approximately 11% of Canadian farm operators were born outside of Canada. Primary and secondary farmers reported similar percentages.

However, there were significant provincial differences. Notably in British Columbia, 30% of all farm operators and 35% of primary farmers were born outside Canada. Reporting the lowest percentages of operators born outside Canada were Newfoundland (1%), Saskatchewan (3%) and Quebec (4%).

Farm Operators Born Outside Canada, 1991

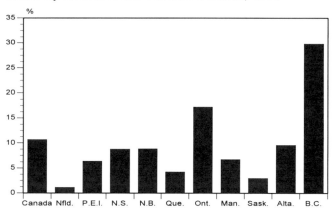

Profile of General Working Population[1] and All Farm Operators[2] by Occupation, 1991

| | | | | | | | Farm Operators | | | | | |
| | | General working population | | | All operators farmers[3] | | | Primary farmers[3] | | | Secondary farmers[4] | | |
	Units	Total	Male	Female	Total	Male	Female	Total	Male	Female	Total	Male	Female
Canada													
Number of persons	no.	14,429,705	7,932,640	6,497,065	390,725	290,020	100,705	241,305	192,370	48,930	149,415	97,650	51,770
Per cent of total	%	100.0	55.0	45.0	100.0	74.2	25.8	100.0	79.7	20.3	100.0	65.4	34.6
Education													
Under Grade 9	%	7.7	9.2	5.8	20.2	22.9	12.2	24.1	26.2	16.1	13.8	16.6	8.6
Grades 9-13	%	40.1	40.4	39.7	45.3	45.3	45.1	47.6	47.2	49.2	41.5	41.6	41.2
Post-secondary non-university	%	26.4	25.1	28.2	21.2	19.6	25.7	18.3	17.2	22.7	25.8	24.3	28.6
University	%	25.8	25.4	26.3	13.4	12.2	17.0	9.9	9.4	12.0	19.0	17.5	21.7
Average years of schooling	years	12.9	12.8	13.0	11.3	11.1	12.0	10.8	10.7	11.5	12.1	11.9	12.6
Work activity													
Average weeks/year worked[5]	weeks	41	42	40	46	46	43	47	47	45	44	45	41
Average hours/week worked[6]	hours	33	36	29	51	57	35	57	62	41	41	47	30
Age													
Under 35 years	%	46.5	45.2	48.1	19.9	19.3	21.7	18.7	18.6	18.8	21.9	20.6	24.4
35 - 54 years	%	42.9	42.7	43.1	48.1	46.7	52.2	43.4	41.9	49.3	55.7	56.1	54.9
55 years and over	%	10.6	12.1	8.8	32.0	34.0	26.2	37.9	39.4	31.9	22.4	23.3	20.7
Average age	years	37	38	36	47	48	46	49	49	48	45	45	44
Birthplace/ Mobility													
Not born in Canada	%	19.6	19.9	19.3	10.7	10.0	12.7	11.0	10.0	14.9	10.2	9.9	10.7
Moved in the past 5 years	%	50.5	49.5	51.7	16.2	14.9	19.8	11.7	10.8	14.9	23.5	23.0	24.4
Farm characteristics													
Average gross farm receipts in 1990[5]	$	...	...	...	95,390	97,728	88,658	124,935	128,460	111,074	47,676	37,183	67,470
Average total farm area	acres	...	...	...	608	636	530	771	807	630	346	299	435
Average total farm capital	$	...	...	...	498,997	507,605	474,206	590,553	604,056	537,468	351,137	317,593	414,410

1 Includes persons aged 15 years and over participating in the labour force.
2 Data relate to up to three operators per farm as recorded on the 1991 Census of Agriculture questionnaire.
3 Refers to farm operators with an agricultural occupation.
4 Refers to farm operators with a non-agricultural occupation.
5 The data are reported for the year preceding the Census year.
6 Refers to the week prior to Census day.
... Figures not appropriate or not applicable.
Source: 1991 Agriculture-Population linkage database, 1991 Census of Population database

PART 2: HISTORICAL FARM OPERATOR PROFILES, 1986-1991

First-listed Operators

Although 37% of Canadian farms reported more than one operator in the 1991 Census of Agriculture, this section refers only to the person reported in the first position on the questionnaire. This allows comparison with previous censuses, when only one farm operator was reported per farm.

Unlike the previous section, no analysis by sex is presented. Because most female operators were listed in the second and third positions on the 1991 Census of Agriculture questionnaire, an analysis of first-listed operators reveals little about women who operate farms. A complete comparison of farm operator characteristics over time by sex will only be possible when results of the next Census of Agriculture are compared to those from 1991.

Share of farm operators reporting an agricultural occupation declined

Between 1986 and 1991, the percentage of Canadian primary farmers declined from 68% to 65%.

All provinces registered declines except Newfoundland and Nova Scotia.

Primary Farmers Declined

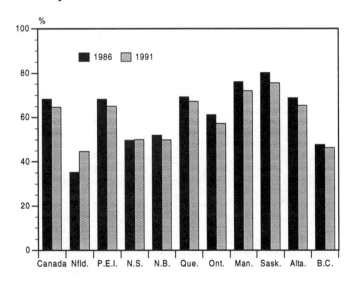

Seventy-six per cent of Saskatchewan farm operators reported an agricultural occupation in 1991, the highest of any province. Newfoundland at 45% and British Columbia at 46% of farm operators, reported the lowest.

Primary farmers operated larger farms

Primary farmers operated much larger farms than secondary farmers – larger in total farm area, gross farm receipts and total farm capital. In fact, average gross farm receipts in 1990 reported by primary farmers ($114,220) were 231% higher than for secondary farmers. The average farm area, at 758 acres, was 162% larger and farm capital, at $553,419, was 82% higher.

The increase in gross farm receipts since 1985 was 26% for primary farmers and 4% for secondary farmers.

The contrast in average gross farm receipts between the agricultural and non-agricultural occupational groups was most pronounced in Atlantic Canada and much less pronounced in the Prairies. This was because farms operated by primary farmers in Atlantic Canada had higher average gross farm receipts than in the Prairies. In all provinces except Saskatchewan, the average gross farm receipts of primary farmers exceeded $100,000; in most of Eastern Canada they exceeded $125,000. The average gross farm receipts for secondary farmers were all less than $45,000 in 1990 in all provinces.

Characteristics of Farms by Primary and Secondary Farmers[1]

	Primary farmers	Secondary farmers
Total farm area (acres)		
1986	691	262
1991	758	289
% change	9.7	10.3
Gross farm receipts (in 1990 $)		
1985	90,778	33,113
1990	114,220	34,510
% change	25.8	4.2
Total farm capital ($)		
1986	441,278	215,868
1991	553,419	303,627
% change	25.4	40.6

1 Data in table refers only to first person reported on the 1991 Census form to allow for comparisons with previous censuses.

Farm operators and general population show increases in average years of schooling between 1986 and 1991

Farm operators had, on average, 11.1 years of schooling in 1991, or 5% more than in 1986. Secondary farmers had 11.9 years, while primary farmers had 10.6 years. By comparison, the general working population averaged 12.9 years of schooling in 1991 or 4% higher than in 1986.

In 1991, British Columbia farm operators averaged 12.1 years of schooling, the highest of all provinces. Quebec (at 10.1 years) and Manitoba (at 10.6 years) had the lowest average years of schooling.

Average Years of Schooling for Primary and Secondary Farm Operators[1]

	1986	1991	% change
General working population	12.4	12.9	4.0
All operators	10.6	11.1	4.7
Primary farmers	10.2	10.6	3.9
Secondary farmers	11.4	11.9	4.4

1 Data in table refers only to first person reported on the 1991 Census form to allow for comparisons with previous censuses.

Average Years of Schooling for Farm Operators

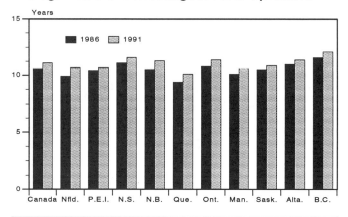

In all provinces, the average years of schooling for farm operators climbed between 1986 and 1991, consistent with the trend towards higher education in the general working population.

As well, the percentage of operators reporting less than a Grade 9 education dropped from 29% in 1986 to 23% in 1991, a 21% decline.

Farm operators getting older

Most operators (48%) were between 35 and 54 years old at the time of the 1991 Census. The share of operators in this age category has remained in the 46% to 52% range for a number of censuses. In 1991, 43% of primary farmers fell in this middle age category compared to 57% of the secondary farmers.

The significant story is that changes are taking place in the younger (under 35 years) and the older (55 years and over) age groups.

The share of operators under 35 years declined from 20% in 1986 to 16% in 1991 – a decline of 20%. The decline was slightly less for secondary farmers.

For older operators (55 years and over), the change from 1986 to 1991 for primary farmers was a 10% increase (from 38% in 1986 to 42% in 1991). Secondary farmers remained unchanged at 25%.

Age Categories of Farm Operators[1]

	Less than 35 years		35-54 years		55 years+	
	1986 %	1991 %	1986 %	1991 %	1986 %	1991 %
All operators	19.7	16.2	46.3	48.1	34.0	35.7
Primary farmers	19.5	15.1	42.4	43.3	38.1	41.6
Secondary farmers	20.2	18.2	54.5	56.9	25.2	24.9

1 Data in table refers only to first person reported on the 1991 Census form to allow for comparisons with previous censuses.

Long-term trend or short-term fluctuation?

This phenomenon of a decline in the share of younger farm operators and the increase in the share of older farm operators between 1986 and 1991 was also observed between 1981 and 1986. In the 1966 and 1971 Censuses the share of younger operators was only 15% (slightly less than the 16% in 1991) while the share of older operators was 32% and 33% (compared to 36% in 1991).

A decrease in the proportion of younger farm operators occurred in all provinces. British Columbia had the highest proportion of older primary farmers with 49% at 55 years and older and only 10% under 35 years. The decline in the share of farm operators under 35 years since 1986 was most pronounced in Newfoundland (78%) for primary farmers; those in Quebec were the youngest in 1991 with 20% under 35 years. This was a decline of 8% since 1986.

Primary Farmers Under 35 Years of Age

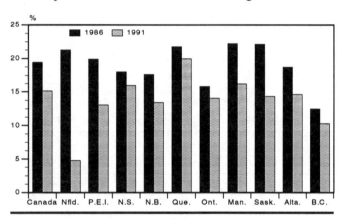

Primary farmers least mobile

Primary farmers were not a highly mobile occupational group; only 11% moved between 1986 and 1991. By contrast during the same five-year span 23% of secondary farmers moved, 50% of the general population moved.

British Columbia's primary farmers were the most mobile, with 20% moving. Primary farmers in New Brunswick, Newfoundland, and Prince Edward Island were the least mobile. In each of these provinces, fewer than 8% of these farmers reported moving between 1986 and 1991.

Mobility of General Working Population and Farm Operators[1]

	1981-1986 %	1986-1991 %	% change
General working population	48.6	50.5	3.9
All operators	16.9	15.3	-9.5
Primary farmers	14.3	11.0	-23.1
Secondary farmers	22.6	23.1	2.2

1 Data in table refers only to first person reported on the 1991 Census form to allow for comparisons with previous censuses.

Generally, primary farmers were even less mobile in 1991 than in 1986. Only 11% moved between 1986 and 1991 compared to 14% between 1981 and 1986.

However, at the provincial level, British Columbia primary farmers were more mobile (20% moved between 1986 and 1991 and 18% between 1981 and 1986.)

Mobility of Primary Farmers

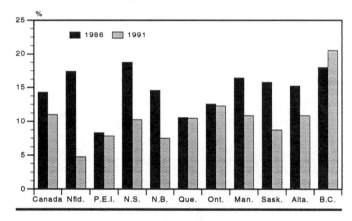

Post-censal Surveys

Catalogue 11-001E (Français 11-001F) ISSN 0827-0465

Tuesday, June 29, 1993

1991 ABORIGINAL PEOPLES SURVEY – LANGUAGE, TRADITION, HEALTH, LIFESTYLE AND SOCIAL ISSUES

HIGHLIGHTS

- Close to one-third of the North American Indian, Métis and Inuit population aged 5 and older reported being able to carry on a conversation in an Aboriginal language. The proportion was 36% for adults aged 15 and older and 21% for children aged 5 to 14

- Among Aboriginal adults aged 15 and older, 3% reported having tuberculosis. For the Canadian population aged 15 and older, the incidence of tuberculosis was less than 1%

- Among the Aboriginal population aged 15 and older, 67% identified unemployment, 61% alcohol abuse and 25% suicide as a social problem in their community

- Aboriginal adults aged 15 and older proposed more policing, family service counselling, improved community services and more employment as solutions to their communities' social problems

Language, Tradition, Health, Lifestyle and Social Issues
1991 Aboriginal Peoples Survey

The information in *Language, Tradition, Health, Lifestyle and Social Issues* (89-533, $45) was obtained from the 1991 Aboriginal Peoples Survey.

Data tables include information for Canada, the provinces and territories, 11 selected census metropolitan areas, and on and off Indian reserves and settlements; data are tabulated for adults and children by both total Aboriginal population and by specific Aboriginal group.

 Statistics Statistique
Canada Canada

Canadä

This release highlights information on language, tradition, health, lifestyle and social issues collected from 625,710 persons who reported in the 1991 Aboriginal Peoples Survey that they identified with an Aboriginal group. That is, they considered themselves North American Indian, Métis or Inuit.

Those who identified with an Aboriginal group represented approximately 63% of the total number of people who, in the 1991 Census of Population, reported having Aboriginal origin(s) and/or being registered under the Indian Act of Canada.

One-third spoke an Aboriginal language

Close to one-third (171,090) of the North American Indian, Métis and Inuit population aged 5 and older were able to speak an Aboriginal language well enough to carry on a conversation. Among adults aged 15 and older, 36% (139,375) were able to speak an Aboriginal language compared with 21% (31,715) of children aged 5 to 14.

Among North American Indians . . .

For the population aged 5 and older who identified as North American Indian, 34% spoke an Aboriginal language. However, among North American Indians living on Indian reserves and settlements, almost 60% indicated that they spoke an Aboriginal language, with Cree (46%) and Ojibwa (17%) being the most frequently reported spoken languages.

Of the 253,760 North American Indians aged 5 and older living off reserves, 19% reported that they spoke an Aboriginal language, with Cree (44%) and Ojibwa (20%) being the most frequently reported spoken languages.

Among Aboriginal children aged 5 to 14 who identified as North American Indian, the difference in reported ability to speak an Aboriginal language between those living on and off Indian reserves and settlements was even more pronounced than among the adult population. Of the 40,500 children who identified as North American Indian living on Indian reserves and settlements, 44% reported speaking an Aboriginal language compared with 9% of children who identified as North American Indian living off reserves.

Among the adult population aged 15 and older who identified as North American Indian living on Indian reserves and settlements, 65% reported speaking an Aboriginal language. Of the 186,295 adults who identified as North American Indian living off reserves, 23% reported being able to speak an Aboriginal language.

Ability to Speak an Aboriginal Language, 1991

	Total	Number	%
Total Aboriginal population aged 5 and older	**537,060** [1]	**171,090**	**31.9**
North American Indian	396,335	133,800	33.8
Living on Indian reserves and settlements	142,575	84,665	59.4
Living off reserves	253,760	49,140	19.4
Métis	116,140	16,305	14.0
Inuit	30,050	21,700	72.2
Aboriginal children aged 5 to 14	**148,160** [1]	**31,715**	**21.4**
North American Indian	107,970	24,035	22.3
Living on Indian reserves and settlements	40,500	17,945	44.3
Living off reserves	67,465	6,095	9.0
Métis	31,985	1,580	4.9
Inuit	9,245	6,190	67.0
Aboriginal adults aged 15 and older	**388,900** [1]	**139,375**	**35.8**
North American Indian	288,365	109,765	38.1
Living on Indian reserves and settlements	102,075	66,720	65.4
Living off reserves	186,295	43,045	23.1
Métis	84,155	14,725	17.5
Inuit	20,805	15,510	74.5

1 An individual may identify with more than one Aboriginal group; therefore the individual groups do not add to the total.

Cree and Michif were spoken by the Métis

Of the 116,140 persons aged 5 and older who identified as Métis, 14% reported speaking an Aboriginal language. Among Métis children aged 5 to 14, this proportion was lower (5%). For Métis adults aged 15 and older, 18% reported speaking an Aboriginal language; of these, 70% spoke Cree and 6% Michif.

Three of four Inuit spoke an Aboriginal language

The majority of Inuit aged 5 and older reported that they spoke an Aboriginal language. Among the 30,050 Inuit aged 5 and older, 72% spoke an Aboriginal language, with 96% reporting that they spoke Inuktitut. Unlike the North American Indian and Métis groups, there was little difference in the ability to speak an Aboriginal language between Inuit children and adults. Two-thirds (67%) of Inuit children aged 5 to 14 spoke an Aboriginal language, compared to 75% of Inuit adults aged 15 and older.

Rheumatism and arthritis were the most commonly reported health problems

Of the 388,900 persons aged 15 and older who identified with an Aboriginal group, 31% were told by health care professionals that they had a chronic health problem. Thirty-three per cent of Métis, 30% of North American Indians and 23% of Inuit reported a chronic health problem.

Fifteen per cent of Aboriginal adults aged 15 and older reported having arthritis or rheumatism. The proportion was 10% for Inuit and 17% for Métis. According to the 1991 General Social Survey, arthritis or rheumatism among the Canadian population aged 15 and older was 14%. Differences in age distribution have been adjusted to permit comparisons between the two populations.

The presence of diabetes was reported by 6% of Aboriginal adults aged 15 and older, compared with 2% of Canadian adults aged 15 and older (adjusted for differences in age distribution) who reported diabetes in the 1991 General Social Survey. Approximately 9% of North American Indians living on Indian reserves and settlements and 2% of Inuit adults reported diabetes as a chronic health problem.

Three per cent of Aboriginal adults aged 15 and older reported that they had tuberculosis. For the Canadian population aged 15 and older, the incidence of tuberculosis was less than 1% in 1991. Among adults who identified as North American Indian living on Indian reserves and settlements, 3% reported tuberculosis as a chronic health problem; among Inuit adults, 7% reported tuberculosis.

Chronic Health Problems, 1991

	Total		N.A.I.[1] on Indian reserves and settlements		N.A.I.[1] off-reserves		Métis		Inuit	
	number	%	number	%	number	%	number	%	number	%
Total Aboriginal population 15 and older	388,900	100.0	102,075	100.0	186,295	100.0	84,155	100.0	20,805	100.0
Diabetes	23,255	6.0	8,635	8.5	9,790	5.3	4,670	5.5	405	1.9
High blood pressure	44,735	11.5	13,110	12.8	20,635	11.1	9,555	11.4	1,995	9.6
Arthritis, rheumatism	57,995	14.9	14,410	14.1	27,870	15.0	14,375	17.1	2,150	10.3
Heart problems	25,580	6.6	6,940	6.8	11,695	6.3	5,905	7.0	1,275	6.1
Bronchitis	32,650	8.4	6,190	6.1	17,040	9.1	8,875	10.5	1,035	5.0
Emphysema/shortness of breath	22,155	5.7	6,785	6.6	9,685	5.2	4,835	5.7	1,120	5.4
Asthma	22,135	5.7	4,545	4.5	11,375	6.1	5,755	6.8	690	3.3
Tuberculosis	11,655	3.0	3,445	3.4	4,970	2.7	2,075	2.5	1,350	6.5
Epilepsy, seizures	5,910	1.5	1,640	1.6	2,870	1.5	1,030	1.2	380	1.8

1 North American Indian.

Social problems facing aboriginal communities . . .

The Aboriginal population aged 15 and older were asked for their opinion on the social problems facing Aboriginal people in their communities.

Unemployment was identified by 67% of adults as a problem in their community. It was a problem for 78% of North American Indians living on Indian reserves and settlements and for 75% of Inuit adults.

Alcohol abuse was a problem reported by 61% of adults. Among North American Indians living on Indian reserves and settlements, 73% reported alcohol abuse as a social problem.

Twenty-five per cent of adults reported suicide as a problem in their community. Slightly more than two-fifths (41%) of Inuit reported that suicide was a problem in their community.

. . . and reported solutions

Aboriginal adults aged 15 and older were asked to propose solutions to the social problems that they felt existed in their communities. Their proposed solutions included increased policing, family service counselling, improved community services and more employment.

Among adults who identified as North American Indian living on Indian reserves and settlements, 17% proposed more policing and 14% suggested family service counselling as possible solutions to social problems within their Aboriginal communities.

Of Inuit adults, 13% proposed improved community services and 12% proposed more employment as possible solutions to the social issues that they felt existed in their communities.

Social Problems Facing Aboriginal Communities, 1991

	Total		N.A.I.[1] on Indian reserves and settlements		N.A.I.[1] off- reserves		Métis		Inuit	
	number	%	number	%	number	%	number	%	number	%
Total Aboriginal population 15 and older	**388,900**	**100.0**	**102,075**	**100.0**	**186,295**	**100.0**	**84,155**	**100.0**	**20,805**	**100.0**
Social issues[2]										
Suicide	98,690	25.4	35,195	34.5	38,005	20.4	18,200	21.6	8,575	41.2
Unemployment	261,100	67.1	79,900	78.3	112,195	60.2	56,330	66.9	15,505	74.5
Family violence	152,435	39.2	44,975	44.1	67,820	36.4	32,805	39.0	9,040	43.5
Sexual abuse	95,400	24.5	29,555	29.0	40,605	21.8	19,350	23.0	7,305	35.1
Drug abuse	186,425	47.9	60,010	58.8	80,390	43.2	38,060	45.2	10,195	49.0
Alcohol abuse	237,680	61.1	74,715	73.2	104,280	56.0	49,520	58.8	11,980	57.6
Rape	58,120	14.9	16,735	16.4	24,725	13.3	12,305	14.6	5,190	24.9

1 North American Indian.
2 Persons reporting that they feel [social issue] is a problem in the community where they are now living.

Solutions to Social Problems Proposed by Aboriginal Peoples, 1991

	Total		N.A.I.[1] on Indian reserves and settlements		N.A.I.[1] off-reserves		Métis		Inuit	
	number	%	number	%	number	%	number	%	number	%
Total Aboriginal population 15 and older	**388,900**	**100.0**	**102,075**	**100.0**	**186,295**	**100.0**	**84,155**	**100.0**	**20,805**	**100.0**
Proposed solutions										
More policing	39,425	10.1	17,810	17.4	13,200	7.1	6,245	7.4	2,380	11.4
Shelters for abused women	22,390	5.8	6,790	6.7	10,600	5.7	3,910	4.6	1,215	5.8
Family service counselling	40,815	10.5	14,255	14.0	16,495	8.9	8,705	10.3	1,805	8.7
Counselling services (other than family)	34,895	9.0	8,690	8.5	17,075	9.2	7,385	8.8	2,330	11.2
Improved community services	38,260	9.8	10,465	10.3	17,140	9.2	8,515	10.1	2,795	13.4
More employment	30,385	7.8	7,170	7.0	14,055	7.5	7,225	8.6	2,450	11.8
Improved education	28,835	7.4	3,615	3.5	16,450	8.8	8,180	9.7	1,415	6.8

1 North American Indian.

1991 Aboriginal Peoples Survey

A large-scale survey of people who reported Aboriginal ancestry and/or who reported being registered under the Indian Act of Canada was conducted after the 1991 Census. This survey, the Aboriginal Peoples Survey, was developed in consultation with Aboriginal organizations and government departments. From those people who identified as North American Indian, Métis or Inuit, the survey collected information on such issues as employment, education, language, tradition, health, lifestyle and social issues, mobility, housing, disability, and income and expenses.

Incompletely Enumerated Indian Reserves and Settlements

There were 78 incompletely enumerated Indian reserves and settlements during the 1991 Census. These reserves and settlements represent approximately 38,000 persons. Because the Aboriginal Peoples Survey (APS) sample was selected from the 1991 Census, these 78 reserves and settlements are not included in the APS tables.

An additional 181 Indian reserves and settlements, representing approximately 20,000 individuals, were incompletely enumerated during the APS because enumeration was not permitted or was interrupted before all questionnaires could be completed.

Another 14 Aboriginal communities, representing approximately 2,000 persons, were also incompletely enumerated for the APS.

Lists of these incompletely enumerated Indian reserves and settlements and other Aboriginal communities can be found in Language, Tradition, Health, Lifestyle and Social Issues (89-533, $45).

Catalogue 11-001E (Français 11-001F) ISSN 0827-0465

The Daily
Statistics Canada

Monday, September 20, 1993

1991 ABORIGINAL PEOPLES SURVEY – SCHOOLING, WORK AND RELATED ACTIVITIES, EXPENSES AND MOBILITY

HIGHLIGHTS

- Use of Aboriginal languages in elementary and secondary schools increased among younger generations

- Unemployment among Aboriginal adults was 25% in 1991, two and one-half times the national rate

- Fourteen per cent of Aboriginal people reported having participated in activities such as fishing for food, or bartering goods and services for food, to support themselves and their families

- In 1990, 5% of Aboriginal adults had a total income of over $40,000, compared with 15% of Canada's adult population

- Contrary to a commonly held view, Aboriginal people do not move more frequently than Canada's total population. In 1991, 15% of Aboriginal people had recently moved, compared to 16% of Canada's total population

---

Schooling, Work and Related Activities, Income, Expenses and Mobility
1991 Aboriginal Peoples Survey

Data tables in *Schooling, Work and Related Activities, Income, Expenses and Mobility* (89-534, $60) include information for Canada, the provinces and territories, and 11 selected census metropolitan areas. Data are tabulated for adults and children by both total Aboriginal population and by specific Aboriginal group.

 Statistics **Statistique**
Canada **Canada**

Canadä

This release highlights information on schooling, work and related activities, income, household expenses and mobility that was collected in the 1991 Aboriginal Peoples Survey. Respondents in this survey identified with an Aboriginal group, that is, they considered themselves to be North American Indian, Métis or Inuit.

Those who identified with an Aboriginal group (625,710) represented approximately 63% of the people who, in the 1991 Census of Population, reported having Aboriginal origin(s) and/or being registered under the *Indian Act* of Canada.

The Aboriginal Peoples Survey was first conducted following the 1991 Census; therefore, historical data for most information presented today do not exist for comparative purposes.

Use of Aboriginal languages in elementary schools increased among younger generations

Among Aboriginal adults aged 15 to 49, only 11% of those who attended elementary school were taught in an Aboriginal language at any time during their elementary school years. However, among children aged 5 to 14, 25% were taught in an Aboriginal language.

The largest difference between the two age groups occurred for North American Indians living on Indian reserves or settlements. Among North American Indian adults (aged 15 to 49) who reported attending elementary school, 18% had been taught in an Aboriginal language. Among North American Indian children, however, 49% had been taught in an Aboriginal language in their elementary school years.

Formal education levels for Aboriginal people were lower compared with Canada's total population

One-third of the Aboriginal population aged 15 to 49 reported some postsecondary education and 17% reported less than Grade 9 (including no schooling). By comparison, just over half of Canada's total population aged 15 to 49 reported some postsecondary education and only 6% reported less than Grade 9. For the Aboriginal population in the same age group, North American Indians living off reserves (11%) and the Métis (12%) had the lowest proportions reporting less than Grade 9, followed by North American Indians living on reserves (28%) and the Inuit (38%).

Among older Aboriginal people aged 50 to 64, 22% had some postsecondary education and 53% had less than Grade 9. By comparison, one-third of Canada's total population aged 50 to 64 had some

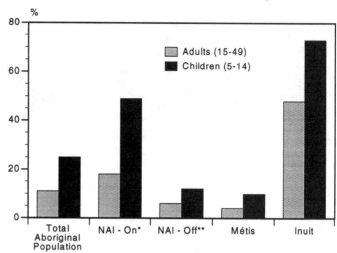

Use of Aboriginal Language in Elementary School,

Legend: Adults (15-49), Children (5-14)

*   NAI - On: North American Indian Living on Indian Reserves and Settlements.
**   NAI - Off: North American Indian Living off Reserves.

postsecondary education and 26% had less than Grade 9.

The most notable differences in levels of schooling between Canada's total population and the three Aboriginal groups occurred with the North American Indians living on Indian reserves and settlements and the Inuit. Among those aged 15 to 49, 28% of North American Indians living on reserves and settlements, and 38% of Inuit, reported less than Grade 9. Among those aged 50 to 64, 70% of North

Level of Schooling, 1991

	Less than Grade 9		Some post-secondary	
	Age 15-49	Age 50-64	Age 15-49	Age 50-64
	%			
Total Aboriginal Population	17	53	33	22
NAI - On	28	70	25	15
NAI - Off	11	44	38	28
Métis	12	45	34	25
Inuit	38	76	26	15
Canada's Total Population	**6**	**26**	**51**	**33**

Note: NAI - On: North American Indian Living on Indian Reserves and Settlements.
NAI - Off: North American Indian Living off Reserves.

American Indians living on reserves and settlements and 76% of the Inuit reported less than Grade 9.

Adults who identified with an Aboriginal group were asked about their experience during their school years. Among those aged 15 to 49 who had attended elementary school, 11% (34,860) had lived in residential schools during all or part of their elementary school years. By contrast, among the 50 to 64 age group, just over one-third (15,080) had lived in residential schools during all or part of their school years.

Almost one-quarter of Aboriginal adults aged 15 to 49 (80,670) took on-the-job or classroom training during 1990 and/or 1991. Among those who participated in training courses, 62% had taken one course and 13% had taken two courses.

Unemployment higher among those who identified with an Aboriginal group

Unemployment among Aboriginal adults aged 15 and older was almost 25% in 1991; by comparison, the unemployment rate was 10% for Canada's total population. Among Aboriginal groups, North American Indians living on Indian reserves and settlements reported the highest unemployment (31%), over three times the national rate, while the Métis reported the lowest rate at 22%.

The higher unemployment rates among Aboriginal people reflect, in part, a higher proportion of people living in rural and remote areas where employment opportunities are limited. When respondents were asked about barriers to finding employment, most

Aboriginal people reported limited opportunities as the major barrier. Of the 127,680 Aboriginal adults who looked for work during 1990 and/or 1991, almost two-thirds (83,685) reported that few or no jobs were available, 41% stated that their education or work experience did not match the available jobs and 16% reported difficulty finding employment because they were Aboriginal people.

Unemployment Rate, 1991

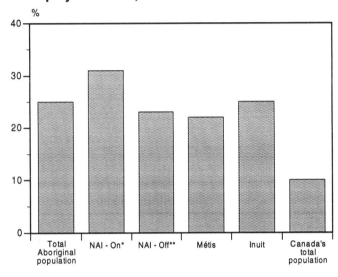

* NAI - On: North American Indian Living on Indian Reserves.
** NAI - Off: North American Indian Living off Reserves.

Barriers to Finding Employment, 1991

	Total Aboriginal Population	NAI-On	NAI-Off	Métis	Inuit
Number looking for work	127,680	31,790	61,840	28,215	7,250
			%		
Problems finding a job					
Few or no jobs in area	66	75	61	62	71
Education or work experience did not match jobs	41	41	41	43	38
No one available to look after children	8	8	8	8	9
Not enough information about available jobs	26	32	25	22	24
Because of being an Aboriginal person	16	22	16	12	12

Note: NAI - On: North American Indian Living on Indian Reserves and Settlements.
NAI - Off: North American Indian Living off Reserves

Total Income, 1990

	No Income	Under $2,000	$2,000 to $9,999	$10,000 to $19,999	$20,000 to $39,999	$40,000+
			%			
Total Aboriginal Population	13	12	29	23	18	5
NAI - On	11	18	36	22	12	2
NAI - Off	14	10	26	23	20	7
Métis	13	10	26	24	20	6
Inuit	17	10	30	20	16	7
Canada's Total Population	9	6	20	22	28	15

Note: NAI - On: North American Indian Living on Indian Reserves and Settlements.
NAI - Off: North American Indian Living off Reserves.

Proportion who worked for income was highest among the Inuit

Just over 59% (229,905) of Aboriginal adults worked for income during 1990 and/or 1991. The Inuit had the highest proportion (68%) who worked for income, followed closely by the Métis at 65%. Among Aboriginal adults who worked for income, 29% worked at more than one job during the period.

Traditional activities continued to play an important role in the support of Aboriginal people and their families

Almost 20% (73,390) of Aboriginal adults were involved in additional work-related activities for which they received money to support themselves and their families during 1990 and/or 1991. These included traditional activities such as carving, trapping and guiding.

Fourteen per cent (53,595) also reported that they participated in other activities to support themselves and their families for which they did not receive money. These activities included fishing for food, and bartering goods or services for food.

Just over 8% (32,680) of Aboriginal adults reported that they had, at one time, owned or operated a business. Among this group, 57% owned or operated a business in 1991.

1990 total income was lower among Aboriginal people

Among Aboriginal adults, 13% reported no income during 1990 while 5% reported a total income of $40,000 or more. By comparison, among Canada's total population aged 15 and older, 9% reported no income during 1990 and 15% reported total income of $40,000 or more.

Among North American Indian adults who were living on Indian reserves and settlements, only 2% reported a total income of $40,000 or more in 1990. Among Inuit adults, 17% reported no income in 1990.

Employment income was lower among Aboriginal people

Of the 388,900 Aboriginal adults aged 15 and older, 60% (231,865) reported employment income in 1990. Among those, 17% reported employment income of under $2,000, and only 8% reported employment income of $40,000 or more. By comparison, among Canada's total population aged 15 and older, 8% reported having employment income of under $2,000 during 1990, and 18% reported $40,000 or more.

Among North American Indian adults who were living on Indian reserves and settlements, only 3% reported having employment income of $40,000 or more in 1990.

Employment Income, 1990

	Under $2,000	$2,000 to $9,999	$10,000 to $19,999	$20,000 to $39,999	$40,000 +
			%		
Total Aboriginal Population	17	30	21	24	8
NAI - On	20	36	23	18	3
NAI - Off	16	28	20	27	9
Métis	14	29	23	26	8
Inuit	20	33	18	21	8
Canada's Total Population	8	21	20	33	18

Note: NAI - On: North American Indian Living on Indian Reserves and Settlements.
NAI - Off: North American Indian Living off Reserves.

During 1990, 29% of Aboriginal adults reported receiving social assistance

Among Aboriginal adults, 29% (111,020) had received social assistance during 1990. This percentage rose to 42% among North American Indian adults living on Indian reserves and settlements.

Five per cent of Aboriginal adults received an allowance for postsecondary studies. This percentage was smallest among the Inuit: only 2% reported that they had received a postsecondary allowance during 1990.

Income From Sources Other Than Employment, 1990

	Social Assistance	Post-secondary Allowance	Training Allowance	Worker's Compen-sation
			%	
Total Aboriginal Population	29	5	4	2
NAI - On	42	5	4	2
NAI - Off	25	6	4	3
Métis	22	4	4	3
Inuit	23	2	5	2

Note: NAI - On: North American Indian Living on Indian Reserves and Settlements.
NAI - Off: North American Indian Living off Reserves.

Fifteen per cent of Aboriginal adults had moved recently-slightly less than the proportion of movers in Canada's total population

Contrary to a commonly held view, Aboriginal people do not move more frequently than Canada's total

Movers for 12 month period prior to survey

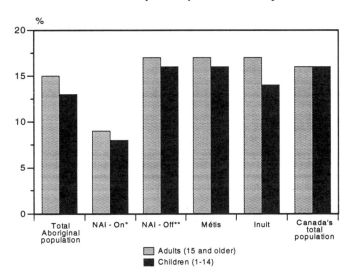

*   NAI - On: North American Indian Living on Indian Reserves.
** NAI - Off: North American Indian Living off Reserves.

population. Only 15% of Aboriginal adults had moved during the 12 months prior to the survey. According to the 1991 Census, 16% of Canada's population in the same age group moved during the 12 months prior to the Census.

Among adult North American Indians who were living on Indian reserves and settlements, only 9% had moved during the 12 months prior to the survey.

A similar pattern is noted when comparing Aboriginal children aged 1 to 14 with Canada's total population of the same age group. Among Aboriginal children, 13% had moved during the 12 months prior to the survey, while 16% of children in Canada had moved in the 12 months prior to the Census.

1991 Aboriginal Peoples Survey

A large-scale survey of people who reported Aboriginal ancestry and/or who reported being registered under the Indian Act of Canada was conducted after the 1991 Census. This survey, the Aboriginal Peoples Survey, was developed in consultation with Aboriginal organizations and government departments.

From those people who identified as North American Indian, Métis or Inuit, the survey collected information on such issues as employment, education, language, tradition, health, lifestyle and social issues, mobility, housing, disability, income and household expenses.

Incompletely enumerated Indian reserves and settlements

There were 78 incompletely enumerated Indian reserves and settlements during the 1991 Census. These reserves and settlements represent about 38,000 people. Because the Aboriginal Peoples Survey (APS) sample was selected from the 1991 Census, these 78 reserves and settlements are not included in the APS tables.

An additional 181 Indian reserves and settlements, representing about 20,000 people, were incompletely enumerated during the APS because enumeration was not permitted or was interrupted before all questionnaires could be completed.

Another 14 Aboriginal communities, representing about 2,000 people, were also incompletely enumerated for the APS.

Lists of these incompletely enumerated Indian reserves and settlements and other Aboriginal communities can be found in Schooling, Work and Related Activities, Income, Expenses and Mobility (89-534, $60).

Catalogue 11-001E (Français 11-001F) ISSN 0827-0465

Tuesday, October 13, 1992

1991 HEALTH AND ACTIVITY LIMITATION SURVEY – DISABILITY, AGE AND SEX

HIGHLIGHTS

● 4.2 million Canadians – 15.5% of the population – reported some level of disability in 1991

● Disability increased with age – 7% of children under 15 experienced some level of disability, compared to 14% of adults aged 35 to 54 and to 46.3% of those aged 65 and over

● Severity of disability also increased with age – 2.9% of children with disabilities had a severe disability, compared to 32.4% for those aged 65 and over

● 93.7% of people with disabilities lived in private households in 1991 compared to 6.3% who lived in health-related institutions

● Among Canadians with disabilities aged 15 to 64, living in households, mobility disabilities (limited ability to walk, move or stand) were reported most often, at 52.5%, followed by agility disabilities (limited ability to bend, dress or handle small objects) at 50.2%

 Statistics Statistique
Canada Canada

Canadä

The Daily, October 13, 1992

This release from the 1991 post-censal Health and Activity Limitation Survey (HALS) profiles the age and sex characteristics of Canadians with disabilities, as well as the nature and severity of their disabilities.

Persons with disabilities

In 1991, 4,184,685 people in Canada – 15.5% of the population – reported some degree of disability. While this rate was significantly higher than the 13.2% disability rate measured in 1986, most of the increase occurred among those reporting a mild disability. The increase among this group can be attributed at least partly to an aging population as well as to a change in survey methodology which enabled more comprehensive enumeration of persons with disabilities related to a mental health condition or handicap, or learning disabilities. As well, an increased awareness of disability in society in recent years may have made people more willing to report their activity limitations and the barriers they encountered in their everyday activities.

What is a Disability?

The 1991 Health and Activity Limitation Survey (HALS) uses the World Health Organization's definition of disability, which is:

> *...any restriction or lack (resulting from impairment) of ability to perform an activity in the manner or within the range considered normal for a human being.*

Adults were asked questions about various limitations in activities related to daily living (sensory, mobility, agility or other physical and psychological abilities) in order to determine if a disability was present.

Parents reported on the existence of general limitations, chronic conditions, attendance at a special school or special classes and the use of technical aids for children under the age of 15. A positive response in any of these categories was taken as an indication that a disability existed.

The answers to the questions on disability represent the respondents' perception of the situation and are therefore subjective.

Disability increased with age. Among children under the age of 15, 7% were reported to have a disability. Within the adult population, the disability rate among persons aged 15 to 34 was 8%. This rate increased to 14% for persons aged 35 to 54 and to 27.1% for those aged 55 to 64. Among those aged 65 and over, the rate increased to 46.3%.

The severity of a disability also increased with age. Among children with disabilities under the age of

Disability Rate

	Disability Rate (%)	
	1991	1986
CANADA	**15.5**	**13.2**
Newfoundland	10.0	13.1
Prince Edward Island	16.9	14.7
Nova Scotia	21.3	16.9
New Brunswick	17.7	15.5
Quebec	12.5	11.2
Ontario	16.0	13.9
Manitoba	17.6	15.7
Saskatchewan	19.1	13.9
Alberta	17.0	11.9
British Columbia	16.7	13.8
Yukon	11.1	8.7
Northwest Territories	12.6	8.8

Disability Rates by Age Groups

	Disability Rate (%)	
	1991	1986
Total - All Ages	**15.5**	**13.2**
0 - 14	7.0	5.2
15 - 34	8.0	5.7
35 - 54	14.0	11.7
55 - 64	27.1	26.1
65 and over	46.3	45.5

Persons with Disabilities Residing in Households and Health-Related Institutions by Level of Severity, 1991

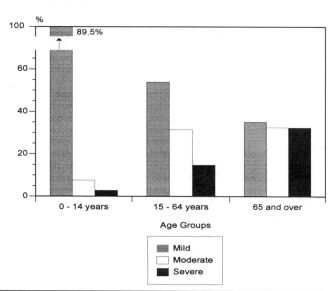

15, 2.9% were reported to have a severe disability. This rate was 14.8% among persons aged 15 to 64 and 32.4% for those 65 and over. (For a full description of the measurement of severity, see the note on page 175.)

Where persons with disabilities lived

Most persons with disabilities lived in private households, with the remainder living in homes for seniors and health-related institutions. Of persons reporting disabilities in 1991, 93.7% lived in private households and 6.3% lived in homes for seniors and health care institutions. This reflected little change from 1986.

Among persons with disabilities aged 15 to 64, 97.9% resided in private households, while the remaining 49,325 (2.1%) lived in homes for seniors and in health care institutions. In the age group 65 and over, the proportion remaining in private households decreased to 85.3%, while those living in institutions increased to 14.7%.

Among those aged 65 and over, 17.3% of females lived in homes for seniors and health care institutions, compared to 10.7% of males. This difference may result from the higher life expectency of females which contributes to a lower probability of a spouse being present to provide support to a female senior with disabilities living at home.

It is the severity of disability that is a significant factor in moving from a private household into a home for seniors or a health care institution. Among the population with disabilities aged 15 to 64 living in households, 14.1% reported having a severe disability compared to 48.8% of those living in homes for seniors and health care institutions. For those individuals aged 65 and over, 25.4% living in a private household reported a severe disability compared to 73.6% among persons with disabilities living in institutions.

Persons with Disabilities Residing in Households and Health-Related Institutions, 1991

	Population with Disabilities		Persons with Disabilities Residing in	
	Number	Disability Rate %	Households %	Institutions %
Both Sexes	**4,184,685**	**15.5**	**93.7**	**6.3**
0 - 14	389,355	7.0	100.0	*
15 - 64	2,346,455	12.9	97.9	2.1
65 and over	1,448,875	46.3	85.3	14.7
Females	**2,217,640**	**16.2**	**92.2**	**7.8**
0 - 14	156,365	5.7	100.0	*
15 - 64	1,182,145	12.9	98.2	1.8
65 and over	879,130	48.4	82.7	17.3
Males	**1,967,045**	**14.8**	**95.5**	**4.5**
0 - 14	232,990	8.1	100.0	*
15 - 64	1,164,310	12.8	97.6	2.4
65 and over	569,745	43.4	89.3	10.7

*   *Children in institutions were not included in the 1991 survey. In 1986, there were an estimated 2,400 children with disabilities in institutions.*

Persons with Disabilities Residing in Households and Health-Related Institutions by Level of Severity, 1991

	Total		Persons with Disabilities Residing in			
	Number	%	Households	%	Institutions	%
0 - 14	**389,355**	100.0	**389,355**	100.0	*	*
Mild	348,300	89.5	348,300	89.5	*	*
Moderate	29,555	7.6	29,555	7.6	*	*
Severe	11,500	2.9	11,500	2.9	*	*
15 - 64	**2,346,455**	100.0	**2,297,135**	100.0	49,320	100.0
Mild	1,261,825	53.8	1,248,500	54.3	13,325	27.0
Moderate	737,345	31.4	725,430	31.6	11,915	24.2
Severe	347,285	14.8	323,205	14.1	24,080	48.8
65 and over	**1,448,875**	100.0	**1,235,955**	100.0	212,920	100.0
Mild	508,095	35.1	487,420	39.4	20,675	9.7
Moderate	470,745	32.5	435,155	35.2	35,590	16.7
Severe	470,035	32.4	313,380	25.4	156,655	73.6

---

*   *Children in institutions were not included in the 1991 survey. In 1986, there were an estimated 2,400 children with disabilities in institutions.*

Children with disabilities

As with the adult population, rates of disability among children increased with age. In 1991, 85,070 or 4.6% of children aged 4 years and under were reported to have a disability. This rate increased to 7.4% for children aged 5 to 9 and to 9% for those aged 10 through 14.

Reported disability rates for males were higher than for females – 8.1% versus 5.7%. This higher rate holds true for the three age groups within the child population.

The majority of children had a mild disability. This remained constant over the three age groups. Among males, 10.7% had moderate or severe disabilities as compared to 10.3% of females. (Disability among children was measured in a number of different ways; see the note on page 175.)

Children with Disabilities Residing in Households by Level of Severity, 1991

	Total		0 - 4		5 - 9		10 - 14	
	Number	%	Number	%	Number	%	Number	%
Both Sexes								
Mild	348,300	89.5	75,330	88.6	120,945	87.7	152,025	91.4
Moderate	29,555	7.6	7,185	8.4	11,850	8.6	10,520	6.3
Severe	11,500	2.9	2,555	3.0	5,130	3.7	3,815	2.3
Females								
Mild	140,285	89.7	33,955	91.3	47,695	89.2	58,635	89.3
Moderate	11,130	7.1	2,365	6.4	3,870	7.2	4,895	7.4
Severe	4,950	3.2	870	2.3	1,925	3.6	2,155	3.3
Males								
Mild	208,015	89.3	41,375	86.4	73,250	86.8	93,390	92.8
Moderate	18,425	7.9	4,820	10.1	7,980	9.4	5,625	5.6
Severe	6,550	2.8	1,685	3.5	3,205	3.8	1,660	1.6

Children with Disabilities Residing in Households, 1991

	Population with Disabilities	Disability Rate %
Both Sexes - 14 and Under	**389,355**	**7.0**
0 - 4	85,070	4.6
5 - 9	137,925	7.4
10 - 14	166,360	9.0
Females - 14 and Under	**156,365**	**5.7**
0 - 4	37,190	4.1
5 - 9	53,490	5.9
10 - 14	65,685	7.3
Males - 14 and Under	**232,990**	**8.1**
0 - 4	47,880	5.0
5 - 9	84,435	8.8
10 - 14	100,675	10.6

Difficulty in speaking and being understood decreases as age increases; among children aged 0 to 4, this difficulty was reported for 26.9%. Among those aged 10 to 14, the rate had decreased to 12.3%. Almost 30% of children with disabilities aged 5 to 9 and 10 to 14 attended special schools or special classes within regular schools. Among children with disabilities, a chronic condition (long-term) was reported for more than half (56.2%).

Children with Disabilities Residing in Households by Selected Characteristics, 1991

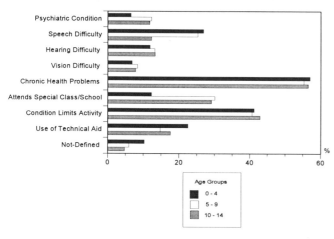

Adults with disabilities aged 15 to 64 living in households

Among persons with disabilities aged 15 to 64, 97.9% or 2,297,135 resided in private households. Within

Adults (Aged 15 - 64) with Disabilities Residing in Households by Level of Severity, 1991

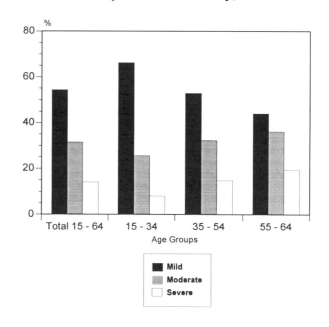

Adults (Aged 15 - 64) with Disabilities Residing in Households, 1991

	Number of Persons with Disabilities	Disability Rate %
Both Sexes - 15 - 64	**2,297,135**	**12.7**
15 - 34	675,055	7.9
35 - 54	992,835	13.7
55 - 64	629,245	26.6
Females - 15 - 64	**1,160,810**	**12.7**
15 - 34	346,615	8.1
35 - 54	501,095	13.8
55 - 64	313,100	26.0
Males - 15 - 64	**1,136,325**	**12.6**
15 - 34	328,435	7.7
35 - 54	491,740	13.6
55 - 64	316,150	27.3

the adult population, the disability rate among persons aged 15 to 34 was 7.9%. This rate increased to 13.7% for persons 35 to 54 and to 26.6% for those aged 55 to 64.

Of this group, 54.3% reported having a mild disability, 31.6% a moderate disability and 14.1% a severe disability. Within this age group, there were significant differences in reporting severe disabilities. Eight per cent of those 15 to 34, and 19.4% of persons aged 55 to 64 reported a severe disability.

Mobility (52.5%) and agility (50.2%) disabilities were most often reported by adults aged 15 to 64. However, of those aged 15 to 34, the most often reported disability was "Other". In this age group 43.1% of persons with disabilities reported that they perceived they were limited because of a learning disability, a mental health condition, a mental handicap, or because of how they were labelled by others. (For an explanation of the different types of disabilities identified among adults aged 15 and over; see the note on page 175.)

Seniors with disabilities

Of the estimated 1,448,875 seniors with disabilities, 85.3% lived in private households. The probability of moving into a home for seniors or a health care institution increased with age. Among persons aged 65 to 74, 95.4% lived at home but for those aged 85 and over, the percentage still living at home had decreased to 53.9%.

Females aged 65 and over were more likely to move from a private home to a home for seniors or a health care institution. Among those aged 65 and over, 17.3% of females lived in homes for seniors and health care institutions, compared to 10.7% of males. Within the age group 85 and over, 49.5% of females, compared to 37% of males, lived in a home for seniors or a health care institution.

Adults (Aged 15 - 64) with Disabilities Residing in Households by Nature of Disability and Age Groups, 1991

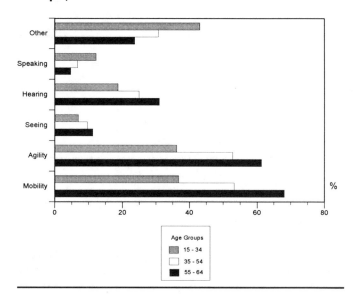

Women, who tend to live longer, were less likely to live with a spouse and more likely to live alone in a private household, a hospital or a special care institution.

Seniors (Aged 65 and Over) with Disabilities Residing in Households and Health-Related Institutions, 1991

	Seniors with Disabilities	Seniors with Disabilities Residing in	
	Number	Households %	Institutions %
Both Sexes			
Total, 65 and Over	1,448,875	85.3	14.7
65 - 74 Years	732,715	95.4	4.6
75 - 84 Years	507,830	83.6	16.4
85 Years and Over	208,330	53.9	46.1
Females			
Total, 65 and Over	879,130	82.7	17.3
65 - 74 Years	400,835	95.3	4.7
75 - 84 Years	327,180	82.3	17.7
85 Years and Over	151,120	50.5	49.5
Males			
Total, 65 and Over	569,745	89.3	10.7
65 - 74 Years	331,880	95.5	4.5
75 - 84 Years	180,655	86.1	13.9
85 Years and Over	57,210	63.0	37.0

Regardless of age among seniors, having a severe disability was consistently a major factor in the decision to move from a private household to a home for seniors or a health care institution. Severe disabilities were so prevalent among seniors living in these types of facilities that a separate measurement scale of severe disability was developed for this group. (For a full explanation of this scale, see to the note on page 175.)

Seniors (Aged 65 and Over) with Disabilities Residing in Households and Health-Related Institutions by Level of Severity, 1991

	Seniors with Disabilities		Seniors with Disabilities Residing in			
	Number	%	Households	%	Institutions	%
Total, 65 and Over	1,448,875	100.0	1,235,955	100.0	212,920	100.0
Mild	508,095	35.1	487,420	39.4	20,675	9.7
Moderate	470,745	32.5	435,155	35.2	35,590	16.7
Total Severe*	470,035	32.4	313,380	25.4		
Severe Level 1					46,070	21.6
Severe Level 2					49,065	23.1
Severe Level 3					61,520	28.9
65 - 74 years	732,715	100.0	698,830	100.0	33,885	100.0
Mild	336,500	45.9	330,510	47.3	5,990	17.7
Moderate	253,560	34.6	247,445	35.4	6,115	18.1
Total Severe*	142,655	19.5	120,875	17.3		
Severe Level 1					7,290	21.5
Severe Level 2					7,195	21.2
Severe Level 3					7,295	21.5
75 - 84 years	507,835	100.0	424,800	100.0	83,035	100.0
Mild	149,125	29.4	140,800	33.2	8,325	10.0
Moderate	163,145	32.1	147,170	34.6	15,975	19.3
Total Severe*	195,565	38.5	136,830	32.2		
Severe Level 1					18,625	22.4
Severe Level 2					19,025	22.9
Severe Level 3					21,085	25.4
85 years and Over	208,325	100.0	112,325	100.0	96,000	100.0
Mild	22,470	10.8	16,110	14.3	6,360	6.6
Moderate	54,045	25.9	40,545	36.1	13,500	14.1
Total Severe*	131,810	63.3	55,670	49.6		
Severe Level 1					20,160	21.0
Severe Level 2					22,840	23.8
Severe Level 3					33,140	34.5

*   *The category "severe" was reported as a total for seniors with disabilities residing in households and was subdivided into three levels for seniors with disabilities living in health-related institutions.*

Reporting of all types of disabilities was substantially higher among the population 65 and over living in institutions. The most notable was in the proportion of seniors reporting a disability in the category of "Other". Among seniors living in institutions, 65.2% perceived that they were limited because of a learning disability, a mental health condition, a mental handicap, or because of how they were labelled by others, compared to 25.7% of seniors living in households. Speaking disabilities were also reported in greater numbers among persons aged 65 and over living in institutions (29.3%) compared to those living in households (5.1%).

Seniors (Aged 65 and Over) with Disabilities Residing in Households and Health-Related Institutions by Nature of Disability, 1991*

| | Total | | Seniors with Disabilities Residing in | | | |
	Number	%	Households	%	Institutions	%
Total	**1,448,875**	**100.0**	**1,235,955**	**100.00**	**212,920**	**100.00**
Mobility	1,075,560	74.2	886,600	71.7	188,960	88.7
Agility	941,455	65.0	750,615	60.7	190,840	89.6
Seeing	384,395	26.5	298,370	24.1	86,025	40.4
Hearing	605,530	41.8	508,035	41.1	97,495	45.8
Speaking	125,705	8.7	63,220	5.1	62,485	29.3
Other	456,305	31.5	317,390	25.7	138,915	65.2

*   *Individuals may report more than one type of disability. Therefore, columns do not add to the totals.*

Nature of Disability

Different types of disabilities were identified among adults aged 15 and over:

mobility — *limited in the ability to walk, move from room to room, carry an object for 10 metres or stand for long periods.*

agility — *limited in ability to bend, dress or undress oneself, get in or out of bed, cut toenails, use fingers to grasp or handle objects, reach or cut one's own food.*

seeing — *limited in the ability to see newsprint or to see someone from four metres even when wearing corrective glasses.*

hearing — *limited in the ability to hear what is being said in a conversation with one or more people, even when wearing a hearing aid.*

speaking — *limited in the ability to speak and be understood.*

other — *limited because of a learning disability, a mental health condition, a mental handicap, or because of labelling by others .*

Respondents' answers to disability questions represent their perception of the situation and are therefore subjective.

Severity of Disability

A severity scale for adults has been developed using the responses to the screening questions. The scoring is first derived by adding together the individual severity scores of all screening questions, counting one point for each partial loss of function and two points for each total loss of function (i.e., a complete inability to perform a function). The total score is then categorized as follows:

mild	—	*less than 5 points*
moderate	—	*5 to 10 points*
severe	—	*11 or more points*

The category "severe" is further divided as follows for persons with disabilities living in health care institutions:

level 1	—	*11 to 17 points*
level 2	—	*18 to 25 points*
level 3	—	*26 to 42 points*

In deriving a score to measure the disability of children, a point is given each time a "yes" answer is given to one of a series of questions on the HALS survey. The score is then calculated by adding all the points and categorized as follows:

mild	—	*1 to 2 points*
moderate	—	*3 to 4 points*
severe	—	*5 or more points*

Who Was Surveyed?

Households: *Individuals were pre-identified through their response to the disability questions on the long-form 1991 Census questionnaire. The disability questions asked respondents to indicate if they were limited in the kind or amount of activity they could undertake because of a health problem or condition or if they had a long-term disability or handicap. Previous use of these questions confirmed that they would identify the population with severe disabilities as well the population with less severe disabilities. However, in some cases, those who had less severe disabilities would answer "no" to the census disability question. Therefore, a sample of individuals who answered "no" to the census disability question was also selected and then screened either in or out of the survey on the basis of more detailed questions.*

Health Care Institutions: *Individuals in health care institutions were also selected to ensure representation of persons with disabilities. The types of institutions included were: nursing homes; residences for senior citizens; hospitals (general, maternity, etc); chronic care hospitals; psychiatric institutions; and treatment centres and institutions for the physically handicapped. Respondents were selected from those residents who were living in the institution on February 1, 1991, and who had been in an institution for a continuous period of six months or more. Institutions were stratified and samples selected according to type and size within each province. Individuals were sampled from within each selected institution.*

Persons excluded: *For operational reasons, the survey excluded residents of penal institutions, correctional facilities, military camps, campgrounds and parks, soup kitchens, merchant and coast guard ships and children's group homes. Aboriginal persons living on reserves were covered separately by the Aboriginal Peoples' Survey.*

The data presented in this release have been weighted to estimate the total population with disabilities.

Catalogue 11-001E (Français 11-001F) ISSN 0827-0465

Tuesday, July 27, 1993

1991 HEALTH AND ACTIVITY LIMITATION SURVEY – EMPLOYMENT AND EDUCATION

HIGHLIGHTS

- 2.3 million Canadians between 15 and 64 years of age – 13% of the working age population – reported some level of disability in 1991. In 1986, 1.8 million Canadians in this age group (10%) reported disabilities

- In 1991, 48% of working age Canadians with disabilities were employed (1.1 million), up from 40% in 1986. Among persons without disabilities, the percentage employed increased to 73% in 1991, from 70% in 1986

- A larger percentage of Canadians with disabilities had at least some post-secondary education in 1991 (35%) than in 1986 (31%). Forty-nine per cent of the population without disabilities had this level of education in 1991

- Among individuals with a university degree, the percentage employed was lower for persons with disabilities (67%) than for persons without disabilities (87%)

Adults with Disabilities: Their Employment and Education Characteristics
1991 Health and Activity Limitation Survey

The information in *Adults with Disabilities: Their Employment and Education Characteristics*, (82-554, $60) as obtained from the 1991 Health and Activity Limitation Survey.

Data tables include information for Canada, the provinces and territories, and 17 selected census metropolitan areas; data are tabulated for persons with and without disabilities between 15 and 64 years of age.

Statistics   Statistique
Canada   Canada

Canadä

This release highlights information on the employment and education characteristics of 2.3 million Canadians who reported in the 1991 Health and Limitation Survey (HALS) that they had some level of disability or limitation in activity. These persons, aged 15 to 64, were among the 4.2 million persons with disabilities who reported some level of disability in 1991.

Profile of the working age population

The working age population with disabilities had an older age distribution than the population without disabilities. Among the 1991 population with disabilities, 30% were aged 15 to 34 years; in the population without disabilities, 50% were in this age group.

Within the 1991 population with disabilities, 54% (1,248,500) reported mild disabilities, 32% (725,430) reported moderate disabilities, and 14% (323,205) reported severe disabilities.

Persons with Disabilities, 1991

Age	Total	Males	Females
All Levels of Severity			
15-64	2,297,135	1,136,325	1,160,810
15-34	675,055	328,435	346,615
35-54	992,835	491,740	501,095
55-64	629,245	316,145	313,100
Mild			
15-64	1,248,500	651,110	597,395
15-34	447,305	220,310	227,000
35-54	524,380	283,070	241,315
55-64	276,815	147,730	129,085
Moderate			
15-64	725,430	329,910	395,520
15-34	173,605	78,540	95,065
35-54	321,430	140,035	181,390
55-64	230,400	111,335	119,065
Severe			
15-64	323,205	155,305	167,900
15-34	54,140	29,590	24,555
55-54	147,030	68,640	78,390
55-64	122,030	57,075	64,955

Persons with Disabilities

In 1991, 4.2 million Canadians of all ages – 16% of the population – reported some degree of disability. This release focuses on the group of persons typically referred to as the "working age population" – that is, persons aged 15 to 64, excluding institutional residents.

Among persons of this age group, the number with disabilities increased from 1.8 million in 1986 to 2.3 million in 1991, representing an increase in the percentage of Canadians of working age with disabilities, from 10% in 1986 to 13% in 1991. This increase is partly due to an aging population and partly to a change in survey methodology, which provided a more comprehensive enumeration of persons with mental health conditions or handicaps and of persons with learning disabilities. As well, an increased public awareness of disability in recent years may have made people more willing to report the limitations in activity and the barriers they encounter in everyday activities.

The increased enumeration of persons with mild disabilities likely contributed to the increase in employment and education levels among the population with disabilities.

Persons with disabilities made gains in employment

While there are still major differences between the rates of employment of persons with disabilities and persons without disabilities, the percentage of persons with disabilities who were employed increased to 48% (1.1 million) in 1991 from 40% in 1986. A smaller increase in the percentage employed occurred among persons without disabilities, from 70% in 1986 to 73% in 1991.

Women led the increase in percentage employed in both these populations. The percentage of women with disabilities who were employed increased from 31% in 1986 to 41% in 1991. Among women without disabilities, the percentage with employment increased from 60% to 66%.

The percentage of men with disabilities who were employed also increased, from 50% in 1986 to 56% in 1991; for men without disabilities, the percentage employed was unchanged at 80%.

While 48% of all persons with disabilities were employed in 1991, this percentage varied according to the level of severity of disabilities. Persons reporting mild disabilities were far more likely to be employed (62%) than those with moderate disabilities (37%) and those with severe disabilities (19%). Between 1986 and 1991, the number of employed persons with disabilities increased by 396,000; 82% of this increase (325,000) was among persons with mild disabilities.

Employment percentages among persons with disabilities were higher than the national average in Prince Edward Island, Ontario and the Western provinces; this was also the case for the employment percentages of persons without disabilities. The highest percentage of employment of persons with disabilities was reported in Regina, while the lowest was reported in Sudbury.

The 1991 Health and Activity Limitation Survey included questions addressing barriers to employment of persons with disabilities. The survey results indicated the following:

● 4% of employed persons with mild disabilities believed that they had been refused employment during the last five years because of their condition; this percentage increased to 10% for persons with moderate disabilities and to 19% for persons with severe disabilities;

● 3% of employed persons with mild disabilities, 7% of those with moderate disabilities and 9% of those with severe disabilities believed that they had been refused a promotion because of their condition, and equal proportions believed that they had been dismissed from a job because of their condition;

● 16% of employed persons with mild disabilities, 38% of those with moderate disabilities and 54% of those with severe disabilities believed that an employer would consider their condition to be a disadvantage in employment;

● As to the potential for advancing in their present jobs or for changing jobs, 22% of respondents with mild disabilities, 54% of those with moderate disabilities and 69% of those with severe disabilities indicated that it would be difficult or very difficult.

The unemployment rate of Canadians with disabilities was 14% in 1991

The unemployment rate (i.e., percentage of unemployed in the labour force) among Canadians with disabilities was 14% in 1991, down from 15% in 1986. The unemployment rate among Canadians without disabilities was 10% in 1991, unchanged from 1986. There was a difference between the 1991 unemployment rates for women (16%) and men (13%) with disabilities, but there was little difference between the rates for women (9.7%) and men (9.9%) without disabilities.

Unemployment rates among Canadians with disabilities also varied by level of severity. The 1991 unemployment rate was 12% among persons with mild disabilities, 17% among persons with moderate disabilities and 28% among persons with severe disabilities.

Survey data on barriers to employment in 1991 reveal that, among those who were unemployed at the time of the survey:

● 12% of those with mild disabilities, 23% of those with moderate disabilities and 28% of those with severe disabilities believed that they had been refused employment because of their condition during the last five years;

● 3% of those with mild disabilities, 7% with moderate disabilities and 12% with severe disabilities believed that they had been refused a promotion because of their condition;

● 10% of persons with mild disabilities, 23% with moderate disabilities and 30% with severe disabilities believed that they had been dismissed from a job during the past five years because of their condition;

● 29% of persons with mild disabilities, 55% with moderate disabilities and 72% with severe disabilities believed that an employer would consider their condition to be a disadvantage in employment.

Labour Force Status of Persons Aged 15 to 64 Years

	Persons With Disabilities			
	1991		1986*	
	Number	%	Number	%
Both Sexes	**2,297,135**	**100.0**	**1,757,055**	**100.0**
Labour Force Participation Rate		56.3		47.7
Employed	1,106,205	48.2	709,740	40.4
Unemployed	186,300	8.1	127,850	7.3
Unemployment Rate		14.4		15.3
Not in Labour Force	1,004,625	43.7	889,660	50.6
Females	**1,160,810**	**100.0**	**873,285**	**100.0**
Labour Force Participation Rate		48.5		37.1
Employed	472,640	40.7	268,595	30.8
Unemployed	90,310	7.8	55,075	6.3
Unemployment Rate		16.0		17.0
Not in Labour Force	597,860	51.5	536,765	61.5
Males	**1,136,325**	**100.0**	**883,770**	**100.0**
Labour Force Participation Rate		64.2		58.2
Employed	633,565	55.8	441,145	49.9
Unemployed	95,990	8.4	72,780	8.2
Unemployment Rate		13.2		14.2
Not in Labour Force	406,765	35.8	352,895	39.9

	Persons Without Disabilities			
	1991*		1986	
	Number	%	Number	%
Both Sexes	**15,859,035**	**100.0**	**15,179,720**	**100.0**
Labour Force Participation Rate	80.8		78	.0
Employed	11,558,940	72.9	10,623,180	70.0
Unemployed	1,255,365	7.9	1,217,900	8.0
Unemployment Rate		9.8		10.3
Not in Labour Force	3,022,770	19.1	3,338,645	22.0
Females	**7,949,635**	**100.0**	**7,641,245**	**100.0**
Labour Force Participation Rate		73.3		68.0
Employed	5,253,610	66.1	4,593,255	60.1
Unemployed	574,770	7.2	599,415	7.8
Unemployment Rate		9.9		11.5
Not in Labour Force	2,112,180	26.6	2,448,575	32.0
Males	**7,909,400**	**100.0**	**7,538,480**	**100.0**
Labour Force Participation Rate		88.3		88.2
Employed	6,305,335	79.7	6,029,925	80.0
Unemployed	680,595	8.6	618,485	8.2
Unemployment Rate		9.7		9.3
Not in Labour Force	910,595	11.5	890,070	11.8

*   Respondents not stating their labour force activity are not shown, but are included in the totals.
**   Totals may not add due to rounding.

Fewer Canadians with disabilities were not in the labour force in 1991

Between 1986 and 1991, the percentage of working age Canadians with disabilities who were not in the labour force declined from 51% to 44%, to one million people. In 1991, by contrast, only 19% of Canadians without disabilities in this age group were not in the labour force. Women were less likely than men in both populations to be in the labour force. In 1991, 52% of women with disabilities and 36% of men with disabilities were not in the labour force. Among Canadians without disabilities, 27% of women and 12% of men were not in the labour force.

Differences in the percentage of persons not in the labour force also existed between levels of severity reported by persons with disabilities. In 1991, the percentage of persons not in the labour force was 29% among persons with mild disabilities, 55% among persons with moderate disabilities and 74% among persons with severe disabilities.

Among the population with disabilities who were not in the labour force in 1991, 59% or almost 600,000 persons reported being completely prevented from working. For those with mild disabilities, this percentage was 35%; it increased to 66% for those with moderate disabilities and to 86% for those with severe disabilities.

Questions on barriers to employment in 1991 revealed that, among people with disabilities who were not in the labour force at the time of the survey:

- 5% of those with mild disabilities, 9% of those with moderate disabilities and 9% of those with severe disabilities believed that they had been refused employment because of their condition during the last five years;

- 2% with mild disabilities, 3% with moderate disabilities and 3% with severe disabilities believed that they had been refused a promotion because of their condition;

Labour Force Status of Persons Aged 15 to 64 Years

	1991		1986*	
	Number	%	Number	%
All Levels of Severity**	**2,297,135**	**100.0**	**1,757,055**	**100.0**
Labour Force Participation Rate		56.3		47.7
Employed	1,106,205	48.2	709,740	40.4
Unemployed	186,300	8.1	127,850	7.3
Unemployment Rate		14.4		15.3
Not in Labour Force	1,004,625	43.7	889,660	50.6
Mild Disabilities	**1,248,500**	**100.0**	**907,375**	**100.0**
Labour Force Participation Rate		70.9		58.2
Employed	774,970	62.1	449,700	49.6
Unemployed	109,630	8.8	78,090	8.6
Unemployment Rate		12.4		14.8
Not in Labour Force	363,905	29.1	361,755	39.9
Moderate Disabilities	**725,430**	**100.0**	**580,740**	**100.0**
Labour Force Participation Rate		44.8		43.2
Employed	271,525	37.4	213,680	36.8
Unemployed	53,515	7.4	37,170	6.4
Unemployment Rate		16.5		14.8
Not in Labour Force	400,395	55.2	322,220	55.5
Severe Disabilities	**323,205**	**100.0**	**268,935**	**100.0**
Labour Force Participation Rate		25.6		21.9
Employed	59,710	18.5	46,360	17.2
Unemployed	23,160	7.2	12,595	4.7
Unemployment Rate		27.9		21.4
Not in Labour Force	240,330	74.4	205,685	76.5

*   1986 respondents not stating their labour force activity are not shown, but are included in the totals.
**   Totals may not add due to rounding.

- 4% of persons with mild disabilities, 7% with moderate disabilities and 10% with severe disabilities believed that they had been dismissed from a job during the past five years because of their condition;

- 40% of persons with mild disabilities, 71% with moderate disabilities and 82% with severe disabilities believed that an employer would consider their condition to be a disadvantage in employment.

Post-secondary education increases among persons with disabilities

In 1991, individuals with at least some post-secondary education represented 35% of the population with disabilities, an increase over 1986 (31%). Forty-nine per cent of the population without disabilities had at least some post-secondary education.

Educational Distribution of Persons With and Without Disabilities, 1991

	Persons with Disabilities	Persons without Disabilities
	%	
Highest Level of Schooling		
Total	100.0	100.0
No Formal Schooling	1.7	0.4
1 to 8 years	18.1	7.7
Secondary	44.9	43.1
Some Post-secondary Studies	10.8	12.9
Certificate/Diploma	18.7	22.3
University Degree	5.9	13.6

The proportion of persons with disabilities having at least some post-secondary education varies by level of severity. In 1991, 39% of persons with mild disabilities, 32% of persons with moderate disabilities and 28% of persons with severe disabilities had at least some post-secondary education.

What is a disability?

The 1991 Health and Activity Limitation Survey (HALS) uses the World Health Organization's definition of disability: "... any restriction or lack (resulting from impairment) of ability to perform an activity in the manner or within the range considered normal for a human being."
Adults were asked questions about various limitations in activities related to daily living (sensory, mobility, agility, or other physical or psychological abilities) to determine the presence of a disability. The answers to the questions on disability represent the respondents' perception of the situation and are, therefore, subjective.

Severity of disability

A severity scale for adults has been developed using the responses to the activity limitation questions in HALS.
Each respondent receives a severity score by adding together the individual's responses to all activity limitation questions: one point is scored for each partial loss of function and two points are scored for each total loss of function (i.e., a complete inability to perform a function). The total score is then categorized as follows:

mild:	less than 5 points
moderate:	5 to 10 points
severe:	11 or more points

Among persons with a university degree, the percentage employed was lower for persons with disabilities (67%) than for persons without disabilities (87%). In the population with disabilities who had a university degree:

- 74% of persons with mild disabilities were employed;

- 61% of persons with moderate disabilities were employed;

- 31% of persons with severe disabilities were employed.

Among persons with a university degree, the percentage unemployed in 1991 was similar for persons with and without disabilities: 6% compared to 5%.

The percentage of persons with a university degree who were not in the labour force was substantially higher for persons with disabilities (27%) than for persons without disabilities (8%).

Data Comparability

Users of Census data should take into account factors which could affect the comparability of 1991 Census data with those from previous Censuses.

Changes in the Completeness of Enumeration: *No national census can obtain a complete enumeration of the population. Variations in the completeness of enumeration can occur from one census to another. Estimates of the completeness of the 1991 Census are now available.*

Non-permanent Residents: *In 1991, the Census counted both permanent and non-permanent residents of Canada. Non-permanent residents are persons who held student or employment authorizations, Minister's permits or who were refugee claimants; the 1991 Census enumerated some 223,410 non-permanent residents in Canada, representing slightly less than 1% of the total population. Users should be especially careful when comparing data from 1991 and previous Censuses in geographic areas where there is a concentration of non-permanent residents, particularly the major metropolitan areas of Quebec, Ontario and British Columbia.*

Incompletely Enumerated Indian Reserves: *Some Indian reserves and Indian settlements (a total of 78) were incompletely enumerated during the 1991 Census. Data for 1991 are therefore not available for those reserves and settlements. Because of the missing data, users are cautioned that for affected geographic areas, comparisons (e.g. percentage change) between 1986 and 1991 are not exact. For larger geographic areas (Canada, provinces and territories, census metropolitan areas) the impact of the missing data is quite small.*

Exclusion of Institutional Residents: *The analysis is based on data collected from a sample of 20% of households which completed the long form questionnaire. As with the 1986 and 1981 Censuses, the data do not include institutional residents. The total number after weighting (26,994,000) is slightly smaller than the 100% data (27,297,000).*

Upcoming Data Products and Services from the 1991 Aboriginal Peoples Survey

Aboriginal Peoples Survey Workshop

1-Disability 2-Housing (89-535)

Community Profiles (available in electronic format)

Microdata File

North American Indians: A Statistical Profile

The Métis: A Statistical Profile

The Inuit: A Statistical Profile

Upcoming Data Products and Services from the 1991 Health and Activity Limitation Survey

Selected Characteristics of Persons with Disabilities Residing in Households, *1991 (82-555)*

A Workshop on the Health and Activity Limitation Survey

Public Use Microdata Files: Adults in Households
                                 Adults in Institutions

ORDER FORM
Statistics Canada

MAIL TO:	PHONE:	FAX TO:	METHOD OF PAYMENT:

MAIL TO:

✉

**Marketing Division
Publication Sales
Statistics Canada
Ottawa, Ontario
Canada K1A 0T6**

(Please print)

PHONE:

☎ **1-800-267-6677**

Charge to VISA or MasterCard. Outside Canada and the U.S. call (613) 951-7277. Please do not send confirmation.

FAX TO:

📠 **(613) 951-1584**

VISA, MasterCard and Purchase Orders only. Please do not send confirmation. A fax will be treated as an original order.

METHOD OF PAYMENT:

(Check only one)

☐ **Please charge my:** ☐ VISA ☐ MasterCard

Card Number |_|_|_|_|_|_|_|_|_|_|_|_|_|_|_|_|_|

_____ |_|_|_|
Signature   Expiry Date

☐ **Payment enclosed** $ _____

Please make cheque or money order payable to the *Receiver General for Canada – Publications*.

☐ **Purchase Order Number** |_|_|_|_|_|_|_|_|_|_|_|
(Please enclose)

_____
Authorized Signature

Company _____

Department _____

Attention _____ Title _____

Address _____

City _____ Province _____

Postal Code _____ Phone ( ) _____ Fax ( ) _____

Please ensure that **all information** is completed.

Catalogue Number	Title	Date of Issue or Indicate an "S" for subscriptions	Annual Subscription or Book Price			Quantity	Total
			Canada $	United States US$	Other Countries US$		$

SUBTOTAL	
DISCOUNT (if applicable)	
GST (7%) (Canadian clients only)	
GRAND TOTAL	

► **Note: Catalogue prices for U.S. and other countries are shown in US dollars.**

► GST Registration # R121491807

► Cheque or money order should be made payable to the *Receiver General for Canada – Publications*.

► Canadian clients pay in Canadian funds and add 7% GST. Foreign clients pay total amount in US funds drawn on a US bank. Prices for US and foreign clients are shown in US dollars.

PF 093238 ♻

THANK YOU FOR YOUR ORDER!

 Statistics Canada   Statistique Canada

 Canada